Big Man on Campus

Big Man on Campus

JOHN THOMPSON AND THE GEORGETOWN HOYAS

Leonard Shapiro

A JOHN MACRAE BOOK

Henry Holt and Company   New York

To Vicky, Jennifer, Emily and Taylor,
to Mom and Pop, to Chuck and Naoma—
What Rocks!

Published by Henry Holt and Company, Inc.,
115 West 18th Street, New York, New York 10011.
Published in Canada by Fitzhenry & Whiteside Limited,
195 Allstate Parkway, Markham, Ontario L3R 4T8.

Library of Congress Cataloging-in-Publication Data
Shapiro, Leonard, 1947–
    Big man on campus: John Thompson and the
Georgetown Hoyas / by Leonard Shapiro.—1st ed.
        p.   cm.
    Includes index.
    1. Thompson, John, 1941 Sept. 2–
2. Basketball—United States—Coaches—Biog-
raphy.   3. Georgetown Hoyas (Basketball team)—
History.   I. Title.
GV884.T48S53   1991
796.323′092—dc20
[B]   90-49044
                                          CIP

Henry Holt books are available at special discounts
for bulk purchases for sales promotions, premiums,
fund-raising, or educational use. Special editions or
book excerpts can also be created to specification.

    For details contact:
    Special Sales Director
    Henry Holt and Company, Inc.
    115 West 18th Street
    New York, New York 10011

First Edition

Designed by Kate Nichols

Printed in the United States of America
Recognizing the importance of preserving
the written word, Henry Holt and Company, Inc.,
by policy, prints all of its first editions
on acid-free paper.∞
10 9 8 7 6 5 4 3 2 1

Illustrations

These photographs appear courtesy of The Washington Post unless otherwise indicated:

Title page spread: Thompson and the Georgetown bench (*Georgetown University*).
Opener: *Left to right:* Thompson with Eric Smith. The coach talks strategy in the 1982 NCAA title game. Pacing the sidelines at McDonough.
  1: Deserted playground (*Steve Goff*).
  2: *Bottom:* Thompson at Providence College (*Providence College Library*).
  3: Thompson with Red Auerbach (*The Boston Celtics*).
  4: *Top:* Thompson and Dean Smith (*AP/Wide World Photos*). *Bottom:* Donald Washington signs to attend North Carolina as Dean Smith, Washington's sister and Thompson look on.
  5: *Left to right:* Georgetown's pressure defense. Craig Shelton, 1980.
  6: *Left to right:* Billy Lynn (*Georgetown University*). Mike Stokes (*Georgetown University*). Merlin Wilson scores.
  7: *Left to right:* Thompson, 1975 ECAC Tournament. Derrick Jackson (*Georgetown University*).
  8: *Left to right:* Tom LaGarde in 1976 Olympic game against Italy (*UPI*). 1976 U.S. Olympic basketball team accepting gold medals (*UPI*).
  9: Craig Shelton.
  10: Four Big East coaches: Carnesecca (*AP/Wide World Photos*), Boeheim (*Syracuse University*), Evans (*University of Pittsburgh*) Massimino (*AP/Wide World Photos*). Sleepy Floyd against Missouri, 1982.
  11: *Left to right:* Patrick Ewing grapples with the net. Ewing fights off Ralph Sampson and Craig Robinson, 1982 (*AP/Wide World Photos*).
  12: North Carolina celebrates after defeating Georgetown in 1982 NCAA championship (*AP/Wide World Photos*).
  13: Michael Graham fights for loose ball (*AP/Wide World Photos*).
  14: Hoyas applaud after losing NCAA title game to Villanova, 1985.

What's a Hoya? In the days when all Georgetown students were required to study Greek and Latin, the University's teams were nicknamed 'The Stonewalls.' A student of the classics started the cheer 'Hoya Saxa,' which translates into 'What Rocks!' The name proved popular and the term Hoyas was eventually adopted for all Georgetown teams.''

From the 1990 Georgetown basketball media guide

Big Man on Campus

I think John Thompson is a fraud as an academician. I have another view of Michael Graham. John Thompson used the guy to win a national championship. All of a sudden he didn't go to class. Is he saying that for a year the guy was a good student, did his work, did his studying, went to class? . . . He basically abandoned this kid. I don't think that's the work of a guy who theoretically cares. . . . My differences with John Thompson did not start with access. I could care less about talking to his players. Most of them had nothing to say anyway. My differences started because of their style of play. A thug game. Cheap shots. . . . The more serious problem I had is the way they play and the way they take on this 'academic integrity,' yet they graduate people who can't speak."

—*Curry Kirkpatrick,*
Sports Illustrated

The worst journalists are skeptics and cynics with no common sense. When you run into an authority figure that fights them, it's a sick thing, almost a pack reaction to strike back. There are coaches who will wine you and dine you. Then there's John Thompson, who's never wined, dined or romanced anybody. . . . He establishes his terms and either you accept them or you don't. . . . He's a tough guy who has created his own world, for whatever reasons. . . . I don't think I can understand what he's gone through. I ain't black. I didn't live it. I can't feel it, I don't understand it. I go at him understanding that. . . . He's too smart to be a racist. He doesn't make all his decisions based on race. I think he makes decisions based on what's best in his world.''

—*Dave Kindred,*
The National Sports Daily

Opener

I FIRST MET JOHN THOMPSON MORE THAN TWENTY YEARS AGO, a few months after I had joined *The Washington Post* as a young reporter. I'd been assigned a story on Thompson and his star player at St. Anthony's High School in Northeast Washington, D.C., and I had called him to arrange an interview at the school. Come after practice, he said, and we can talk. Two hours after I had opened my notebook, John Thompson had stopped speaking and I was stunned, amazed by what I had just heard.

Over the years, there were many more lengthy sessions with this huge mountain of a man whose soft baby-fat face remains an incongruous trick of nature. Provocative ideas and a unique way of getting across his message make communication lively and clear. Often, he stops the conversation and asks, "You understand what I'm saying?" And I did. We spoke often, first at St. Anthony's and later when he took the head coaching job at Georgetown in 1972, the first black coach in the history of the school.

In his early tenure at Georgetown, I had almost total access to Thompson and his players. Though I moved on to covering professional football and then to a position as the paper's sports editor, I stayed in touch with him, occasionally covering a game or writing about his team. He allowed me to watch some of his practices. He helped set up interviews with his players. He took me on a recruiting trip when he was wooing a young Baltimore-area player to show me how difficult it was to attract white athletes to his program. He was both a source and a sounding board.

One Sunday morning, he drove me around town for a guided tour of Washington's basketball playgrounds. He introduced me to some of the best players, talked about the traditions of places with such exotic names as Turkey Thicket, Candy Cane Lane and Luzon, and outlined the simple etiquette of his boyhood haunts—"winners stay on, losers walk." More important, he talked about the concept known as *bogarding*, a distinctly Washington term that, in retrospect, goes a long way toward defining John Thompson's philosophy of life.

Neither Thompson nor anyone else was exactly certain of the origin or even the spelling of *bogarding*, but almost everyone I talked to on the playground agreed that Humphrey Bogart's tough-guy, take-no-stuff-from-no-one demeanor was a good place to start. Bogarding on a basketball court meant you held your ground, stuck out your chest and strutted your stuff at all times, right or wrong. If you called a foul on the man guarding you and he disagreed, you simply would not give in, no matter how long it took to settle the argument. If one of your teammates was hogging the basketball, you'd tell him to his face, even if you were only 5-foot-9 and he stood 6-foot-10 and outweighed you by 75 pounds. If you'd been patiently waiting to get into a game and someone tried to get ahead of you or replace you with one of his pals, you'd stand firm to the point of physical risk to get your way.

Bogarding meant taking control of the situation, walking and talking with arrogant authority and being prepared to back it up, on and off the basketball court. It was playground power, pure and simple. John Thompson learned all about that at a very early age, and, in a sense, he has been bogarding his way through life ever since.

I saw one vivid example of it during a game that may very well have marked the turning point for his program and his career. In December 1979, his Georgetown team was playing the University of Maryland, a longtime rival and big-time top-twenty school, when Thompson got involved in a shouting match with another colorful and controversial coach, Lefty Driesell. Thompson cursed him with language that would not have been appreciated by the Jesuit priests at his own institution of higher learning. Perhaps inspired by Thompson's emotional outburst, Georgetown went on to beat Maryland that night for the second straight year, a 12-point victory that served notice that the Hoyas were now a major force both in Washington and nationwide. His profane verbal barrage at Driesell, heard clearly and distinctly by hundreds of people at the D.C. Armory and widely reported in the media, also exploded the myth that he was a high-topped goody-two-sneakers, the St. John of Washington Basketball whose only mission in life was to educate deprived young black athletes he had rescued from the street.

"You see," he said, winking at me that night, "I told you I could be a bastard."

John Thompson bogarded his way past Lefty Driesell and into the national consciousness shortly thereafter, taking that 1980 team all the way to the NCAA Final Eight before losing to the University of Iowa in a heartbreaking 1-point loss decided in the final seconds. I covered that game, too, saw the hurt in Thompson's face on a night his team had come so close to breaking through to the promised land of the Final Four. But I also saw the steely resolve in his eyes as he dissected the loss later on. He told me he was certain there would be more chances, that this loss was simply a momentary detour on the road to a national championship.

Before long he was exactly right, and his team's brawling brand of basketball has been mostly responsible. For most of Thompson's tenure as the biggest man on the Georgetown campus, his teams have been known to come at opponents in waves, with flailing arms in your face, elbows in your gut and an occasional punch in your nose. In years past, particularly during the Patrick Ewing era of the early 1980s, they played a confrontational style of basketball that enhanced their image as a swaggering bunch of bullies, an image that even now makes Georgetown jackets and T-shirts the fashion of choice among gang members, drug dealers and punks from coast to coast, not to mention countless decent kids from Harlem to Watts who dream of playing for the big man with the perpetual scowl on his face and the trademark white towel draped over his shoulder.

Thompson was asked once what he looked for in a basketball player. "What I want," he said, "is everything. I want the talent, a kid who can run and leap and shoot, but I want him to have enough intelligence, discipline, character or whatever so that he'll walk when I tell him to, run when I want him to, pass if that's what I want. Without talent, all the character in the world won't do it, but talent alone isn't enough. There are great individuals and teams with lots of talent who don't win. I tell the kids that it's as though we're putting on a play. I'm the director. I'm going to pick the script and I'm going to give them their roles. They're the actors. Their job is to go learn those roles—that's what practice is about. When we go out on the court, that's our stage. Out there, they're supposed to perform as we practiced. I don't want anybody making up new lines, putting on their own act."

The prototype Thompson team would include a dominating big man in the middle, a hulking big forward to help on the boards, a versatile small forward with a feathery outside touch and the ability to go strong to the hoop as well, a sharpshooting off guard and a heady, penetrating point guard who can get the ball to all the proper places and take the tough shot himself if necessary. The bench would be four or five players deep, and every man on the court also would be expected to play tough, belly-to-belly, end-to-end defense for forty minutes. As far back as his

North Carolina's James Worthy
sandwiched by Patrick Ewing
and Fred Brown in 1982 NCAA
title game. (AP/Wide World
Photos)

high school coaching days in the late 1960s, Thompson preferred to jam the ball inside to a big man, crash the boards nonstop and run a controlled, disciplined fast break when the opportunity presented itself. On defense, his teams were always superbly conditioned and kamikaze oriented—diving on the floor for every loose ball, trapping and pressing fullcourt and capable of smoothly switching back and forth from a variety of zones and man-to-man formations designed to befuddle their foes.

His greatest teams took the floor in the first half of the 1980s, with 7-foot Patrick Ewing the man in the middle and the most dominant player of his time, a terror on offense around the basket and a menacing shot-blocking presence to anyone who dared challenge his authority down the lane. Just when an opponent thought he had broken clear of Georgetown's suffocating press, there was Ewing and his B-29 wingspan, swatting a two-on-one fast break right back in his face.

Thompson's 1983–84 national championship team epitomized The Georgetown Way, and its performance in the Big East tournament that same season was a classic example of the intimidating style of play that sent shivers of fear throughout college basketball. In the team's opening game it routed Providence by 20 points. In the semis, it bumped off St. John's by 11, despite 25 points from all-American Chris Mullin, a human pinball bouncing off Hoya defenders all night. And in the final, it survived an all-out blitz by Syracuse all-American Pearl Washington to win in overtime by 11. That game also was marred by a nasty punch thrown by Georgetown's freshman hatchet man, Michael Graham, a bad boy long before the Detroit Pistons used a similar style to dominate the NBA over the last few years. Ewing's performance over those three games was stunning—25 of 32 shots from the floor, 69 total points, 28 rebounds, 13 blocked shots and countless angry glares, dirty looks and well-placed elbows.

"Georgetown has the panzer divisions and the swift tanks and the *Luftwaffe* and the long bombs," moaned St. John's coach Lou Carnesecca. "They just completely destroy people and yeah, they scare the hell out of you."

Even today, the tradition continues, in the presence of another dominant 7-footer, Alonzo Mourning, a free-spirited soul who delights in taunting foes with a very sharp tongue and an occasional hair-trigger temper that was on display for all the world to see last summer. Playing for the U.S. national team, Mourning threw a punch in a game against Puerto Rico during the Goodwill Games in Seattle, then got involved in another melee two weeks later against Greece in the world championships in Buenos Aires. Clearly, the beat goes on.

Thompson's players come mostly from black America, some with subpar high school grades and educational skills that would seem certain to spell failure at such an elite, prestigious Jesuit university as Georgetown, a school with an impeccable academic reputation for producing diplomats, doctors, lawyers and leaders of industry, commerce and high finance. Yet, when his players leave Thompson and his program after four years, 98 percent—sixty-one of sixty-three through 1990—have earned their diplomas, an enviable record in almost two decades of big-time college sports rocked by scandals as diverse as point shaving, blatant cheating to recruit athletes, academic fraud to keep them in school, the use of illegal and illicit drugs and more felonies and misdemeanors, right on up to rape, armed robbery and murder, than occurred in all of amateur American sports before 1973.

Thompson's methods often go against the grain. In the early years when I covered his team, school publicists begged for attention, but how times have changed. For most of the last decade, he has not allowed freshmen to be interviewed by the media. His practices are held behind locked doors. His teams are sequestered in secret locations before big games and important tournaments. All interview requests must be approved by the head coach. He trusts few people, but he seems intensely loyal to many of his friends. His program is criticized for having been almost entirely black, yet Mary Fenlon, his longtime academic coordinator and assistant coach and perhaps his best friend and alter ego, is white, as are his chief recruiter, his longtime trainer, and his top assistant coach on the Olympic team, a college teammate who worked as an assistant at Georgetown for ten years.

Thompson is the man behind "Hoya paranoia," a phrase made popular in the early 1980s by the national media when Thompson's team rose to prominence. The Hoyas won one national championship, lost two others in memorable confrontations against North Carolina and Villanova and should be a top-ten team for years to come, as long as Thompson stays.

Basketball has made him rich: He has a long-term, six-figure coaching contract that ranks him as the highest-paid man at the university, and his salary is supplemented by outside income from television, a summer camp and a $200,000-a-year contract with the Nike shoe company to promote its products and serve as a national spokesman. He is said to earn close to $1 million a year, and in the summer of 1990 he turned down an offer to become general manager and a minority owner of the Denver Nuggets, a job that could have earned him over $6 million in the next five years.

For most of the last two decades, Thompson also has been a prominent figure on the national college basketball scene. He is a past president of the National Association of Basketball Coaches. He was an assistant coach on the gold-medal-winning 1976 Olympic team and head coach of the 1988 team that lost in the semifinals to the Soviet Union in Seoul, South Korea, a defeat that led to a firestorm of criticism for Thompson's tactics on and off the court.

Ever since he stepped on the mostly white Georgetown campus, Thompson has been a lightning rod for controversy, and over the past several years it has only intensified. He was at the center of the storm for his stand on Proposition 42, a measure initially passed by the National Collegiate Athletic Association in 1989 that would have eliminated financial aid to athletes unable to meet minimum academic standards for athletic eligibility. In a widely publicized action, he walked out of a game in protest of Proposition 42, sat out another game, then led the effort to rescind a measure he believed was specifically directed toward denying black athletes their fair share of the American Dream. That walkout, and the national debate that followed, led to the modification of Proposition 42 at an NCAA convention in 1990.

In the summer of 1989, Thompson appeared on national television and calmly told Ted Koppel and millions of "Nightline" viewers that he recently had met with one Rayful Edmond, at the time the drug kingpin of Washington and a young man whose gang Washington police believed may have been responsible for more than thirty drug-related murders. Thompson had heard that two of his own players, Mourning, then a freshman, and sophomore John Turner, not only had met Edmond at a local nightclub but also had played basketball with him often around town. "What I was attempting to do, Ted, is what I do, what I thought was my responsibility," Thompson told Koppel that night. "Not to wait until something happened that would hurt one of the kids, not to have a body laying there where it's saying somebody had been using drugs." It may have been the ultimate form of bogarding, Thompson telling—not asking, but insisting—this dangerous and vicious man to stay away from his boys.

A few weeks after Thompson had made national headlines with his Koppel appearance, I set off on a trip to begin the research for this book. I was seeking answers about a man I had considered a friend through most of the 1970s, a man I still admired through the 1980s, even though we had drifted apart as our careers headed in different directions, and different tax brackets. Because I was determined to consider him in all his guises and John Thompson would know this, I didn't know exactly what his response to the book might be. Yet I was surprised when I heard that certain people close to him were told not to speak with me. John put it this way in that deep baritone voice of his after telling me by telephone that he was planning to write a book himself: access to him and his team "would be like Ford cooperating with General Motors."

A few individuals didn't cooperate, but eighteen months and two hundred and fifty interviews later it was clear to me that the basketball world, including its key members and many former Georgetown players, considered Thompson a public personality. Only a few sources, concerned with their future relations with the coach, asked for anonymity, which I have honored.

Even as many of my colleagues at the *Post* insisted that the John Thompson I thought I knew so well had changed dramatically, I had always defended him. And on a sultry, simmering evening in the summer of 1989 I was doing it again, sitting with two of his former Providence College teammates in the living room of a little house on a quiet East Providence street.

Jimmy Ahern had raised his family in this house. He was born and grew up in Rhode Island, and he had gone on to a long career as one of the state's top high school basketball coaches after playing at hometown Providence College in the early 1960s. He had invited another old teammate, Jim Benedict, to come over this evening to talk with me about the John Thompson they remembered from more than twenty-five years earlier. Thompson had been a 6-foot-10 center for the Providence College Friars, a team that had been ranked as high as number three in the country before the start of Thompson's senior season in 1964.

Thompson was one of two black starters and a cocaptain; Ahern was a sixth man and Benedict a starting guard. Ahern was a year behind Thompson, Benedict a sophomore when Thompson was a senior. Ahern was a flashy, fiery 6-foot guard with a bit of a temper who was more than occasionally a resident in the doghouse of the head coach, Joe Mullaney, a brilliant tactician and still an active coach into his mid-sixties. Benedict was a 6-foot-4 guard with a deadly outside shot who had learned the game on the playgrounds of his native Hartford, Connecticut. He had gone to Providence hoping to emulate the success of another Hartford hero, Johnny Egan, a legendary player for the Friars whom Bob Cousy once described as the best college guard he'd ever seen.

Ahern, now a coach and schoolteacher, and Benedict, now a hospital administrator, have remained friends over the years. Ahern said he had heard from Thompson occasionally, and once had even permitted him to hold practice in his high school gym when Georgetown came north to play Providence a few years back. "Look, here's a picture of me and Patrick Ewing," he said proudly. "John came over here one night, sat in the same chair you're sitting in. He's good people, real good people."

Benedict had not been close to Thompson when they played. Thompson was a senior with a big reputation, on campus as well as nationally; Benedict was a hungry sophomore, eager to prove that he could play big-time college basketball. Still, Benedict had followed Thompson's career after college closely, watching his Georgetown teams play on television and sometimes going over to the Providence Civic Center to watch, though he never stayed to talk with his old teammate. He also said he tried to read all he could about a man who had become one of the most controversial figures in all of sports. There was much to read.

Benedict had also watched John Thompson talk to Ted Koppel about his meeting with the drug dealer on television that night, and was troubled by what he heard, just as he said he had been troubled by John Thompson almost from the day Thompson was hired to coach the basketball team at Georgetown in 1972.

Early in the evening, Benedict and Ahern both talked with some affection about John Thompson. Ahern recalled the time he had gotten upset with Joe Mullaney in practice and been thrown out of the gym by the coach. When the traveling squad for an upcoming game had been posted, Ahern's name wasn't on it. "In my mind, that's when John Thompson started coaching," Ahern said. "He said to me, 'Jimmy, don't worry, I'll talk to him.' John was a senior. He was the captain. I went on the trip because Big John talked to Joe Mullaney.

"I hear all this stuff about how prejudiced he is supposed to be," Ahern went on. "To me, there's no conceivable way. He's the finest gentleman I ever met. He was more of a student than a player. And he really studied the game. . . . The year we won the NIT championship [National Invitation Tournament, Thompson's junior season, 1962–63], that was the best basketball team I have ever seen."

Benedict, still basketball lean with a full but neatly trimmed salt-and-pepper beard, initially recalled that John Thompson was more than just a basketball star. "What I enjoyed about him was that being black was just one part of John's life," Benedict said. "Being academically prepared, someone you'd view as a real good student, was another side of John. He was a listener, a perceptive listener. . . . John drove him-self to be a total person, the kind of guy who says, 'I'm not just a black person or a black athlete, I'm going to be the kind of person Providence College wants me to be.' Black wasn't important. 'What other attributes do I have that will springboard me to something else?' John used to organize forums on campus—not just for athletes, for everyone. 'Let's talk about this issue—not just black issues, everything,' he'd say."

Still, as the evening wore on, Ahern began to sit back in his chair and listen as Benedict warmed to the subject. What began as an in-terview quickly turned into a heated discussion, and Jim Benedict's position on John Thompson shifted dramatically as I tried to play devil's advocate and defend my old friend.

"I watch him on TV, I watch how he handles his players, and I was always perplexed as to how did he wind up at Georgetown University, a blue-blood school, a place that really doesn't need a basketball team," he said. "I watched, and I always said to myself, 'Why does it have to be all black?' "

A little later on:

"My point is balance," he said, his voice rising. "John Thompson does not speak to balance. If you think he does, I'll tell you you're wrong. I know a lot of Georgetown graduates, and they haven't sold it to them. There is a group that doesn't like it. It's important that is known. You ought to talk to them about it.

"If you were to say to me today, 'Do you think John Thompson is making a concerted effort for a balance in society, to make things happen in a progressive way?' I would have to say no. He's talking one way. A guy like John has an obligation to look in terms of balance. His obligation is only commensurate with what the school's obligation is. If George-town is willing for John to have autonomy and do what he does, that's fine. But that doesn't make it right for me."

The discussion lasted for more than two hours. When it was over, Benedict stood up, shook hands with his old teammate Jimmy Ahern and wished me the best of luck.

"I don't know John Thompson," he said. "I played with him a long time ago and I didn't really know him then. But I know where he came from. I know the kind of education he got. And I know what I see now and what I hear and read. I hope you find the answers you're looking for. I hope you'll tell the truth."

On that summer night not so long ago, Jim Benedict raised questions about John Thompson that many people, both passionate and casual followers of college basketball, have been asking about the Georgetown coach for years.

And over the course of researching this book, I learned that some of his former players and close associates also wonder about John Thompson.

Craig Shelton, a player who led Georgetown to the brink of that Final Four appearance in 1980, wonders why his former coach never returned his phone calls when Shelton wanted to come back to school to finish the degree he never got.

Several other players and former friends wonder why Thompson never lifted a finger to help them find better jobs, never used his considerable influence to help them advance professionally in basketball or their various careers, seemed to turn his back on them once they were out of his program and out of school, once they could no longer be of any help to him. Said one former player, "He always told us not to let the white man exploit you, but some of us think it wasn't the white man who exploited us, it was John Thompson."

Many people who knew him back when will tell you that Thompson has changed for the worse. A childhood friend now describes him as "one of the most paranoid, duplicitous guys I've ever seen. I personally have never sensed the depth of caring about his kids. He's more about the numbers, the stats and the money, and that's it."

Greed, power and control are what John Thompson is all about, some say, and money is always a motivating factor. In 1983, a game matching Patrick Ewing against Virginia's Ralph Sampson was televised on a cable outlet rather than network television, in part because Thompson asked for and received a $50,000 perk from a soft-drink company sponsor that paid him to do a few clinics as an inducement to give his approval to the cable deal. It wasn't illegal, just avaricious.

And power and control were the central issues in his decision not to leave Georgetown in 1990 to take over as general manager of the Denver Nuggets, a deal that would have provided $6 million and partial ownership after five years. In truth, the money was not all that much more than he could make at Georgetown over the same time span. Still, when he was told he would have to inform the team's ownership of any major trade or acquisition beforehand—the better to satisfy the shareholders of a publicly held corporation that owned 62 percent of the team—he decided to pull out and reject the offer. At Georgetown, John Thompson answered to no one.

One Denver executive involved in the discussions with Thompson described him as a "nasty, arrogant son of a bitch." Then he went on to say he had no doubt that Thompson also could have turned his franchise around because that's exactly what the job would have required. "He would have put his nose to the grindstone and outworked everyone, just like he does now," said the executive. "That was never an issue."

There are so many questions about the man, and so many contradictions.

Who is John Thompson and how did he get this way? Is he the compassionate coach who once seemed to hug a player to death after the pour soul threw a pass to an opponent that cost his team a national championship, or the out-of-control maniac hit with three straight technical fouls and tossed from a nationally televised game against Syracuse during the 1989–90 season for screaming at the referees?

Is he the man North Carolina's Dean Smith describes as "a great coach, a better human being," or a racist bully who intimidates anyone who dares get in his way and teaches a confrontational style of basketball?

Is he a master manipulator of the media who shouts, "Racism, racism," whenever hc comes under criticism, or a man who simply believes in his own privacy and the sanctity of The Team?

Critics ask, If he's such a stickler about education, why does he allow so many marginal students into his program?

Critics ask, If he's so concerned about the plight of blacks in Amer ca, why isn't he more visible and more active in his own community, and why does he steer all his business toward a predominantly white sports management firm that also represents most Georgetown players once they turn professional?

Critics, ironically, ask why his teams are predominantly black. Why his teams play so rough-and-tumble. Why he insists on such a soft early-season schedule. Why he won't play the top Division I programs in his own Washington area, ending years of traditional rivalries in the early 1980s. Yet the answers are obvious.

Why do so many people admire John Thompson?

Why do so many others get hot at the mention of his name?

Is he a cut above the average, or just another greedy capitalist coach in the swamp that is big-time collegiate sports?

Is he St. John, or a devil of a coach?

Does anyone really know John Thompson?

When I started looking for answers, I thought I did. Now I know a good deal more.

The tall young boy and a few of his friends from the neighborhood have come to the playground looking for a game. As they walk toward the basketball court, the white man who supervises the park blocks their path. No one, least of all John Thompson, forgets.

FOR THE LAST NINE YEARS OF HER LIFE, ANNA THOMPSON lived with her youngest child and his family, first in the modest little house John Thompson owned near Catholic University, then in the big place in Northwest Washington that was given to her son, the basketball coach, by alumni of Georgetown in 1980 as an inducement to keep him from moving to another school.

What must Anna Thompson have thought about that house at 4881 Colorado Avenue, with its high ceilings and big rooms and a swimming pool out back, nestled in an exclusive section of the city? The school had paid $350,000 for the house, then rented it to the coach before transferring it to his name two years later in lieu of a pay raise. It was the kind of house Anna Thompson knew very well back when John, the youngest of her four children, was growing up, and up and up.

For $5 a day, until she was in her fifties and went back to school to learn how to be a practical nurse, she had cleaned houses like that all over town, toiling as a domestic to help her husband, John, make ends meet, to buy food for John junior and his three big sisters, to put clothes on their backs and educate them in the strict Catholic values they had always believed in. John senior and Anna had moved to Washington from their roots in southern Maryland. John senior had been taken out of elementary school to work in the fields to support his own family, and never did learn how to read or write. Later on, he would ask people to read to him out loud from the newspapers about his son's exploits on the basketball court. He would also tell his son, "Boy, you get an education because that's something the white man can never take away from you."

Anna Thompson was lucky. She was allowed to go to school and had earned a teaching certificate from a two-year college. But when the family moved to Washington in the 1930s, she found out she couldn't teach in the District of Columbia schools without a four-year degree. And so she did the best she could, washing and ironing and dusting in the big houses of the fancy people on the other side of Rock Creek Park, the city's forested dividing line, where black folks only ventured to go to work.

Washington was a sleepy southern town when John Thompson was born on September 2, 1941. Segregation was still the order of the day even in the nation's capital; blacks used separate rest rooms and water fountains and had their own beaches. At Griffith Stadium, Washington's two major-league franchises, the baseball Senators and football Redskins, were both lily-white operations owned by men who employed blacks to sweep the bleachers and clean the toilets, but couldn't even dream of having a black man run the bases or the football, let alone coach the team.

It did not take long for young John Thompson to learn about life in a segregated society. When the family traveled back to southern Maryland to visit relatives and old friends, he could never understand why he had to sit in the back of the Catholic church, or wait until the white folks took Communion before he had his turn.

"Don't get caught up in that," Anna Thompson told her son. "The world can be very mean sometimes. Just go ahead and ignore it. The people who run the church aren't the same as what is being taught in the church."

Thompson was asked once how his parents explained segregation to him. "Life was explained to me in a limited fashion," he said. "You are young and black and growing up in a segregated situation, you learn not to expect certain things. . . . As you grew older and as you expanded your views and your education, you became very puzzled and angry by a lot of that. My parents did talk about it, but they didn't harp on it."

By all accounts, Thompson's parents didn't have much time to harp on it. They both put in long, hard hours. John senior was out of the house at 5:00 A.M. most mornings and went off to his job at a tile factory, his hands hard and callused from working all day with ceramic and marble. He also was a skilled mechanic, and he took great pride in knowing that the white man who owned the tile factory trusted him with the office keys.

George Leftwich, who played basketball with John years later at Archbishop John Carroll High School, recalled that "Mr. Thompson was kind of an old-fashioned guy. He was real quiet, and when he did say something, he talked real fast—'Gottagettowork, gottagonow'—like a lot of black men of that generation. When I knew them, he was an old man. John's mother reminded me of my own grandmother—very nice, very friendly, very plain. People knew when you went to my grandmother's house, she'd always open the door, let you in and give you a cup of coffee or a doughnut. There was always a cherry pie waiting to be eaten. Mrs. Thompson was just like that. They were good people."

As John grew up, the family lived at first in the Anacostia section of Washington, in a segregated public housing project. But they stayed all over town in the 1940s and '50s, at one point moving in with Anna's sister Mary in her house on W Street. John slept on a couch in the kitchen.

There was not much money to go around—years later Thompson said he realized looking back that his parents never bought anything for themselves, but that he did not feel deprived. There was always food on the table, there were always secondhand clothes to wear, there was always a gift on his birthday and Christmas. One year, he was given a reconditioned toolbox at Christmas because he liked to fix things around Aunt Mary's house. She started calling him Mr. Fix It. "If Fix It can't fix it, it can't be fixed," she'd say. When John took that toolbox into the backyard, he noticed that the paint started coming off on his hands. "Honey," Anna Thompson told him, "Santa just must have painted it."

John and his father got great pleasure in going to the ballpark. In fact, baseball was John's favorite sport as a child, and he would beg his father to take him to the games. He was a big fan of the Cleveland Indians, if only because they had broken the color line in the American League by signing Larry Doby. Black people pulled for the Indians, just as they had pulled for Jackie Robinson and the Brooklyn Dodgers, and for Joe Louis any time he fought.

Living in the Anacostia projects presented some inane complications. There were so many rules. For one, families had to keep their income below a certain level in order to qualify for the low-income housing. When Anna Thompson left for work, she'd tell her children not to talk to strangers, and, more important, to tell anyone who asked that she'd just gone out to the store for groceries. She didn't want anyone to know she was making extra money, because that sort of information had a way of getting back to the housing authority people, and there were waiting lists to get an apartment.

Once, John Thompson and his father wanted to put a fence up behind their apartment to grow a little grass and a few flowers. "The man from the office came and told us to take it down because it was against the rules," Thompson once recalled. "Sometimes when people talk about how bad it looks around the projects—no grass and everything—they don't realize how it is."

John was sent off to Catholic schools as a child, and he struggled almost from the start. He had difficulty reading and was initially labeled a "slow learner." He also had a mischievous streak, probably talked too much in class and was generally disruptive.

The nuns at Our Lady of Perpetual Help elementary school separated the children by grade and behavior pattern. Bright children, or those perceived to be bright, sat in the front row, the gold star row. In the middle were the blue star rows for the average kids. In the back of the room they put a picture of an infant on one chair and called it the baby row. That's where John Thompson often sat, and he didn't like it much. Anna Thompson liked it less when he was sent home for lipping off or sassing a nun.

Some parents allowed their children to be whacked by their teachers. "I learned the Lord's Prayer because a nun took a ruler and beat the hell out of me," Thompson said years later. "That ruler had steel on the edge of it, and I quickly learned the prayer.

"I didn't like them, and they didn't like me," Thompson said. "I remember . . . one day when one of the nuns came in the morning after a big boxing match and said, 'The black one won.' That was a long time before black was beautiful."

Finally, the nuns at Our Lady of Perpetual Help were convinced that John Thompson was mildly retarded, and at the end of the fifth grade he was asked not to return the following year. "Don't you believe that," John's sister Mary told Anna Thompson. "That boy is not retarded. Don't let them convince you of that."

One nun did tell Anna Thompson that her son did well on tests when someone read him the material, and that gave her some hope. She was a strong, determined woman, and was not about to give up on her baby boy. Instead, she made a few inquiries and got him enrolled in one of Washington's first reading clinics, paying for a private tutor out of the family's meager earnings. She also read to him at home, acting out the parts as her son sat there transfixed by the words and the stories. And whenever he became discouraged, she repeated a little poem to him, one she must have recited a thousand different times.

You can do anything you think you can.
It's all in the way you view it.
It's all in the start you make, young man.
You must feel that you're going to do it.

Rejected by the Catholic school system, John Thompson wound up in the still-segregated Washington public schools. He was put in the sixth-grade classroom of a veteran teacher named Sametta Wallace Jackson, a tall woman who loved her job and talked of things the young boy had never even heard of. Opera, for heaven's sake.

"She came into the classroom the first day and put her big foot up on the desk," Thompson once said. "She told everyone to laugh—one time—and never to mention her feet again." She had other rules. "Good odor or no odor," she told her pupils. "Good hair or no hair, comb it or cut it off." Sametta Jackson also took an interest in John Thompson. She noticed that he had some vision problems, perhaps an explanation for his reading difficulties. She worked closely with the boy, teaching him to read and trying to convince him of his own self-worth. Still, at the end of the first year, he did not meet the public school standard for moving on to the seventh grade.

Even then, John was taller than most of the children in his class, and Sametta Jackson knew it would be difficult for him to repeat the sixth grade without being teased and taunted by his schoolmates. On days when the class practiced for graduation ceremonies, she sent him out of the room on one errand or another so that he would not be embarrassed. John Thompson repeated the sixth grade, and between the tutoring and the individual attention Sametta Jackson gave him, he learned how to read and write and finally moved on to junior high school and the seventh grade. Years later, he went out to visit her in a nursing home and thanked her for what she had done for him.

At about the same time he was catching on at school, John Thompson was also developing in another area. Tall and skinny in grade school, he was shooting up at an astounding rate. By the age of twelve he was already 6 feet tall, and when he got to Brown Junior High School in Northeast Washington not far from his home, coaches and classmates began to take notice. At age thirteen he stood 6-foot-6. His baseball glove soon was pushed to the back of the closet and basketball began to take on new importance. Being the tallest meant usually being picked in playground games, and while the skinny and somewhat awkward boy could hardly be described as a polished player, word was spreading around town about the big kid who could touch the rim without hardly trying. Soon, John Thompson was becoming a playground regular on the asphalt courts of Spingarn High School, and was even being chosen to play by some of the older boys in their after-school games.

Bob Grier, who went on to work with Thompson as an assistant coach at Georgetown in the mid-1970s, recalled seeing him for the first time. "Some of us older guys were playing and then somebody quit and we saw John lying there, noticed how long he was and asked him to play," Grier said. "One of the guys there was a little heavy, so John, who was a pretty sharp kid in those days, said he'd guard the fat kid. That fat kid, who wasn't as slow as he looked, proceeded to take John to the cleaners."

The playgrounds provided one outlet, and Thompson also soon became a regular at Police Boys Club No. 2 on First Street in Northwest Washington. The club had been started in 1951 when the neighborhood had one of the highest rates of juvenile delinquency in the city. The first supervisor was Jabbo Kenner, a former prizefighter and a man who cared deeply about "all my kids." There were hundreds of them over the years who showed up after school every day to pound the ball off the battered wooden court, to play in winter and summer leagues and to take the sage advice of the man they all called Mr. Jabbo. There were others who helped him coach and teach, including Bill Butler and Julius Wyatt, both of whom still work with children around Washington and point to John Thompson as their pride and joy. To this day, Thompson occasionally drops in at the club to see his old friends, and to offer his own advice or a coaching tip to the kids of No. 2.

The Boys Club also was the training ground for some of the city's finest young players. A few years ahead of John Thompson, a youngster named Elgin Baylor played at No. 2, as did another future Hall of Famer, David Bing. Both went on to star in high school, college and the National Basketball Association; both were products of the same streets that spawned Thompson and so many more talented players.

Baylor was known on the playground of Washington as Rabbit, and he could do things with a basketball that his peers could only dream about. Long before Julius Erving and Michael Jordan redefined the game, Baylor left them gasping with his midair show, his dazzling moves and his finger-roll touch. When word got out that Baylor was about to show up at a certain playground around town, crowds quickly gathered to see him play. Baylor's battles with other playground legends in the 1950s are talked about by old-time Washingtonians to this day.

One of those players was James "Sleepy" Harrison, a college dropout but a Ph.D. in playground ball. "They called me the best in the city," he once said. "And I don't mean to be bragging when I say it. I taught John, and I taught Dave Bing, and Austin Carr, and a lot of others. We were always tough on those kids. We didn't give them nothing. We made them appreciate losing so they would know how great it was to win. I guess you could say I was a stepping-stone to these guys' success."

So was Jabbo Kenner.

"Mr. Jabbo was always good to us kids, too," Thompson told *Sports Illustrated* in 1984. "Sent some of his boys from the club up here to play ball for me. I'd have to tell him, 'Mr. Jabbo, you can't bring tuna fish and coats to these kids now. They're NCAA athletes.' 'John,' he'd say, 'I don't care nothing about no NCAA. These my boys. They poor boys. Don't have nothing.' And he'd drive his old wreck of a station wagon right on campus. Park it behind the gym. 'Where's my boys? Where's my children?' Have some of every damned thing packed in the back. Canned food. Bread. Shoes. Don't know where in the world he'd collect all that stuff. Brought a pair of pimp shoes once. Heels six inches high with some kind of fluid in them and little goldfish swimming around. I said, 'Hey, Mr. Jabbo. These are pimp shoes. Where'd you find these things?' 'Got to take care of my kids, John. Where you hiding my boys?' "

For Big John Thompson, there was no place to hide. He played on the team at Brown Junior High for a coach, Kermit Trigg, who "taught us that athletics is supposed to be more than recreation or recognition," Thompson said. "It was the form of security I needed. He gave us an identity through athletics, and he said you have to do things other than athletics to be successful."

Cutty Mitchell, who now owns a prosperous Washington dry cleaning business and also helped coach Thompson at Brown, recalled that "when I first saw him, he was extremely tall. There was no question he'd play basketball. We had a lot of big boys; our team even without John probably would have averaged about six-two a man. His last year there we were undefeated in the city, and there were many high school coaches around town who were interested in John. They'd be calling me up on the phone. In junior high, I'd have to say John was pretty much a loner. He came and went by himself. But he spent a lot of time on that playground."

Frank Bolden, a longtime basketball coach in the D.C. school system, first noticed John Thompson at a track meet when the youngster was in the ninth grade. "We were at McKinley High School and John jumped over the bar at about five-seven with no effort at all," Bolden said. "He had no technique. There was no western roll, no flip that they use now. He just jumped that bar like he was going over a fence. He was maybe six-eight or six-nine. I was coaching at Cardozo High School then, and I thought to myself, I'd like to get that boy on my team."

Other coaches noticed, too. One of them was Ben Smith, a track coach at Archbishop John Carroll, a Catholic high school near Catholic

University. Smith also worked as a teacher in the D.C. public schools. One day he mentioned Thompson to Bob Dwyer, the basketball coach at Carroll, and Dwyer encouraged him to ask Thompson to come over to the school for an interview.

Dwyer was an insurance man who had coached the team at Carroll on a part-time basis since 1952 and was regarded as one of the finest coaches in the city. He also was one of the first in the mostly white Catholic League to play a black public school, and he began recruiting black athletes to Carroll long before it became a widespread practice in the city. He wasn't so much a crusader as he was a realist. The black players constantly worked at the game; their skills seemed at a much higher level.

The year before, Dwyer had brought in Tom Hoover, a 6-foot-9, 260-pound man-child who had been declared ineligible by the D.C. schools because he was attending Dunbar High School but living in another school's district. Hoover entered Carroll on scholarship, and the day Ben Smith brought John Thompson over to visit Carroll, Dwyer asked the young player to take the floor and go one-on-one with Hoover.

"Hoover was a much more physical guy, rougher, tougher," Dwyer said. "But Hoover didn't try to rough him up. I just sat there and watched them. It was obvious this kid Thompson was going to be a good ballplayer. He was well coordinated for his age. I said to him, 'Would you like to come here, John?' He said, 'I'm not going to say yes or no, I'll think it over, but I kind of think I would.' I told him I could tell him one thing: 'If you come here, you'll be an all-American high school player, I'm sure of that. If you work. It all depends on you.' And he assured me that he would work."

Dwyer had a few anxious moments when he found out another Catholic school, St. John's, coached by the wily Joe Gallagher, also was making a strong pitch to land Thompson. When Dwyer got wind of it, he sent Ben Smith back to Thompson's house to talk to his parents.

"Ben had gotten to know the family, and they trusted him," Dwyer said. "So he went over to see Thompson and his mother and father and he came back a few days later and said to me, 'Mr. Dwyer, I don't care if Casey Stengel goes over there, John Thompson is coming to Carroll.' "

Thompson's tuition—about $200 a year—was paid out of a fund Dwyer had wangled from the archdiocese to allow him to go after some of the city's best black athletes. And when Thompson arrived at Carroll in the fall of 1957, he found himself surrounded by some startling talent. There was Hoover, a rugged rebounder and physical specimen who was the first player in the Catholic League who could dunk a basketball.

There was Edward "Monk" Malloy, a young scholar with a deadly shooting touch. There was George Leftwich, who had transferred over from McKinley Tech, another inner-city public school. Like Hoover, he'd been declared ineligible at Dunbar because he didn't live in the district. He spent the second semester of his freshman year at McKinley Tech but was not doing very well academically. A friend from the neighborhood was a senior at Carroll and recommended the school to Leftwich, whose father also liked the idea that his son would get more discipline at Carroll, even if the family was not Catholic.

"When I went for the interview to get in," said Leftwich, now the head basketball coach at the University of the District of Columbia, "the priest asked me why I wanted to go to school there. I told him I felt I wasn't getting certain things in the public schools, that I wanted a better education. After the interview, I happened to see John, and I asked him if the guy had asked him the same questions. John said yeah, that he told him he wanted to go there to play basketball. John says to me, 'That was a very big mistake. That is not what he wanted to hear.' That priest definitely left an impression on both of us.

"His name was Father McDonnell, and he was the dean of discipline. The man took his job seriously. He never smiled in all the time I knew him there. And he rendered harsh judgment and swift punishment."

Life was not easy at Carroll for the young black basketball players, nor was it particularly pleasant for blacks in the city. Though American schools had been ordered to integrate by the Supreme Court in 1954, Washington was still racially divided. "If you were black and crossed Rock Creek Park, you were stopped by the police," Leftwich said. "If you didn't work there, you didn't belong there. On the black side of town, my dad drove a cab. There were white cab companies and black cab companies. The white company was Diamond Cab, and people would always joke that "this guy was as hungry as a Diamond on U Street [a street in the heart of the black community]."

Leftwich recalled that there were occasional racial incidents in the predominantly white, working-lower-middle-class school. "One day one of the white students called me a nigger," he said. "I had not been around many whites before that—this was in the tenth grade, in 1958. I remember wondering to myself, How do I handle this? I knew that if you got in a fight in school, they'd kick you out, and if I got kicked out, my old man would go crazy. But I couldn't just let this guy get in my face. So I pushed him, hoping that people would come and break it up. Fortunately that's what happened, and Father McDonnell wasn't too far behind."

The priest, it seems, was everywhere. "He'd whack you or send you to jug [detention] after school," Leftwich said. "You'd have to just stand there, or clean the erasers and wash the blackboards. We weren't allowed to wear khakis or jeans to school, not even to games. Father McDonnell would go to games and go through the stands checking your pants. I'd stay in the locker room after games for thirty-forty minutes just to make sure I wouldn't get caught."

On the basketball court, there were other problems. Because Carroll was starting three black players in an era when most predominantly white schools had none, the team was often the target of abuse from the stands, especially when it began winning regularly, dominating most opponents.

"I was sitting on the bench at the University of Maryland when Hoover was playing and I'm telling you the stuff we heard coming out of those stands professional athletes don't have to take," Dwyer said. "People screaming at us. I'd get threatening calls at home. My wife was threatened. The kids were getting the same calls before games. One year we played Cardozo [a predominantly black public school] and Leftwich, Hoover and Thompson got calls from people telling them what would happen to them if they won the ball game."

During Thompson's sophomore and junior years, most of the abuse was directed toward Hoover, a year older. Unlike Thompson, who was shy and somewhat introverted, Hoover was a gregarious and emotional player, a body banger who never in his life backed down from a confrontation on or off the court.

"Hoover was the greatest high school rebounder I've ever seen," Dwyer said. "He really helped John a lot. John was pretty timid underneath, but practicing against Hoover every day toughened him up. Hoover was a street kid, in trouble all the time, but he didn't lead Thompson down the same path. Whenever I would mention Hoover's troubles, John would get a sly smile."

Monk Malloy, now a priest and the president of the University of Notre Dame, recalled an incident after a football game. Hoover, still in uniform, was being heckled by a local bully. "With one punch, Tom decked him," Malloy said. Not long after that incident, Hoover was in Malloy's neighborhood dressed in a coat and tie and saw Malloy playing basketball. He went over to the court and "all of a sudden," Malloy said, "I see the same bully coming up. 'You want to take me on now when you don't have any equipment on?' he says to Tom. Tom gives me his jacket and tie and with five punches just completely mauls him. Finally the kid gets up and says, 'You beat me fair and square,' and off he went."

Tom Hoover went on to play briefly in the NBA and now works for the New York State Athletic Commission. He lives in Manhattan and still considers Thompson one of his closest friends. "I was a little more outgoing than the rest of those guys," he said. "Hell, there were people in our own school who didn't want black kids there. I can remember a conversation between a priest at Carroll and Bob Dwyer. The priest told him he shouldn't have that many black kids on his team. When we played, people in the stands would spit on us and yell, 'Nigger.' Players would hold us and punch us, they'd spit at me trying to provoke me into throwing a punch so they could get me out of the game. Sometimes other players would call me a nigger to my face. John always tried to calm me down, and George Leftwich did the same.

"John was a good player in high school. He could score, and I took care of the rest of it. I'd played football, so it wasn't hard for me to get in there and mix it up. John was finesse. I was brute strength."

And Monk Malloy, like Hoover a year ahead of Thompson, helped in other ways. He was a born leader "and in every sense of the word he kept us together as a team," Leftwich recalled. Malloy was known as the Mayor of Turkey Thicket, a playground near his house, because no one was allowed into games there unless he gave his permission. Malloy came from a white middle-class family—his father worked for the D.C. Transit system and often would help drive members of the team in his car whenever they traveled to a game or tournament out of the area.

"Monk's father was always around," Thompson said years later. "I usually went to the games in his car—he always drove, we didn't have a team bus. It was Monk's father who helped me make the adjustment to an environment that was new to me."

There was a memorable trip to a game in Philadelphia. "In Delaware, we stopped at a place and they refused to serve us—only the white players," Monk Malloy said. "We sat there and sat there and finally the manager came over and said that he would serve myself and my father but the other ones would have to get their food outside. . . . I never forgot that. I was so offended—these were my friends." Ed Malloy, Sr., made an indelible impression on Monk's black teammates when he marched them all out of the restaurant, hungry or not. "My father had a real sense of anger about that kind of treatment and the embarrassment since these were my friends," Monk Malloy said. "They didn't make much of it, we didn't talk much about it, but it was a reminder of the times we were in."

Monk and Leftwich became best friends, often sharing meals at each other's homes. Monk Malloy also recalled going over to John Thompson's house more than occasionally, and being welcomed with open arms. Often in the summer, the friends would wind up traveling to various playgrounds around the city in search of competition.

"Leftwich would call Monk, Monk called me, someone would pick us up and we'd go," said Billy Barnes, a sixth man at Carroll during Thompson's senior year. "Sometimes we'd hitchhike to games. John came with us a few times. Occasionally we'd go to Chevy Chase Playground because Red Auerbach would bring some of his guys down from the Celtics. I'd be lucky to get in the games, I was so small. There'd be great games when Elgin Baylor showed up. Nobody could check Elgin. White guys showed up, black guys, it didn't matter. In basketball, there were no racial barriers. If you were good enough, you played, and as long as you won, you stayed on the court. The only thing you had to watch out for was where you went for a soda after the games."

In the summer between his sophomore and junior years, Thompson was told by Dwyer that his game, and the team, would be helped if he could become a better outside shooter. Leftwich recalled that Thompson would go to a playground every day that summer and shoot virtually every time he touched the ball, much to the chagrin of his teammates. "John didn't care," Leftwich said. "He had a practice plan, and that's how he was going to do it. He'd shoot so much his team would just quit on him and he'd come over to the sideline and say, 'Need four more, anybody want to play?' "

All that practice definitely paid off. In Thompson's sophomore season, the young Carroll Lions were 31–5. They lost the city championship game to Frank Bolden's Cardozo team, then lost in the Knights of Columbus tournament final at Georgetown to Archbishop Molloy of New York City before winning the prestigious Eastern States Catholic Invitational Tournament at Newport, Rhode Island, to end the season. The loss to Molloy would be their last to a high school team until after Thompson and Leftwich graduated in 1960.

In Thompson's junior season, Carroll may well have fielded one of the greatest high school basketball teams of all time. Hoover and Thompson dominated down low, Leftwich ran the offense from the point and Malloy bombed away from the outside when teams tried to deny passes to the bigger men underneath. The fifth man was Walt Skinner, a defensive specialist and a decent passer who also made significant scoring contributions. That year, Carroll won all 30 of its games against high school opposition and split 4 games with college freshman teams, laying the groundwork for a 55-game winning streak, a Washington-area record that still stands. Hoover, Thompson and Left-wich were named first-team all-metropolitan by the local papers that season, and Malloy was second-team.

"It was tough knowing you had to play a team like that," said Joe Gallagher, who is still the St. John's coach. "The first time we played them, we must have gotten beat by fifty. The next time, I held the ball on them. People were booing and hooting, but I didn't care. I wanted to give my kids a chance and at least not get embarrassed. Thompson was a pretty good player for his size. For a guy that big, he was not that tough, not a physical player at all. It seems strange that a guy who projects such a strong, hard-nosed image now would not be that way as a player."

"We just rolled over people that junior year," Leftwich recalled. "Nobody really came close. I can remember the Gonzaga team cele-brating because they had only lost by sixteen. I remember hearing them cheering in their locker room."

Monk Malloy still recalls that season as a special time. "One of the reasons we got a lot of notoriety was that we were, in a sense, a symbol of the hopes of the city to show that integration could work," he said. "It was real clear to me the press tried to make a lot of the fact that my senior year three blacks and two whites started; the year before that it was four blacks and one white, and the same in John's senior year. But we were successful and we had a positive image as a team. We shared the glory."

The next year, though Malloy had gone off to play at Notre Dame and Hoover had taken his large body to Villanova, it was more of the same, with Thompson taking on Hoover's rebounding responsibilities and Leftwich called upon to add more points on offense. A sophomore named John Austin, another fine shooter, also transferred to the school (though he would eventually transfer from Carroll to nearby DeMatha), and he later became the first black player to enroll at Boston College.

Austin and Thompson knew each other from the neighborhood. A few years later, when Austin became a Catholic, John Thompson, Jr., was listed as his godfather. Austin's girlfriend also was friendly with a young lady who attended Sacred Heart Academy, a small all-girl Cath-olic school. Her name was Gwen Twitty, and soon after they were introduced, John and Gwen were an item. Like Thompson, she was shy and somewhat introverted, and she also was a serious student. A friend who knows them both said, "They were like an old married couple right from the start. They were so alike it was almost scary." They went together through high school and college, Gwen often traveling to New

York and Philadelphia to watch him play, and were married at Gwen's family church, St. Gabriel's, after Thompson's first year with the Boston Celtics in the summer of 1965.

In the opener of the 1959–60 Carroll High School season, the Lions rolled over Chamberlain High, 71–41. They won their next game 71–31 over Anacostia, and then defeated the Georgetown freshmen, 88–62. In the 7th game of the season, Carroll beat the Villanova freshmen by 4, and 7 games later the Lions routed a talented Maryland freshman team, 95–72, a team they would beat again, by 4 points, in their last regular-season game. Their closest call of the season came in the finals of the annual Knights of Columbus tournament in a packed gym on the Georgetown campus. That tournament always attracted some of the best Catholic schools from up and down the East Coast and occasionally even the Midwest. In the championship game the Lions were going for their 51st straight victory, but they were having difficulty with St. Catherine's, a team from Racine, Wisconsin. With Carroll trailing by a point late in the fourth quarter, Leftwich made a long jump shot from the top of the key after a pass from the corner by Walt Skinner with only four seconds left on the clock. Carroll won, and The Streak went on. "I have a picture of it," Leftwich said. "Any time I get down, I look at it."

When the season ended, Carroll held a fistful of records. They had won 55 straight against all competition, including college freshman teams. For the three years Thompson and Leftwich had started, Carroll was 103–8 against all comers, 86–3 against high school teams. They had won the Washington Catholic League title three straight years, the city championship twice, the Knights of Columbus tournament twice, and the Eastern States Catholic Invitational Tournament in Newport, Rhode Island, three times. Leftwich and Thompson both were named to the all-metropolitan team, and both were selected by *Scholastic* magazine as high school all-Americans as well, two of the top twenty players in the country.

The little boy who could barely read a sentence in the fifth grade had made himself into a student-athlete. A statistic more meaningful than his scoring average showed that John Thompson had also been forty-eighth in a class of almost three hundred, and was now being called and contacted by coaches eager to get him to continue his education—and, of course, play basketball—at colleges all across America.

Anna Thompson had been right: "You can do anything you think you can. . . ."

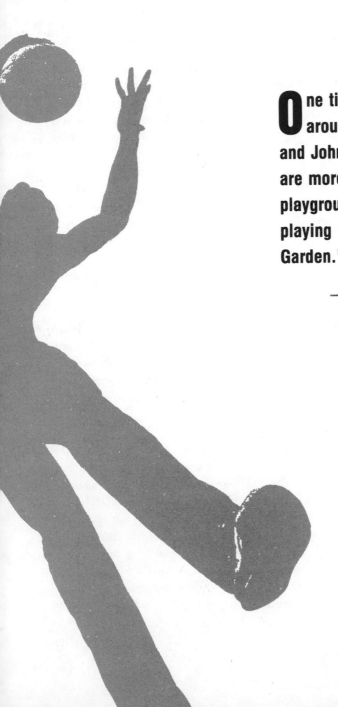

One time we were walking around black Philadelphia and John said to me, 'There are more great players on the playgrounds than there are playing in Madison Square Garden.' "

—*Boston mayor Ray Flynn,*
John Thompson's teammate
at Providence College

WHEN FATHER THOMAS AQUINAS COLLINS WASN'T TEACHING the young seminarians at the Dominican House of Studies in Northeast Washington during the late 1950s, he was pursuing another of his lifelong passions. A biblical scholar who had graduated from Providence College in 1934, Father Collins also was a self-proclaimed "basketball nut" who spent many of his precious few off-hours attending high school and college games in the Washington area.

In the winter of 1958, he bought a ticket to the Knights of Columbus basketball tournament at Georgetown University, a showcase event for some of the East Coast's finest Catholic school teams. While teaching at Providence before his posting to Washington, Father Collins had become good friends with Joe Mullaney, the Providence basketball coach, and was always on the lookout for players who might be interested in attending the little Dominican college with the up-and-coming program.

Father Collins wanted to take another look at a youngster named Tom Folliard, the nephew of *Washington Post* White House correspondent Eddie Folliard and a promising player at Gonzaga High School in D.C. By the time the tournament had ended, Father Collins also was intrigued by another player, a tall, skinny sophomore named John Thompson who played center on the Archbishop John Carroll runner-up team.

Father Collins got on the phone to his friend Joe Mullaney. "I've got two kids who might help you. I want to give you their names," Father Collins told Mullaney. Back in the 1950s, much of the recruiting of high school athletes went on this way—word of mouth from alumni in far-flung cities with an interest in enhancing their schools' athletic fortunes. There were none of the present-day recruiting services, no tout sheets or lists of the top players that appear regularly in national and local newspapers. Mullaney did all his recruiting himself, often leaving practice at five thirty in the evening and driving a few hours to catch a high school game in Hartford or Boston, then driving back in the dead of night. "Between scouting and recruiting, I went through more cars than you can imagine," Mullaney said. "Those first few years at Providence, I did it all myself, and so did everyone else. A recruiting budget? I was happy when they paid for the gas."

When he heard about John Thompson, Mullaney asked Father Collins to represent him and make the initial contact, and the priest was more than happy to oblige. Father Collins watched Thompson play several games the following season, and one day he introduced himself to the player and his high school coach, Bob Dwyer, and asked if he could stop by Thompson's house to visit with him and his parents.

"I was warmly received in their home," Father Collins said. "I was very impressed by what I saw. This was not what you would call a ghetto situation. The house was well furnished, immaculate. I remember his mother told me they had lived in a Dominican parish at one point, and that was a good sign for me. I didn't stay that long. I just wanted them to know they had someone in Washington they could talk to if they needed advice, and I told them that Mr. Mullaney was interested in John going to Providence when he graduated."

That summer, Father Collins returned to Providence to teach a summer-school course, and he also arranged for John and his mother to visit the campus. Thompson also told Father Collins he was interested in talking to the star of the Providence team, all-American guard Lenny Wilkens. "Since there were so few blacks on campus, I think John really wanted to find out what it would be like for him there, and that's why he wanted to see Lenny," Father Collins said. "They went off and had a nice chat, and then we all met back at Aquinas Hall, the center of gravity on campus. I was sitting there with his mother. When he spoke to her, it was like a little boy talking, quiet, reverential."

"What do you think, Mom?" Thompson asked her. "Do you like it here?"

Anna Thompson definitely liked it there, and while John Thompson made no commitments to attend at that point, Father Collins said he had a good feeling about the school's chances as Thompson prepared for his senior year at Carroll.

At the end of Thompson's final season, the recruiting intensified, particularly from the Catholic schools. Thompson and his fellow high school all-American teammate, George Leftwich, went out and visited their friend, Monk Malloy, one weekend at Notre Dame, but the coach, John Jordan, didn't seem that interested. "If we'd had a lot of enthusiasm from the coaching staff, maybe they would have come," Malloy said, adding that his father always suspected Notre Dame's coolness may have stemmed from a fear of fielding a team with too many blacks on the court.

Jack Ramsay, then the coach at St. Joseph's, came by the house one day and showed the youngster some conditioning workouts with a jump rope. Thompson also was extremely impressed with the assistant coach and head recruiter at St. John's, Lou Carnesecca, but was not enthralled by his visit to New York. By the spring there also were offers from Syracuse, Cincinnati, Boston College and Holy Cross.

But Providence had another advantage that was spelled out to Thompson by Red Auerbach, the shrewd coach of the world champion Boston Celtics.

In those days, the National Basketball Association still had a territorial draft. If a player went to school within fifty miles of an NBA team, that organization had the first right to draft him.

Auerbach had gone to college at George Washington University in Washington and still had a home in the District. Auerbach often came to games at Carroll and sometimes would drop in on practices. He also worked the playgrounds of Washington in the summertime, looking for up-and-coming talent.

"There was a court right across the street from the Avalon Theater on Connecticut Avenue, and all the great college players would show up and play," Auerbach said. "Bill Bradley, Dave Bing, Elgin Baylor. Sure I saw John in high school. He played on the biggest high school team I'd ever seen. I probably talked to him a few times back then. Was I responsible for him going to Providence? I don't think so."

Still, Mullaney believed the Celtic connection was very much in his favor. "To tell you the truth, I thought I was fighting Boston College and Holy Cross, because they were also in the Celtics' territory," he said. "I'm sure Red somehow got the message across to John. I don't know if he told him directly or said, 'Hey, kid, if you ever want to play for the Celtics, you'd better go to a school around Boston.' But I used the pitch myself when I went recruiting. I would tell kids that ought to be a consideration.

"I went down to Washington and visited and met John and his mother and his sister. I wasn't real confident about getting him because we already had a big guy, Jim Hadnot, and I thought that would be my biggest negative. Would he want to come play with Hadnot, who was two years ahead of John? But that didn't seem to bother John. I think the Celtic thing was very important."

And so was the Dominican thing. "When she got on that campus and saw those good old Dominican fathers, I could tell she felt very comfortable and knew that I would be taken care of," Thompson said. That clinched it. In the spring of his senior year, John Thompson announced that Providence College was his school of choice.

When Thompson arrived on campus in the fall of 1960, Providence was a school of about eighteen hundred students, all male. Most of the courses were taught by priests. There were a handful of blacks, almost all athletes, and many of the students commuted from the city and its outlying suburbs. Mullaney, a native New Yorker who arrived at Providence in 1955, had taken over a program with a weak regional schedule, a local high school gym as its home court and a minuscule budget. He immediately began to hit the road recruiting, using the Celtics as a primary selling point, and started to attract some first-rate players. There were two all-American guards, John Egan and Lenny Wilkens, who both went on to play and coach in the NBA and had helped give the program some national stature. The arrival of Hadnot, a black 6-10 high school all-American from Oakland, California, in 1958, "really helped turn the program around," Mullaney said.

There was a Celtic connection involved with Hadnot as well. He had gone to the same Oakland high school that Bill Russell had attended. Russell, the star center for the Celtics, had lived in the same Oakland neighborhood and had dated Hadnot's older sister in high school. When Hadnot's father died, Russell, by then an established professional superstar, told Hadnot's mother he would help her son pick a school and provide some financial aid as well.

In Boston, meanwhile, Russell had befriended one of the Celtics' most loyal followers, a businessman and former basketball referee named Harold Furash. Russell told Furash about Hadnot, and Furash called up Mullaney, who, it turned out, had also played for the Celtics himself in 1950.

"One day I got a call out of the blue from him saying, 'How would you like to have a six-ten player from the same high school Bill Russell went to?' " Mullaney said. "Harold was the Celtics' biggest fan and I'm sure he's thinking, God, I've got to get this kid somewhere around Boston. Anyway, I'm thinking this is all a pipe dream, but Furash calls me and says, 'The kid wants to visit. Will you fly him in from California?'

"Next thing you know, the kid is on a plane and he visits the school, meets some people and decides he likes it. I guess in the back of his mind he's thinking in four years he'll be with the Celtics, too. I didn't even initiate this, and this kid just falls into my lap."

"The Celtics were definitely a factor," Hadnot said. "I knew about the territorial draft. When you're young and cocky, you think you can play anywhere, and it was a dream of mine to play with Bill Russell. He was my idol. Russell also wanted to make sure I could handle the schoolwork. The summer before my freshman year, I lived in his house in Reading, Massachusetts. Three days a week he brought in a nun to tutor me. When school started, on weekends I'd go back to his house. He even built a room for me. My grades were sent there—he checked them out. One time I got a D in American Literature and he campused me the whole next semester. I couldn't leave Providence, I couldn't even go see the Celtics play."

Hadnot was two years ahead of Thompson and they only played together for one season, but they immediately became friends. Hadnot had met Thompson on his campus visit, recalling that he was "a little shy, real quiet, but a guy we all felt would help the program. I knew Tom Hoover, and he had played with Hoover, so we had something in common. Hell, there weren't many blacks there, let alone guys who were six-ten, so we hit it off right away."

Thompson's decision to attend Providence led to great expectations for Mullaney and his program. Like Hadnot, Thompson also was being touted as the next Bill Russell, and when he averaged 32 points for the 20–2 Providence freshmen, that sort of talk only intensified.

Bill Baird, the freshman coach at the University of Rhode Island, gushed to a local newspaper, "No question, that big kid at Providence College [Thompson] stands head and shoulders over the field, and that's no pun and it's not just because he's a big man. A lot of these big boys play to the crowd but not that fellow. He just goes about his business. He comes on the floor to play basketball and lets somebody else take care of the show. . . . There isn't much he can't do when he's in close, around the hoop. And yet there are a lot of things he can do when he is outside. He drives well for a big man. And his jumping and ball handling are good. When Thompson is on his game, there isn't much the opposition can do about it. He should be a terrific player with the Friar varsity."

Another story written at the end of Thompson's freshman season was headlined "P.C. Freshman Has All the Moves" and went on to describe Thompson as "the equal of any collegiate yearling player in the nation. This 19-year-old graduate of Archbishop Carroll has the potential of the well-rounded big man that coaches dream of. . . . His credentials are impressive. He shoots well with either hand, dribbles competently, an uncommon trait among big men; he rebounds with vigor, defends creditably and he's agile. . . . He has given P.C. fans much cause for gleeful shouting and, at the same time, has kept visiting scouts in a dither. There was, for example, an incident in a recent game. Thompson was dribbling up court while being covered by an opponent about 10 inches shorter. As he reached midcourt, he dribbled behind his back, upsetting the composure of the defender. A visiting scout bent over in mock faint. 'Oh, my gosh,' he said, 'that's adding insult to injury.' "

Years later, Thompson would wind up coaching another "next Bill Russell" himself when he recruited and signed Patrick Ewing of Cambridge, Massachusetts, the most dominating big man of his era. Thompson would also say that with the memory of his own painful early experiences at Providence still on his mind he tried to soften the great expectations for Ewing, shielding him from the fans and the media as much as possible to make his life easier.

Despite the presence of Thompson and Hadnot on the 1961–62 team, the Friars struggled all season. Providence fans got a preview in March 1961, when the freshmen and sophomores took on the juniors and seniors and won, 106–103. Thompson scored 40 for the freshmen and Hadnot had 31 for the veterans, while Thompson's freshman teammate, transfer guard Jim Stone, added 21. The headline in the *Pawtuxet Valley Times* of West Warwick, Rhode Island, declared, "Thompson and Stone Will Make Friar Hoopmen Real Powerful Next Season," and the opening paragraph of the story read, "Wait 'til next year." The last paragraph concluded that "with Thompson and Stone moving up to the varsity next season, the Friars certainly will once again be well-represented against the best of college basketball competition."

The local press was not alone in its praise for Providence. The following fall, both the Associated Press and United Press International ranked Providence fifth in the country in their preseason polls, based on the return of Hadnot, a preseason all-American, and Vinnie Ernst, a brilliant junior guard from Jersey City, New Jersey, the most valuable player in the 1961 National Invitation Tournament in New York, which Providence had won. A clever passer and a ball-hawking defender, Ernst would be joined in the backcourt that season by Ray Flynn, another junior with a soft shooting touch. Jim Stone, who had transferred in from Grambling, was the fifth starter, a 6-footer who had a deadly fallaway jump shot and a weak knee that had not fully recovered from major surgery the year before. Ray Flynn once described him as "the best one-legged player in America."

The Friars got off to a fast start, winning their first four games, but they lost a few games and never could become the dominant team everyone expected that year. Thompson was experimenting with contact lenses early on, but eventually he gave up on them. And the twin-towers concept with the two big men was, by Mullaney's own description, "pretty much of a disaster."

"I don't think Joe knew how to handle it," Hadnot said. "He had his own ideas on how to do it, but we never seemed to get in sync. We didn't really run a structured offense—it was kind of free-lance— and we had no real plays to get me and John the ball to utilize our ability. It seemed like we worked ninety percent of the time in practice on defense. Plus, John was having terrible problems with his eyes that year. His eyes were driving him crazy. Finally, Joe decided to abandon that offense, and John didn't play as much. They moved him outside to the corner. I know that bothered him."

"I guess I didn't coach it well enough," Mullaney said. "Later on in the pros I made it work, but not with those two. Neither one of them was really a facing-forward-type player. They were big men who played it down low, and there wasn't enough room for them to operate the way they wanted to. I was a guard coach—that was my strength— and I just could not make it work with those two big men."

Still, the Friars won 20 games and did well enough to get another bid to the NIT, but when they lost in the first round to Temple, it marked the end of a frustrating season for the players, the head coach and their fans, all wondering why two of the best big men in college basketball couldn't lead them to a national championship. "My sophomore year in college was one of the most testing years of my life," Thompson once told the Providence *Journal.*

Still, he could take comfort from other aspects of college life. Gwen Twitty, his high school sweetheart, visited occasionally, and Thompson was making friends all over campus. There had been a nasty incident his freshman year when a white student from Alabama refused to room with Thompson, but the young Alabaman's attitude was not prevalent on campus, at least not toward a talented black athlete who put on few airs and seemed normal enough. Thompson became close friends with Bill Stein, a white walk-on guard from Waterbury, Connecticut, who later became Thompson's roommate and was his chief assistant coach for ten years after Thompson took the head coaching job at Georgetown in 1972.

Thompson also was befriended by another priest, Father James Stephen Murray, who met him one day at a deli a few blocks from campus and struck up a conversation over lunch. Father Murray, a parish priest at a church near campus, was then learning photography. Thompson was also interested, and Father Murray eventually taught him how to use a camera and work in a darkroom.

"He was a smart guy, very articulate," Father Murray said. "He had a good idea of where he wanted to go and what he wanted to do. We'd talk about those kind of things all the time. He was thoughtful, aware of his role as a black man and a black athlete in a place that idolized him. He knew why he was there, and he always tried to keep things in perspective."

There were other friends, one of whom Thompson had met as a high school sophomore when his Carroll team came north to play in the Eastern States Catholic Invitational Tournament, held in Newport. Aaron Slom, a well-to-do printer in Newport, was on the tournament committee and made it a point to get to know as many of the players and their parents as he could. He met Thompson and told him he would be happy playing at Providence, where Slom had been a rarity himself— a Jewish undergraduate.

"At the tournament, we would have a luncheon," Slom said. "That's how we first got friendly, and yes, I tried to convince him to go to Providence. When he decided to come, we were thrilled. My wife, Rita, and our three sons spent a lot of time with John when he was a student here. We'd have him over for dinner. Rita made brownies for the whole team and brought them to the games. He knew that if he wanted to get away from school, he could always come here. He'd come over, we'd eat, talk, and not just about basketball, about everything. When he first came here, he wanted me to take him where blacks lived in Newport, and we did. I don't think he was lonely. I think he just wanted to know how blacks lived in Rhode Island.

"I never gave John a nickel. When he came here, he got to the house any way he could. Sometimes I'd drive him back. He never asked for a thing; he just wanted our friendship. I consider him one of the finest people I have ever known."

Thompson also made friends with another Jewish family—Boston businessman Harold Furash and his wife, Marty. Furash had also spoken to Thompson about attending Providence, and got to know him better through Hadnot. Thompson was a frequent visitor to their home in the Boston suburbs, spending an occasional weekend there as well.

"The Furashes taught me about the white world," Thompson once said. "We argued all the time, but whenever I really needed someone to talk to, they were there. My mother always called them my parents in Boston."

Marty Furash remembered Thompson as "the best listener I ever met. I talk so much I don't remember half of what I say. John would come up to me and say, 'Now, about what you said three weeks ago, I've been thinking about it and . . . ' He hears everything."

And by his junior season he also was beginning to see everything as well. The contact lenses were replaced by regular glasses, and with Hadnot graduated, Mullaney was able to plant Thompson firmly in the middle of his offense and surround him with outstanding players. One of the best was Ernst, now a senior and considered the best guard in the country. He was a cocky little guy who once called Rita Slom on the telephone and announced, "This is the greatest player in the history of Providence College just calling to say hello."

"Ernst is 5-8," wrote Philadelphia sports columnist Stan Hochman in 1962. "He walks around the hotel lobby in a coat with a velvet collar, a white silk scarf cuddled around his throat and leather gloves on his quick hands. He is blond and articulate and his nose looks like it is made out of Silly Putty. People want to take him home and put him on the shelf along with the other knick-knacks."

Ray Flynn, now the mayor of Boston, was not quite so flashy. He was the proverbial gym rat, a native of South Boston who spent countless solitary hours practicing his jump shot on an empty court. "In every city it's the same," he once told an interviewer. "Everybody else likes to walk around and look at the sights. Not me. I just want to go to the gym and work out. I was at the Palestra [in Philadelphia] at ten thirty this morning. I had to help them set up the baskets. Practiced 'til one in the afternoon. They finally had to wash the floor, so they ran me out. . . . It's the same way up at school. I practice five hours a day. I've got my own private ball, and after practice I'll work out by myself until just before supper time."

Ernst and Flynn provided the Friars' flash and firepower. Thompson anchored the middle and Jim Stone and 6-8 Bob Kovalski were on the wings. At the start of the season, Providence was a methodical, deliberate team, with Mullaney preferring to play a halfcourt game and his combination defenses rather than a fast break. The players were not happy about it.

By the sixth game, Stone became so frustrated he decided to quit. The Friars had already lost twice and Stone, used to a run-and-gun style of play in high school and his first year at Grambling, was miserable. "I just got frustrated," he said. "We had all this talent, all this speed, and Mullaney wanted us to keep doing it his way. He wanted us to pass ten-twleve times before you even took a shot. Joe Mullaney wasn't a screamer, but he was stubborn. I can tell you that John was upset about the style, too. He didn't say much, but you knew he didn't like it. John was also a little more mature than I was, and he could deal with it. He did whatever Mullaney wanted him to do. Not me. I walked."

But Thompson talked him out of it. "We were in the cafeteria at Alumni Hall," Stone said. "He said to me, 'You enjoy the game, you've been doing it all your life. Come back to the team, we need you.' He made me think, and I decided to give it another shot. Mullaney asked me back, too. He was telling people I had begged him to put me back on, but that's not true. He just didn't want the other players to know. I didn't go back for Mullaney. I went back because of John."

At midseason the Friars were a respectable 10–4 after a loss to a mediocre St. Bonaventure team. A few days later, the day before they were about to leave for New York to play defending NIT champion Dayton, the players held a meeting without Mullaney to talk about their problems. The coach had been contemplating lineup changes, but after hearing about the meeting and talking to some of the senior players, he decided to stay with his starting five for a few more games.

Providence had problems from the start. At the half they trailed by 8 points, and five minutes into the second half they were down 48–35. "Flynn and I started yelling to John to pass the ball out and start filling the lane on the fast break," Ernst said. From that point on, this was a vastly different Providence basketball team. At one point, the helter-skelter Friars ripped off 19 straight points, and they went on to an 84–72 victory.

"From then on, we were pretty much a running basketball team," Ernst said. "John wasn't the key guy. To tell you the truth, he was not a great college basketball player. I always felt he complained too much. His eyes bothered him, so he got contacts. He complained that there was too much stickum on the ball. Then he complained that we were passing the ball too low to him. He and Mullaney got along okay. They had a couple of beefs, like everyone did. Everybody expected the world of John when he first got there, but when we first started playing with him, we were kind of disappointed. He tried to work at getting better, and he was so much bigger than most guys that he did all right."

With its new fast-break offense, Providence started to dominate.

In the Friars' next game they drubbed a previously unbeaten Niagara team by 24 points. There was an 18-point win over DePaul, and there were wins by 20 over Seton Hall, 19 over St. Joseph's and 23 over Brown in the season finale, the team's 12th straight victory.

The man from the Newark *Star-Ledger* described the Friars' style of play: "A fast-break, Providence style, consists of Jim Stone or John Thompson taking a defensive rebound and whipping the ball out to the little stick of dynamite [Vinnie Ernst]. Summarily, Ray Flynn charges down the left side of the court, Ernst dribbles down the middle and Stone takes the right. All three are fast. All three are tricky. And all three seem to converge on the Providence basket simultaneously. Then Ernst's prestidigitation with a basketball comes into use, and through some form of black magic, he passes one way while looking the other, and his ultimate receiver has a chippie, a basket too easy to miss. Bingo. Two points for Providence, an aspirin for the other team."

In mid-February the Friars accepted their fifth straight bid to the NIT. They had climbed as high as number ten in the Associated Press poll, and there was some talk that perhaps they would have a chance to make the eighteen-team NCAA tournament. But as Mullaney said, "that was a little risky. The NCAA had a small field and had to take the conference champions from all over the country. We were an independent and there was no guarantee we would get a bid. They didn't make their decision until early March, and by then the NIT was filled. Our fans loved the NIT. It was an easy trip to New York and people made a big weekend out of it. Back then, the NIT had a lot of prestige, and nobody really considered it a comedown."

The New York papers were filled with stories about the tournament teams. The players spent almost a week in the big city, were given souvenir watches and other gifts and were treated like royalty. Madison Square Garden, back then the Mecca of college basketball, was filled for almost every session.

Certainly that was the case in Providence's first game, a 106–96 victory over a University of Miami team that featured a crew-cut sophomore named Rick Barry. Thompson picked up his fourth personal foul less than a minute into the second half, but Mullaney never pulled him from the game until Thompson finally fouled out with 4:04 remaining and his team comfortably ahead. Flynn scored 38, Stone 26 and Thompson 17, while Ernst handed out 11 assists. Barry managed only 14 points and was involved in the game's critical play: With Miami trailing by 4 with less than two minutes remaining, Barry fouled Flynn, his fifth of the game. Knowing he was out of the game, he threw the ball down in disgust and was hit with a technical foul. Flynn made his three foul shots and Providence kept the ball, ending any hope for a Miami comeback.

Ernst hurt his knee late in the game, and before the Friars' semifinal appearance against Marquette, he took a shot of novocaine to deaden the pain. He managed to play most of the game and scored 12 points, including four straight free throws in the final minutes to preserve a 70–64 victory. Once again, Flynn led the Friars with 25 points; Stone added 15 and Thompson 12.

Next up for Providence was Canisius, a decent team from upstate New York that had beaten the Friars earlier in the season. This time it was no contest. Providence opened a 41–32 halftime lead and was never in trouble. Thompson again got his fourth foul early in the second half, but Mullaney moved him out to the corner and shifted Kovalski into the middle. Kovalski also muzzled Bob O'Connor, Canisius's leading scorer, holding him to 6 points in the second half. Flynn, meanwhile, continued his torrid long-distance shooting with 20 points and was named the tournament's MVP. Though Stone was the leading scorer against Canisius with 23, he had to settle for a spot on the all-tournament team, as did Thompson.

In the jubilant Providence locker room afterward, Flynn, a politician even back then, was asked if he thought his team was good enough to win the NCAA tournament. "Bring on Cincinnati and Loyola," he said of the NCAA finalists. "I know they're good, but they're no supermen. I think we'd give either club a heck of a game."

Sports Illustrated described the final game the next week. "Some 5000 noisy Providence fans were among the sellout crowd of 18,499 on hand . . . and they whooped it up with a seemingly endless chant of 'Let's Go Friars,' while a sweet-tooting band, led by a foot-tapping priest, beat out lively tunes. It was a wonder they had even a squeak left when Coach Joe Mullaney removed his starters from the game and happily embraced every Friar he could reach."

The euphoria continued a few days later when the players returned home. More than three thousand were on hand to greet the team bus at the Rhode Island state line and a caravan estimated at nine hundred cars fell in behind the team for the twenty-mile ride into Providence. There was a ceremony at city hall with the governor and mayor and other politicians, then another on campus later in the day with six thousand fans jammed into every corner of Alumni Hall. Mullaney paid tribute to his players for "their loyalty, fine play, what you have done for me and your school."

The Friars had merely posted the best record in the school's history—24–4—and ended the season on a 15-game winning streak, also a school record. And with Thompson, Stone and Kovalski returning, all those giddy fans had no reason to believe the team couldn't do just as well the next season, despite the loss of Flynn and Ernst.

Mullaney also was getting help in another area. The year before, he had hired Dave Gavitt, a Dartmouth graduate who had coached at Worcester Academy in Massachusetts, as an assistant coach. Though Mullaney was still very much in charge, Gavitt helped him with scouting and recruiting and also served as a liaison between the coach and the players, many of whom were only a few years younger than their new assistant. Mullaney was not what is now known as a player's coach. He had little day-to-day contact with them, other than at the two-and-a-half-hour practices. The rest of his time was spent in his cluttered little office in Alumni Hall, shared with five other Providence coaches, or on the road. "That's just how it was back then," he said. "They had a professor for history or philosophy and they saw them in class, and they had a basketball coach and they saw me in practice. I know John is very close to his players now. Maybe that's something that he missed when he was here, but that is how we did it."

Gavitt's presence helped, however. "No question, Dave was very popular with the players," Ernst said. "He was a guy you felt you could talk to."

Gavitt's strongest recollection of John Thompson from those days had little to do with basketball. "The day President Kennedy was shot, we pulled up to the gym steps and there was John, sitting there with a transistor radio in his ear," Gavitt once said. "I sat down next to him and he looked at me and said, 'I just hope to God a black man didn't do this.' "

Less than a week after John Kennedy's death, Providence opened its 1963–64 season with a game against Catholic University, the only time Thompson ever played in his hometown in four years of college. Mullaney was asked about Thompson that week and said, "He has the experience and is playing terrific. He is determined to have a good season and he's looking forward to having the games start."

Providence won that opener easily, and a few weeks later Thompson set a school scoring record, hitting 43 points in a 19-point victory over Fairfield in Providence. Thompson got a standing ovation from the thirty-three hundred at Alumni Hall, many of whom had been chanting "Give the ball to John" when it became apparent he was close to Jim Hadnot's record of 42 points.

The Friars lost by 7 in the opening round of the Holiday Festival to St. Joseph's, then reeled off 14 straight victories before losing to St. Bonaventure in overtime on the road in a game that saw Thompson foul out with six minutes left in regulation. Still, a few weeks later the team was rewarded for its efforts by receiving bids from both the NIT and NCAA tournaments on the same day. Providence chose the NCAA.

"Mostly for the variety of it," said assistant athletic director Rev. Joseph B. Taylor. "We've been to the NIT five times now, and the players, especially the seniors, have wanted to try this other one."

Especially John Thompson. "Right from the start of that season, that's what we wanted to do," Stone said. "John and I were the cocaptains of the team, and we wanted the NCAA. As players we considered it the better tournament, and we felt like we could go a long way. Unfortunately, we had some young guys, and in pressure situations a couple of them didn't show up."

Indeed, Providence lost its first-round East Regional game to Villanova, fifth-ranked in the country and the top team in the East, led by all-American guard Wally Jones. The game was played at Villanova's home court, the Palestra, and the Friars were eliminated, 77–66. In his last game, Thompson scored 18 points but managed only 3 rebounds, and he fouled out with 2:20 left. Thompson's high school teammate, George Leftwich, also started in that game, and he helped the Wildcats pressure Providence into numerous turnovers. A few days later, his college career ended as well, in a loss to Duke.

Leftwich, considered the best high school guard in America when he left Carroll, had been in a terrible car accident during his sophomore season at Villanova and was never the same player. Thompson, on the other hand, had developed into a solid college athlete, a player who averaged 26 points and 14 rebounds his senior season and set school individual and career scoring records. He also was named New England Player of the Year and invited to try out for the 1964 Olympic basketball team.

But when the season ended, John Thompson had other concerns. He was on schedule to graduate, and he spent a good part of the second semester completing the course work that would lead to his degree in economics.

Father Collins, the man who first sounded Thompson out about going to Providence, had him in his class on Christology and the Sacraments. "He was very good about making up all his work," Father Collins said. "I'd say to him, 'You're going to be on a trip for two weeks. Do you have all your assignments?' He'd tell me not to worry, that he'd do the work. And he always did. He was very faithful."

Thompson was hardly a dean's-list student, but clearly he was motivated to leave Providence with a degree. "John once told me about a trip he took to Russia with an American team," Father Collins said. "Darryl Imhof, who played at the University of California, was on that team, and John said one day they were sitting around a hotel lobby talking with each other and the subject of graduation came up. These other kids said to John, 'You mean you are actually going to get a diploma?' John told me that Imhof and he were the only two guys on that team who were going to graduate."

Ray Flynn also recalled that Thompson was deadly serious about his studies. "Nobody gave him anything," Flynn said. "We lived in the same dormitory, St. Stephen's Hall, on the same floor. We had a little library downstairs. Every night he'd be there studying as intensely and seriously as anyone in the building. I'd want to ask him about players, other teams, and he'd get annoyed with me for interrupting his studying."

And while Thompson took basketball seriously as well, Flynn recalled that his old teammate tried to remain on an even keel. "He loved to win, but he didn't get too up or down," Flynn said. "He'd play the game, get his milk and doughnuts afterward and go back to the room. He didn't rehash every play in the game. He would always stay and sign autographs for the kids, but he always had a problem with people who wanted to be with him or around him just because he was an athlete."

Added Ernst, "I always had the sense that he was afraid people wanted to use him. After games, some of the alums would take us out for beers and sandwiches; there were deals with restaurants so you could go out and eat and drink. It was good for them because people would always follow us into those places, and they'd have a big night at the cash register. But John always felt like we were being used, and he didn't like to do it."

Thompson did enjoy working with children. In his senior year he was a student teacher at Central Junior High School in East Providence, and he made a significant impression. He was assigned to a class of children with low IQs, some ranging between 60 and 80.

"I like to see the smiles come across their faces when they finally understand the point being made," Thompson told a Providence *Journal* reporter at the time. "They appreciate the help so much, it gives you a feeling of great satisfaction. I don't know if I have the right temperament or the necessary patience to teach these children, but I want to try."

The same story quoted Thompson's supervising teacher, Julia Sanderson. "He is so tall, such a celebrity, yet he walks down the aisle and gets down on his knees to help a little boy or girl with arithmetic. They all love him so."

Still, for John Thompson, teaching and working with children would have to wait. Pro basketball and the Boston Celtics were beckoning, and the young man described four years before as "the next Bill Russell" would soon be banging bodies with the real Bill Russell.

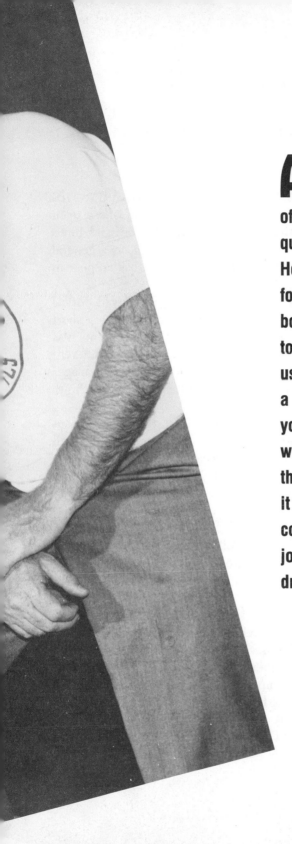

3

As a player, he was not spectacular at any phase of the game. He was an adequate shooter, a good passer. He'd run the court, rebound for you. You tell him to rebound, he'd rebound. Tell him to box out, he'd box out. I used him to give Bill Russell a breather. I'd tell him, 'John, you're not a scorer because we've got four other guys out there who can score. Just get it to those guys.' He never complained. He just did his job. He was a coach's dream.''

—*Red Auerbach, president of the Boston Celtics*

HE WAS THE GENIUS COACH OF A SPORTING DYNASTY, THE little man with a preference for the big victory cigar whose team dominated the National Basketball Association in the 1950s and 1960s and has remained a force almost ever since. As a coach, as a general manager, as a team president, Arnold "Red" Auerbach has no peer in the history of professional basketball.

When John Thompson talks about the people who played critical roles in his life, Auerbach's name is usually at the top of a very short list. "He is in a world of his own," Thompson once said. "As much as anybody that I look back on, he made the adjustments over different periods of time. He passed from era to era extremely well. He manages and handles men, and the other responsibilities that go with coaching, as well as anybody."

For Red Auerbach, no detail was too small, no task too demeaning if it could give him an edge in his life's work, winning basketball games. That's why Auerbach more than occasionally showed up unannounced to watch a high school team play or practice. That's why Auerbach came to the playgrounds of Washington every summer to see the latest star, the newest innovation in the game at what he describes as "the laboratory of basketball." That's why, during John Thompson's four years at Providence College, he'd pick up the telephone on a fairly regular basis and call the school president or the head coach to check up on a 6-foot-10 undergraduate who someday might join his basketball team.

In the summertime, Auerbach asked Thompson, his Providence teammate Jim Stone and assistant coach Dave Gavitt to help him at his basketball camp in Marshfield, Massachusetts. A number of college and professional players were always there, and when they played pickup games every evening while the campers watched in awe, Auerbach also was making mental notes, judging how the college kids played against the pros. Auerbach also spent part of his summer at Kutscher's Country Club in the Catskill Mountains of New York, where many college athletes earned their spending money waiting on tables and carrying suitcases, then squared off in memorable basketball games on the outdoor courts. Auerbach paid close attention to those games, too, dressed in tennis whites and chomping on a stogie.

John Thompson worked several summers as a bellhop at Kutscher's, and Auerbach, who lived in Washington, D.C., in the off-season, often would drive him back and forth to upstate New York. "Listening to his stories, he inspired me, because I knew he'd had it tough, too," Thompson once said. "It was not always easy. He had to come through the ranks, fight his way through and get credibility, and maintain it."

So when the annual NBA player draft came along in the spring of 1964, Red Auerbach had done his homework on John Thompson. He knew that several teams had contacted the Providence star, among them the Baltimore Bullets, the St. Louis Hawks and the Detroit Pistons, all of whom wrote letters to Thompson telling him they were interested in drafting him. But Auerbach, who had steered Thompson toward Providence four years before, had the territorial rights, and he used his third-round choice in the draft to pick a player he'd kept his eye on since the young man's sophomore year in high school.

Auerbach needed a big man to back up Bill Russell, perhaps the greatest center ever to play the game. When Thompson arrived in training camp that fall, he was joining a Celtic team that had already won seven world championships with Russell in the middle, including six straight titles. Only one player—Russell—remained from that first NBA championship team in 1956–57, but everywhere Thompson looked there were future Hall of Famers.

There were K. C. Jones, the smooth floor leader and point guard; Sam Jones, an uncanny outside shooter who taught a generation of players how to use the backboard to their advantage; Satch Sanders, a relentless rebounder with spectacular moves near the basket; Tom Heinsohn, a rugged forward with a deadly running hook shot and the temperament of a saloon bouncer; and John Havlicek, coming off a splendid rookie season and the next great Celtic sixth man. And of course there was Russell, the master of the blocked shot, a dominating rebounder at both ends of the court, the heart and soul of the most successful franchise in the history of the sport.

Auerbach had used his first choice in the 1964 draft to pick Mel Counts, a 7-footer from Oregon State, and took Ron Bonham, a 6-5 forward from NCAA runner-up Cincinnati, in the second round. All three rookies made the basketball team, and Thompson's role was spelled out to him from the start. "I told him he'd be backing up

Russell," Auerbach said. "He knew what his job was, he accepted it and he did everything I ever asked him to do."

If nothing else, John Thompson was a realist. He knew Russell would be the man in the middle for as long as his legs would carry him, and he also was aware he had some limitations as a player, particularly as a rookie in a league dominated by veterans. So Thompson came to practice every day, listened and learned as much as he could from Auerbach off the court and Russell on it.

"Some people say John is a hostile man," Auerbach said a few years ago. "But he is a very caring man. He acts the way he does because he does not want people getting too close. He learned that from me and Russell—be in control, put the other people on the defensive."

Auerbach was in total control of the Celtics, particularly after the team's owner, Walter Brown, died shortly before the start of the 1964–65 season. Auerbach scouted the players, handled the draft, negotiated the contracts, made the trades and coached the basketball team.

"Red thought about winning more than I thought about eating when I was little," Russell wrote in his autobiography, *Second Wind: The Memoirs of an Opinionated Man.* "He ached when we didn't win; his whole body would be thrown out of whack when we lost. . . . He was our gyroscope, programmed solely for winning, and it was difficult for any of us to deviate from the course he set for us.

"But being single-minded about winning didn't mean that Red knew only one road to travel. He was always coming up with a thousand angles. He was open with us about some of them and secretive about others, but that was all right. What really mattered was that we trusted him; we knew his actions were directed solely toward winning and not out of some petty grudge against one of us.

"Red's genius as a coach was mostly his skills as a motivator. He was a master psychologist who knew that there are as many different ways to psyche people as there are personalities. He knew that he had to yell at Heinsohn shrewdly and personally, whereas he bullied Satch Sanders and Don Nelson [acquired as a free agent before the 1965–66 season] in a cruel, offhanded, matter-of-fact way. With K. C. Jones, you had to be honest and leave him alone; he'd do the rest. I watched Red spend time with the Celtics who played the least, the guys at the end of the bench. He expected them not to smolder all season over their lack of playing time, but he always talked to them enough to remind them how important substitutes are to a team. He tended to be more supportive of them than of his regulars."

It was a lesson Thompson learned well years later at Georgetown, when he recruited teams chock-full of high school all-Americans, many of them forced to sit on the bench and fit into roles in his system. Most of those players accepted their status; the ones who didn't soon were gone, because Thompson also learned from Auerbach that the head coach makes the rules, not the players. "I am Georgetown," John Thompson has been known to tell his team, just as Red Auerbach was the Boston Celtics.

There were other lessons, articulated by Auerbach and many of his players over the years. "He taught us not to accept losing," Bob Cousy once wrote. "Society tends to frown on sore losers, but Arnold taught us that was a lot of garbage. Being a sore loser, he kept telling us over and over, was not a bad thing. His idea was that only losers accept losing."

On the court, Auerbach preached fundamentals, conditioning and defense. He was a master at working the referees to his advantage, knowing exactly when it was time for an outburst that might cost him a technical foul but might also be a psychological weapon to get his team back on track. He wanted his players on the floor and on the bench to be totally immersed in the game, just as he was. In the last five minutes of the fourth quarter, he wanted them to know the score, the number of time-outs both teams had left, how many fouls both teams had committed.

"I've never been much for Xs and Os and all kinds of fancy diagrams," Auerbach once wrote. "Throughout my whole career, I believed that the fundamentals of this sophisticated game of ours are still what separates the men from the boys. . . . Keep it simple. That was my rule."

There were more.

"The fast break has to become a way of life," he said. "It's automatic. It's ingrained. Any time our team gets the ball, whether it's on a rebound, interception or whatever, we immediately know where to head on the floor. . . . You want to be ready to fast-break all the time, not just when the situation's perfect. We practiced for hours and hours. . . . If a team knows you're going to fast-break, they probably won't crash the offensive boards because they're afraid they'll look ridiculous if you beat them back downcourt. So when they take a shot, they're stepping backwards instead of forward. There's an immediate advantage. . . . The fast break is just basic fundamentals, based on hustle, conditioning and working as a team.

"Defense is something else again. . . . Defense means work. . . . You work harder because you know eventually you're going to make the other side tired. You're going to wear them down. Then they start throwing bad passes and missing easy shots. You've also got to outlast them. That all comes back to proper conditioning. No matter how powerful you are and no matter how good your players are, there is no substitute for that getting-down-to-the-ground-and-sacrificing type of defense. If you can get great players to do that, then you'll have super players."

Auerbach was talking about the Celtics' philosophy, but clearly all of that material has been incorporated in Thompson's system, from his high school coaching days right on up through his years with Georgetown, along with another of Auerbach's standard operating procedures: making a basketball team a family, keeping private matters inside the family, keeping insiders in and outsiders—particularly the media—outside.

"I had only one rule regarding the press," Auerbach wrote years later. "Certain members of the press would cater to certain players, hoping to develop a pipeline into the team. . . . Whenever I'd find out who the player was who kept feeding the writer little scoops, I'd call him into my office. 'You want to be buddy-buddy with him? Keep it up and you'll have him paying your salary instead of me, because you won't be here. Let's get one thing clear. You are part of the team. The next time we have a secret meeting and something leaks out, it's going to be your neck. . . . You are not going to air your grievances with the press or be a stooge for anybody. No way. This is a team and we stick together. What goes on in our locker room stays in our locker room.' "

Celtic paranoia? Perhaps, but another lesson learned well by Thompson as the years went on and his team retreated into its own private world, eventually spawning the expression "Hoya paranoia" in the early 1980s to describe the Georgetown version of what Auerbach had articulated so many years before.

Away from Auerbach, Thompson also was discovering the realities of professional basketball, an endless season of games and travel, coffee-shop meals and hotel beds not designed for a man 6-10. That first year with the Celtics, Thompson lived with Harold and Marty Furash, his old friends from the days at Providence, in their home in the Boston suburbs. Gwen stayed back in Washington finishing her degree at D.C. Teachers College. By now they were more than just sweethearts, preparing to marry after his first professional season.

The Furashes were known to all the Boston players as part of the Celtic family. "They were all good friends of ours," Sam Jones said. "When I got to Boston, I was only the second black player on the team. Before me it was Russell, and Bill and the Furashes had become good friends. Harold looked out for the black players—he just had that real social consciousness and he understood that it might be tough for us. The only thing I didn't like about the Furashes was their dogs. They had these Dobermans, and you couldn't go in there or out of there unless those dogs wanted you to.

"The Furashes had no children, and they came to every game. They sat right in the same section with all the players' wives. They took care of John—they were like his adopted parents. I believe he made them godparents for one of his children."

Harold Furash does not like to talk about John Thompson other than to say, "I think he was happy here, he enjoyed his time in Boston and we enjoyed him. I don't want to be rude, but unless John Thompson himself calls me to tell me to talk to you, I'd prefer to end the conversation."

Through Harold Furash, Thompson also met Hy Horwitz, another Celtic fan who played golf with Furash and went to the games with him. Horwitz and Furash took it upon themselves to help players adjust to life in Boston, particularly the black players. They found them homes and apartments, introduced them to bankers and merchants, told them where to buy cars and even cosigned notes if that's what it took to close deals.

"It went way back. When most of the black players came to town, they had trouble finding a place to live. Harold and my father would go around asking people in certain neighborhoods if they had any problems with blacks living there," said David Horwitz of his late father. "They helped K. C., Sam, Russell, Satch, John, anyone, really. They'd actually go out looking for for-sale signs. They'd get out of the car, knock on the door and talk to the people, just to make sure they wouldn't have any problems renting or selling to a black basketball player.

"John was a quiet guy, but very opinionated, too. There were always a lot of intellectual discussions, these two old Jewish guys and this young black basketball player. It could have been about basketball, it could have been about anything in life you wanted to talk about. Harold and John still have these discussions to this day."

There were discussions among the players, too. That first year, Thompson and Counts, the tall white kid from the Pacific Northwest, became roommates on the road. Thompson also became close to Satch Sanders, another deeply thoughtful player who had gone to New York University and was now a veteran member of the team.

"John was just a straight-up young man," said Sanders, now an executive with the National Basketball Association. "When people were thinking about socializing, that had very little appeal to him. He was a straitlaced gentleman, and if you wanted conversation, he was the guy to go to. He had a lot to say, but he also was a good listener."

In practice, Thompson squared off against Bill Russell every day. In the beginning, he initially wondered what all the fuss was about, because Russell was not an inspired practice player, preferring to save himself for the brutal grind of the games. Though Auerbach tolerated little foolishness, Russell, the shining star of the NBA, could still get away with more than most, and his cackling laugh often broke the tension of a tough workout.

"In practice, I didn't think he was as good as everyone had said," Thompson said years later. "I'd always been a fan of his, idolized him. Then, in the very first game we played my rookie year in the Boston Garden against the Detroit Pistons, I could not believe it. I just said, 'Oh, my God.' He'd pull your shorts down in practice, he'd laugh at you. But he also knew when the main event started."

Thompson had gotten to know Russell through Auerbach as far back as high school, when Auerbach brought his team down to Washington and Baltimore during the season, and took his players with him to the playgrounds in the summer. The relationship continued when Thompson was at Providence and he occasionally went to Russell's home with Jim Hadnot, his Friar teammate. One time they took along Vinnie Ernst, the peppery little Providence guard, and Russell drove them to Fenway Park to watch the Yankees play the Red Sox. What a sight that must have been, the three tall black men and the little blond white guy crammed into box seats, with kids streaming up the aisles to ask for autographs. Russell, adhering to his lifelong policy of never signing an autograph, always declined, but Ernst and his Providence teammates more than took up the slack. "The kids were just flying down there," Ernst said. "I was at the end of the row so I could run and get the beer and the hot dogs. At my size, I wasn't going to attract the kind of attention those guys did. At least that's what I thought. I hardly saw the ball game."

The Thompson-Russell relationship solidified once Thompson moved to the Celtics. They beat on each other every day in practice;

they had long philosophical talks in the locker room, in the skies over America as they traveled to games, in the Furashes' living room and at Russell's home. Years later, Russell would show up at Georgetown practices and games to talk to the players. He helped Thompson recruit Patrick Ewing, then tutored him on the fine art of blocking shots and playing the pivot. Sometimes they talked basketball, sometimes they talked life. Later still, Russell did the same for Alonzo Mourning, another future NBA star on the Georgetown roster.

"Bill once said about me that we have become philosophical allies," Thompson said. "Russell and I are alike in the sense that he is in search of a way to find the truth. We express it the same way. . . . We talk a lot now. Back then, I listened a lot. He was black before it was fashionable to be black. He named his kids African names. He was the first man I knew to call himself black. He very seldom got involved in marches. I never heard him give any speeches. [But] he has very strong feelings that run deep inside and he does have the courage of his convictions.

"We both appreciate our own privacy. . . . I never asked Russell the real reason he doesn't sign. At times I've seen him look hurt when he doesn't sign. It bothered him that he didn't do it. . . . We've both strived to set up our own standard as opposed to accepting the standards of others. I always felt he came as close as anybody in my life who did what he wanted to do the way he wanted to do it."

On the basketball court that year, Russell was able to do whatever he wanted, leading the Celtics to a 62–18 regular season, a league record, and yet another NBA title, their seventh straight and eighth in nine years. Thompson saw limited action, playing in 64 games, averaging 3.6 points a game and hardly getting off the bench in the playoffs.

It had been an emotional year, particularly for the veteran Celtics and Auerbach. Their longtime owner, Walter Brown, had died a few days before the start of training camp. On opening night of the regular season, uniform number 1 was retired in honor of the Celtics founder and raised to the rafters of the Boston Garden. "We'll win the championship for Mr. Brown's memory," Russell said that night, and eight months later, wearing a black mourning patch on his shirt, he helped fulfill his pledge, though not before some anxious moments and one of the most memorable plays in Celtic history.

The Celtics met the Philadelphia 76ers in the Eastern Conference finals, and the series matching Russell and his longtime bitter foe, Wilt

Chamberlain, went to a seventh game. The Celtics were ahead by a point and had possession in the final seconds, but Russell turned the ball over on an inbounds pass, hitting a guide wire on a basket support as he tried to heave the ball upcourt, giving the Sixers one last chance. Havlicek saved the game, the series and the title when he managed to get a hand on Hal Greer's lob pass, which was intended for Chet Walker near the top of the key. Havlicek swatted the ball over to Sam Jones, and on the radio Celtic play-by-play man Johnny Most screamed into the microphone, "Havlicek steals it! Over to Sam Jones! Havlicek stole the ball! It's all over! It's all over!"

The final series against the Lakers was almost an anticlimax, though Auerbach, always the master psychologist, laid into the team the day before the first game against the Lakers. "They were too frivolous," Auerbach said. "I had to make them realize they could blow that first game as easily as not. Inside, I knew there had to be a letdown." Whatever the case, the Celtics won the series, four games to one, blowing the Lakers out in game five, 129–96. They ran off 20 straight points at the start of the fourth quarter to break the game wide open.

In the locker room, Auerbach reached into his coat pocket and pulled out Walter Brown's St. Christopher medal. "I've never said a word about this before now," he told a television interviewer, "but back in September, Marjorie Brown [Walter's widow] came up to me and told me she wanted me to have this. She hoped it would bring us good luck. . . . It was there in every game, in every huddle, and that's why I'm holding it up in this room right now. This was Walter's championship. We won it this year for him."

John Thompson did not play in that final game, but the frustration of a season on the bench was rewarded with a full $5,000 world championship play-off share, and a few weeks after the final series had ended, on June 19, 1965, he and Gwen Twitty got married. The ceremony was held at St. Gabriel's Catholic Church in Washington, and several of Thompson's teammates from high school, college and the Celtics showed up that day to help the couple celebrate.

By the time the Celtics gathered for training camp the next year, Gwen was pregnant, and the young couple set up housekeeping in a small Cambridge, Massachusetts, apartment. It had not been an easy training camp for John Thompson. He was in a battle for his position with one of his old playground buddies from Washington, Ollie Johnson, the team's first-round draft choice from Russell's old school, the University of San Francisco. Thompson barely beat Johnson out for a spot on the roster, but had to sit on the bench almost the entire season, playing in only 10 games. At one point midway through the year, Auerbach acquired forward Woody Sauldsberry and Thompson was kept on a taxi squad of sorts, permitted to practice but forced to watch many games in street clothes.

Thompson's benchmate on the sidelines much of that year was Ron Watts, a nice Jewish boy from Washington, D.C., who had been an all-metropolitan player at Wilson High School and a star at Wake Forest. The two had known each other from their college days, when both had played on various playgrounds around town, and they became good friends, trying to lift each other's spirits during practices and games. "John realized his limitations," Watts said, "but he also used to say, 'I know I can play in this league if a guy like Joe Strawder of the Detroit Pistons [a nondescript journeyman 6-10 center] can get a lot of minutes.' "

While John was traveling with the team that winter, Gwen gave birth to a son, John Thompson III, on March 11, 1966. She drove herself to the hospital, in fact. "That's the kind of person she is," said George Leftwich, Thompson's Carroll High School teammate. "She likes to tell that story, too. A lot of women in a strange town like that would have twenty-five phone numbers ready so that the first time a little pang shoots, she'd call ten of them and keep the other ones in reserve just in case. But Gwen was very independent. When John left on a trip, she'd rig up a bunch of tin cans on the door as an alarm if anybody showed up who shouldn't be there. She's just like that, a very nice person and her own person. John has always kept her in the background, and she's accepted that. She'd go to Georgetown games and nobody even knew who she was. That's his philosophy: Keep your family out of the public eye. It's been like that all his life."

Thompson was out of the public glare himself for much of that 1965–66 season. He also had some foot problems, though he practiced with the team as much as he could. The Celtics, meanwhile, were on a mission once again. Before the start of the year, Auerbach announced that this would be his last season as the team's coach. He also was serving as the team's general manager, head scout and representative to the NBA Board of Governors, and the strain of fifteen years on the bench had taken its toll. "I'm announcing my retirement now, ahead of time, to let the whole league know they've got one last crack at Auerbach," he said before the start of the season.

Heinsohn had retired the year before, and the Celtics were getting on in age. Russell was thirty-one, Sam Jones thirty-two and K. C. Jones thirty-three. A few days before the start of the season, Auerbach, in a typically shrewd move, picked up Don Nelson, a journeyman 6-6 forward who had been cut by the Lakers in a youth movement. He fit in almost immediately, and the Celtics spent most of the season in first place, with the Sixers close behind. Philadelphia eventually won the Eastern Division by a single game, but the Celtics once again knocked them out of the play-offs in five games, earning their tenth straight trip to the finals, this time against the Lakers.

Los Angeles took the opener in Boston in overtime, and on the off-day between the first and second game Auerbach announced that Russell would be succeeding him and would be a player-coach. If the announcement was timed as yet another Auerbach psychological ploy, it certainly worked. Boston came back to win the next 3 games in the series, though the Lakers managed to win 2 more and force a 7th game.

The Auerbach coaching era ended in one more riveting game, as the Celtics opened a 16-point halftime advantage and led by 10 with thirty seconds to play. Somehow, the Lakers managed to cut the lead to 95–93 with four seconds left, but this time the Celtics got the ball inbounds and held on for the victory and an eighth straight NBA title.

A few days later the players met to vote on play-off shares, and they initially decided to give Thompson a half share because he had missed so many games.

"John was not happy," said Satch Sanders. "He came back into that room and said, 'Hold on here. I'm either a member of this team or I am not a member of this team. If I'm not, I shouldn't get any money. If I am, I should get a full share.' We were all embarrassed. We asked him to step out of the room so we could vote again, and we voted him a full share."

That check would be the final money John Thompson ever earned as a professional basketball player. That season, the NBA decided to expand, adding a team in Chicago for 1966–67 and franchises in San Diego and Seattle in 1967–68. Those teams needed players, and when Thompson was left unprotected by the Celtics, the Chicago franchise took him in the expansion draft. Why not? He was only twenty-five years old, he had spent the last two years learning at the feet of the master, Bill Russell, and his game seemed solid enough to keep him in the league for years. He also was approached by the New Orleans Buccaneers of the fledgling American Basketball Association.

But John Thompson wasn't that interested in playing anymore. He had a wife and a new baby. He despised the travel and wanted no part of being a nomad basketball player, particularly after the Bulls told him to bring his own jocks, socks and sneakers with him when he arrived for camp.

"I'm sure with the Celtics he was frustrated at not playing—hell, we were all frustrated," said Mel Counts, who became a close friend. "I'm sure he was also probably fed up with the travel. The money wasn't that good for guys like us. The stars would make forty or fifty thousand dollars. [Russell was the highest-paid player in the league, earning $100,001, the $1 added to his contract so that he would always be making more than Wilt Chamberlain, who earned $100,000.] My rookie contract was for twelve thousand dollars, and John couldn't have been getting much more than that. It was fun, but it was not an easy life."

And so John Thompson decided that unless Chicago or New Orleans was going to make him a rich man, he was going home to Washington to get on with his life. On September 14, 1966, a United Press International dispatch reported that "John Thompson, a Washington, D.C., product who played at Providence College, was one of three players suspended today by owner–general manager Dick Klein of the Chicago Bulls of the National Basketball Association for violation of contract obligations. In Washington, Thompson said he sent a second unsigned contract back to the Bulls about a month ago and had not heard from them since. The 6-foot-10 Thompson said he considers himself retired unless the Bulls offer him more security."

Years later, Thompson admitted it had been quite a gamble for a young man with a new wife and child, no job and not much else.

"It was a tremendous move, and probably I was too young and dumb to be frightened at the time," he said. "I had been on two championship teams and that was meaningful. I wanted that memory to stay in my mind, but I didn't feel that I wanted to spend the rest of my life as a basketball player. And I didn't feel that in being a basketball player I could do enough meaningful things to fulfill myself as a person. That was just a personal view, with no disrespect for those who did play. I think people have to make personal decisions in their lives and feel that they're making contributions to themselves."

It was time for John Thompson to make his contribution.

4

At first, he was wary of this man from North Carolina, with his fancy suit and his big reputation. But the more Dean Smith talked, the more John Thompson listened. He liked what he heard. Then, and now.

WHEN JOHN THOMPSON RETURNED TO WASHINGTON IN THE summer of 1966, he was not entirely certain what direction his life would be taking. He also needed a job. Armed with his Providence degree and a sense of commitment toward helping the young people of his hometown, Thompson signed on with the United Planning Organization, a program tied to President Lyndon B. Johnson's war on poverty.

He also kept his hand in basketball, returning to his roots by volunteering as a coach at his old stomping grounds, the Police Boys Club No. 2, and helping his old high school coach, Bob Dwyer, by handling Dwyer's St. Anselms team in a summer league. He also started taking part-time courses in guidance and counseling at Federal City College, the forerunner of the University of the District of Columbia, and would eventually earn his master's degree in 1971 after a practicum that included working with inmates at the D.C. Jail.

Before long he was a very busy man, running an urban 4-H program, under the auspices of the Department of Agriculture, designed specifically to help poor youngsters cope with the pressure of growing up in the inner city. He put on basketball clinics, organized activities at playgrounds and recreation centers all around Washington and headed up a small staff of administrators responsible for hundreds of inner-city children.

"Our kids don't need to know how to make Indian headbands, they need to know how to survive in the city," Thompson told *The Wall Street Journal* in 1970. "We teach them how to make their own dinner, sew their own clothes and budget their bus money so they can get to school. We figure these skills will help pull them through the impossible odds they face in their neighborhoods each day."

On the basketball front, things were also falling into place for Thompson. Shortly after he arrived back home from Boston, Thompson and George Leftwich were sitting in Bob Dwyer's living room when Dwyer had an idea. He'd recently heard that St. Anthony's High School, a small school in Northeast Washington, had an opening for a basketball coach. Dwyer was friendly with the St. Anthony's principal and offered to make a phone call to Father John Bailey. Thompson was intrigued because it would allow him to continue his full-time job while coaching part-time after school. The money would help, too.

"I told Father Bailey that John Thompson would do an excellent job for him," Dwyer said. "John went over and interviewed, and he must have done something right, because they gave it to him."

They also gave him the freedom to build the program any way he saw fit. St. Anthony's had about three hundred students, and when Thompson arrived it was in a transitional stage, from a school that drew mostly from the suburbs to one that was beginning to attract blacks from the city. The basketball program was mediocre and the gymnasium barely adequate, with seating for about two hundred, a far cry from Thompson's days at Carroll High, when his team often played before huge crowds in packed arenas.

Still, it was a start. With Thompson's visibility as a former member of the world champion Boston Celtics and with countless contacts around the city, finding players was no problem. St. Anthony's was an independent school, and he could recruit from all over the Washington area. His friends at the Police Boys Club No. 2 were a valuable source of information, and Thompson had tentacles out on playgrounds, junior high schools and recreation centers in every corner of town.

One day, shortly after his first season at St. Anthony's, Thompson was driving through the neighborhood around the school trying to spot some of his players in a pickup game on a local playground. "I'm always on the kids to go out and play on their own," he said at the time. "That's where you really develop your talent." On this particular day, Thompson got lucky. He noticed one of his freshmen playing with some of the neighborhood kids, one of them a tall, skinny boy dressed in a pair of floppy blue overalls "like he'd been pitching hay or something," Thompson said.

Thompson sat in his car and watched for a while. "They were all playing ball," he said, "and he was getting faked out all over the place. The kids were teasing him pretty heavy, but I noticed he was real quick, even when they made him look bad." Thompson eventually got out of his car, introduced himself to the boy and spent a good part of the day teaching him a few fundamentals.

"I told him I'd work with him any time he wanted and then I took him home with me that night," Thompson said. "My wife got out the tape measure just for the heck of it and he was six-foot-four. He was in the eighth grade then and his hands were bigger than mine."

The boy's name was Donald Washington, and Thompson continued to keep his eye on him. Eventually, he asked him to take the entrance exam for St. Anthony's. Washington passed and was enrolled as a freshman for the fall term, a decision that would change both their lives. Washington would eventually grow to 6-foot-8 and become one of the most intensely recruited high school players of his time, leading St. Anthony's into the elite ranks of Washington schoolboy basketball and enhancing Thompson's image as a promising young coach with a keen eye for talent and tactics.

Thompson also was polishing his image in the halls of St. Anthony's High School. His players knew that unless they performed in the classroom, they would not be allowed to practice or play in the games. He checked their work, stayed in touch with their teachers and monitored their grades. He went out and bought new uniforms and blazers for the varsity team and insisted the players wear coats and ties whenever they traveled to another school.

Though he only spent a few hours a day at St. Anthony's, and most of them after school, some faculty members were beginning to take notice. One of them was Mary Fenlon, a former nun who was now a lay teacher of Latin and English. One of her students was on the basketball team, and one day she saw him in the halls and asked him to stay after school to complete an assignment. St. Anthony's had a game that very afternoon, and when several players told Thompson what had happened, he headed toward Miss Fenlon's classroom to see what he could do. Instead of berating the teacher, Thompson stomped into the room and began yelling at the player for not completing his work and lecturing him about the importance of school over basketball. Mary Fenlon tried to tell Thompson that the boy could easily make it up the next day, but Thompson wouldn't hear of it. St. Anthony's played that day without him; John Thompson had lost a player but gained an ally for a lifetime in Mary Fenlon. Soon, she began working with Thompson and his players on academic matters. Eventually, he also hired her as a staff member in the 4-H program, and did the same for Bob Grier, another one of Thompson's longtime friends from back when he was growing up. At one point, in fact, Fenlon and Grier were engaged to be married, and though they eventually broke up, their relationship with Thompson remained constant. Grier became Thompson's assistant coach at St. Anthony's, and, like Mary Fenlon, he would join Thompson on the Georgetown basketball staff in the mid-1970s.

Three years after Thompson took over the program, the St. Anthony's Tonies were becoming a Washington high school power, challenging schools like DeMatha and St. John's for top players and top billing in the weekly polls conducted by *The Washington Post* and the *Evening Star*. Even then Thompson's teams were known for their aggressive, pressing defenses and for jamming the ball inside to a big man.

"What he did at St. Anthony's was the same thing he did to build up Georgetown," said George Leftwich, who was coaching at Carroll at the same time. "He would find forgotten kids, players that other people wouldn't really look at. His friends would call him, guys in the boys' clubs and the rec departments. He always tried to get big people, and his guards were not great ball handlers but fast and aggressive. His theory then and now is the same—we'll just keep coming at you and punching the ball inside. Finesse is not one of his ways of coaching a team. It's not his style. Not now, not then."

"Our practices were brutal," said Felix Yeoman, who played for Thompson at St. Anthony's in 1972 and later at Georgetown. "If you weren't executing the plays, if you were fooling around, he'd put you on the line for what he called hamburger drills, a hundred of them. You run from the baseline to the foul line and back, then to halfcourt and back. That was one hamburger. A killer drill. We did that a lot. We also scrimmaged quite a bit. He would set us up in game situations—you're down three with thirty seconds left, what do you do? We always ended with free throws, because he'd always say when you're the most tired, in the fourth quarter, that's when you have to make those free throws."

The St. Anthony's basketball program also served to unite the school. There were bake and candy sales, and a booster club was started to help raise funds for trips. Large crowds began following the Tonies around the city to watch them play, and the local media were beginning to pay more attention.

Over at DeMatha High School in Hyattsville, Maryland, Morgan Wootten also was beginning to take notice. Wootten had been coaching at DeMatha since 1956, and his team had been a frequent victim of Thompson's Carroll team in the late 1950s. By the 1960s, however, he had built DeMatha into one of the finest high school programs in the country, as evidenced by his team's 46–43 victory in 1965, over a Power Memorial team led by Lew Alcindor (later Kareem Abdul-Jabbar), a victory that ended Power's 71-game winning streak.

Wootten also had become a power broker of sorts. He was in demand as a teacher and clinician; he ran a highly successful summer camp with his friend Joe Gallagher, the St. John's coach, and his team was always sought after for big local tournaments at Christmas and in the postseason. As such, Wootten could generally pick and choose his spots (not to mention his referees), and if he could gain a competitive edge, he'd pounce at the opportunity.

As St. Anthony's also grew in stature, there was much sentiment from the fans and the media for DeMatha and St. Anthony's to play. It never happened, though. Wootten insists to this day that he was never trying to duck Thompson, only that he wanted a game played at a site and time that would be fair and beneficial to both teams.

One year, DeMatha was invited to the O'Connell High Christmas tournament in Arlington, Virginia, just across the Potomac from the city, an event the school had participated in for several years. Wootten said he was reluctant because the tournament usually invited a number of local schools, including several from his own conference, and he did not like the idea of playing those schools once in the tournament, then twice more later in the season. DeMatha had several offers to go out of town, and Wootten was leaning toward accepting one of those invitations. But the O'Connell people assured him that only one other local school—the host team, O'Connell—would be invited, so he accepted.

A few weeks later, Wootten learned that St. Anthony's had also been invited and placed in an opposing bracket, meaning the two teams would probably meet in the tournament final. He told O'Connell officials he did not want to play St. Anthony's in a game that would fill the house at O'Connell but would not benefit DeMatha or St. Anthony's. "I told them St. Anthony's is getting good enough now that if we play them, which I'd be happy to do, we ought to play them for the mutual benefit of our two schools," he said. "We're two Catholic schools. We ought to play each other somewhere else. We'll get a big crowd. So I offered to withdraw and let St. Anthony's play in our place. I could go out of town, the kids liked going on a little trip, and everyone would be happy."

But the O'Connell people wouldn't hear of it. "They called back and said, 'No, no, no. DeMatha has to be here. We're going to withdraw our invitation to St. Anthony's,'" Wootten said. "I told them I didn't want them to do that, but it was too late, they'd already called St. Anthony's. I'm sure that's what started this so-called controversy between John Thompson and myself."

There were other problems. Every year, the M Club, the athletic

70

fund-raising arm at the University of Maryland, held a midseason doubleheader that involved two Catholic high schools and two public schools. St. Anthony's had never been invited, and Thompson blamed Wootten for that as well. "He went to the papers and said I was snubbing him," Wootten said. "That was not true, but that's what he thought."

At the end of the 1969 season, Thompson thought he'd finally get his chance to play DeMatha at the Knights of Columbus tournament at Georgetown at the end of the season. But Wootten instead took his team to play in the Alhambra tournament in Cumberland, Maryland, a three-hour drive from Washington. "We don't feel the Knights of Columbus can be what it has been—a tournament of champions of the best areas of the country," Wootten said at the time. "There are too many local teams invited."

In the summer of 1970, John Thompson got even. The two schools were scheduled to play each other in a summer-league game at the Jelleff Boys Club in Georgetown. Most good high schools entered teams in local leagues in the summer. It would be the first meeting of players from both schools in an organized game, and basketball aficionados from every corner of the city showed up that day to watch. John Thompson did not.

Instead, his assistant, Bob Grier, coached a team that was made up of seven St. Anthony's students, none of them on the varsity. Thompson's real players sat on the bench in uniform the entire game and watched their schoolmates play the DeMatha varsity. It was not a pretty sight.

"What was advertised as a heroic struggle ended as an 82-point DeMatha victory, 108–26, in what winning coach Wootten correctly called a travesty," *The Washington Post* reported the next day, adding that Thompson had been planning it for weeks.

"The seven kids we used are students at St. Anthony's we put on the roster to make it legal," Thompson said that day. "Nobody who will be on the team in the fall played." Thompson said he did it because St. Anthony's was not invited to play at the M Club tournament the previous year.

"Not inviting us deprived my six seniors of one of the most meaningful experiences in their lives," Thompson said. "I know playing in Cole Field House was one of the big thrills of my life. Something like this serves to make the public more conscious. Where where they when we needed support, when we were literally just placed out of the O'Connell Christmas tournament last year? I hope everybody who was there the other night and everyone who was interested was disappointed. Then they'll know how my kids felt."

Twenty years later, Wootten still vividly recalls that game. "Oh gosh, they were hanging on the fences trying to see it," he said. "They had a great team—Donald Washington was still there—and we were pretty good, too. So we put our starting lineup on the floor and five real small kids walked out for St. Anthony's. Our kids looked over at me and I just told them to play. I'm thinking maybe this is just some kind of psychological ploy. So we opened up a pretty good lead and I started substituting. I'm using everybody. And of course the crowd is hootin' and hollerin'; they want the other team to put in the big guys, the real players. They were all over the St. Anthony's coach. In my opinion, those little kids were being humiliated."

Aaron Long was a starter on the St. Anthony's varsity that year, and he also remembers sitting on the bench and not exactly understanding what was happening. "When we showed up for the game, no one had told us a thing," he said. "We thought we were going to play, and then all these other kids from school were getting dressed. We thought they were just going to be there to cheer us on because it was such a big game. So we warmed up like we normally would do and Mr. Grier called the starting lineup out and none of the regular starters was supposed to go out there. We looked at each other and said, 'What do we do now?' Were we going to spot them some points and try to catch them, or what? At first we were mad at Bob Grier, because we didn't know what he was doing. By the time it ended, we had an idea there was something happening that was bigger than all of us and we would just leave it alone.

"Mr. Thompson did talk to us the next day. He told us the statement he was trying to make was that if that many people could show up for the game in a summer league, and that many media people, and so many people were interested, why wasn't there more pressure on St. Anthony's and DeMatha to play during the winter? We didn't mind playing them—as players we wanted to play them. But after we understood what he was trying to do, we stood behind him all the way."

There would be one more attempt to get the teams together. After the Jelleff debacle, Thompson and the principal of St. Anthony's met with Wootten and the principal of DeMatha to see if something could be worked out.

"I said to him, 'John, we can play some games, and we can make some money for the two schools,'" Wootten said. "I told him my schedule was full for that next season but that we would definitely plan on playing the following season and for years to come. We had a pretty good meeting and it was agreed we'd meet again the following year and schedule a game."

So they met again. The same four people got together one day at St. Anthony's and Wootten opened the session by suggesting they try to play at a neutral site like the University of Maryland or Georgetown. Thompson had another idea. "He said he wanted to play at Howard University at nine o'clock on a Saturday night," Wootten said. Howard, one of the nation's most prestigious black colleges, located in a bustling black neighborhood, had a three-thousand-seat arena. But Wootten said he didn't think followers of DeMatha, a mostly white suburban Catholic school in nearby Hyattsville, Maryland, would feel comfortable at Howard. "Things were kind of unsettled in the city back then," Wootten said, "and I told John I didn't think our fans wanted to go down there. He said, 'Well, my kids would be very uncomfortable in an environment like Georgetown or Maryland and that's taking them out of their element.'

"Howard was not satisfactory to us," Wootten said. "We could not get together and work out the total package. But I hold no grudge over the fact that we never played. . . . I never blocked him from a tournament in my life, though I can see maybe he thinks I did on the O'Connell thing. I wasn't trying to bully him or call the shots on anything, but ever since then, I don't think John likes me very much. And that's too bad because I don't have any animosity toward him at all."

The same could not be said for Thompson. In fact, for most of the past two decades he has demonstrated a remarkable lack of interest in recruiting Wootten's players for his teams at Georgetown. Many of them have gone on to excel in major-college basketball and the professional ranks. Adrian Dantley, Kenny Carr, Dereck Whittenburg, Jerrod Mustaf and Danny Ferry are all DeMatha graduates. None were approached by Thompson or his staff about playing at Georgetown.

There were two exceptions. In the late seventies Sidney Lowe was recruited briefly by Thompson's assistant, Bill Stein, before Lowe decided to attend North Carolina State. And in 1990, Wootten got another call from Craig Esherick, Thompson's chief recruiter, telling him Georgetown was interested in a guard named Ken Blakeney, whose mother had called the Georgetown office herself to let them know her son had Georgetown on his list of college choices. Blakeney visited the campus, but Esherick called Wootten a few weeks later and told him the school had signed another player for the position and was no longer interested. Blakeney signed with Duke instead.

"They did everything by the book," Wootten said. "They called about the rules we set up, they called to see if they could talk to the kid, and they called when they were no longer interested, which is exactly what they should do, and I appreciated it."

Did John Thompson ever call?

"No, never heard from him, just the assistant," Wootten said. "I didn't expect to."

One of Wootten's friends related another story. A few years ago, one of Wootten's daughters was attending a social weekend at Princeton, when John Thompson's son, John III, was in school there. They happened to be introduced, and Thompson's son told her, "I shouldn't talk to you, I'm supposed to hate you." He wasn't smiling.

Asked a few years ago about his twenty-year feud with Wootten, Thompson said, "People can live on the earth away from one another."

Thompson's success made St. Anthony's a magnet school for the city's top players and his teams were constantly flirting with the number-one ranking in the Washington area. In 1969–70, Thompson recruited three of the area's finest players—a 6-foot guard named Jonathan Smith, 6-6 forward Greg Brooks and 6-9 center Merlin Wilson, all of whom would eventually end up playing for him at Georgetown. With Donald Washington still around in 1971, the Tonies were virtually unstoppable, and suddenly college coaches were flocking in droves to the tiny school in Northeast Washington to recruit Thompson's players.

Donald Washington was the first jewel in the crown, and Thompson was in total control of his recruiting. During Washington's sophomore year, his father had become seriously ill and required a long hospitalization. That same year, his mother had died. Soon, the youngster had moved in with Thompson and his family, and the coach and Gwen Thompson became his legal guardians.

The Thompsons had undergone a personal tragedy themselves early in Thompson's career at St. Anthony's: A second son had died of complications a few days after his birth and, according to an old friend of the family, "they were just devastated by it. But they are both very strong people, and life went on."

A decade earlier, John Thompson had gone through the recruiting whirl himself, and he was determined not to let it get out of hand with Donald Washington. He designed a set of rules to shield his star player: All contact between a college and Washington had to originate through the school. Thompson took all the phone calls, handled most of the mail before passing it on to Washington and steadfastly refused to give out his ward's grades or College Board scores to a college unless Washington had expressed an interest in going there.

"The most important thing we both want is for Donald to be some-where where people are concerned about him—he needs that," Thompson said at the time. "If he's had a bad game or not doing well in the classroom, I want him to have somebody there he can talk to. . . . But this is Donald's decision. If I feel he's making a mistake, I'm going to voice an opinion—not to would be less than honest. I'm not going to sit there with my mouth shut. But I'm not going to pressure him.

"We're not trying to shelter these kids, but we do want them so they won't lose interest in their schoolwork and their basketball. How can I as a high school coach tell a kid he's doing something wrong or he's not working when seven or eight schools are flying him all over the country, feeding him expensive steaks and telling him he's the best player in the world? The kids lose their perspective. I just want the coaches to be honest with the kids. I don't want a man to come in here and guarantee a boy will start when he's a sophomore or that he'll be a cinch to make all-American. I want someone who'll help them in basketball, but I also want to make sure the kid gets the degree."

Most of the speculation on Washington's eventual choice of schools centered on Providence, his coach's alma mater, and nearby Maryland, the College Park school that Lefty Driesell, a fiery competitor and a colorful character, was pushing into national prominence. Thompson also was good friends with Maryland's black assistant coach, George Raveling, a native Washingtonian who had gone to Villanova while Thompson was still in high school and had helped recruit his friends, Tom Hoover and George Leftwich, to the Philadelphia school.

But Dean Smith, the North Carolina coach, also was interested in Donald Washington, even if Thompson was somewhat skeptical about sending a black inner-city player to a white coach in the South to play for a team that had fielded relatively few black players in its history, and then only within the past few years. Undaunted, Smith came to Thompson's house one night to visit with Washington and his legal guardians.

"I remember coming in on a Sunday afternoon," Smith said. "Don-ald was there, John was there and Gwen was there. And John asked some tough questions. For instance, Donald had scored 890 on the combined SAT, but John wouldn't let anyone know that. He didn't give out any information. He said, 'What's the minimum he can get in with and I'll tell you whether he's interested in your school later on?' Years later, I found out that John wasn't particularly impressed. Donald was okay, but Gwen said, 'Let's listen to Dean again.' "

Bill Guthridge, Smith's longtime assistant coach, was with Smith that day and recalled that Thompson was skeptical about Carolina. "At that time, a lot of people felt the South was not the place to come for black people," Guthridge said. "There were some hard questions about integration and what Donald could expect down here. He was concerned about the black-white situation in Chapel Hill. I remember specifically him asking Coach Smith about who one of our players had for a geology teacher. A lot of coaches were telling them how concerned they were about academics and John was trying to find out whether we really knew our players' professors or if this was just more talk. Dean knew."

Thompson had been impressed, and when it came time for Washington to visit Chapel Hill, he and Gwen went with him. There were more questions, and more of the answers from Smith and his staff that Thompson wanted to hear. Washington also met with Bill Chamberlain, a black player on the Carolina team. "John spent time with Chamberlain, too," Guthridge said. "He asked him questions, about what was it like to be a black player here. I also think John found out that Dean was one of the leaders of integration in Chapel Hill. Back in the sixties, Dean had sat in at a restaurant. He did it with his church. Chapel Hill was a pretty liberal town and it was probably as popular a thing as it could be at that time, but not throughout the state, not with the Jesse Helms people."

Smith eventually won Thompson over, and on May 25, 1971, a few weeks before he was scheduled to graduate from St. Anthony's, Donald Washington signed his letter of intent to attend North Carolina. But that decision did not end Thompson's involvement with his guardian, or with Dean Smith.

During Washington's freshman season, he missed a few classes. Smith found out about it and called Thompson to let him know. "John was here by ten o'clock that night," Smith said. "He got Donald down here at the University Inn, and I've always said if I had the talk he gave him on tape, it would be just unbelievable. He said to him, 'Donald, some of your buddies down here, their dads are presidents of companies. They can goof off and still have a job. You don't have that.' And he went on about education just eloquently. This went on for about four hours. I didn't leave until four A.M."

Donald Washington got the message, at least for a while. By his sophomore season he had moved into the Tar Heels' starting lineup, but he suffered a foot injury that sidelined him for more than six weeks, and before long he had stopped going to class and eventually was dismissed from the university. Smith helped him get a tryout in the American Basketball Association, and Washington eventually wound up playing professionally in France, where he still lives, calling Smith and Thompson occasionally. "I've always felt that Donald was bright and intelligent," Guthridge said. "If he had not broken his foot, he would have been a graduate and a fine professional basketball player."

There was an upside to the Donald Washington failure, however. It was the beginning of a mutual admiration society between Dean Smith and John Thompson, a relationship that has flourished over the years to the point that they prefer not to play each other in the regular season to avoid the aggravation of coaching against a best friend. Smith also was instrumental in helping Thompson get the Georgetown job, used him as an assistant coach on the 1976 Olympic team and pushed him for the head coaching position on the 1988 Olympic team.

Before Georgetown came calling in 1972, however, Thompson was still in demand, both as a coach and as a professional basketball player, long after he had left the Celtics and started coaching at St. Anthony's.

Satch Sanders, Thompson's friend and teammate on the Boston Celtics, got a call from an ABA team asking him to talk to Thompson about resuming his playing career in the late 1960s. The team had written Thompson several letters and left messages at school, but Thompson had never responded. So team representatives called Sanders and asked him to serve as an intermediary.

"It was a Texas team, and they were talking about a two-year guaranteed contract for a lot of money," Sanders said. "I called John up and told him, 'For two years you could make a lot of money and then come back and coach again.' 'Satch,' he said to me, 'I appreciate your interest, but you have to understand I've made a commitment to these kids and their parents and I can't stop doing that.' I thanked him for being so clear about it, and I understood him completely. You had to respect the man."

There also was an offer from the University of Michigan. The head coach, Johnny Orr, was looking for a black assistant, and he called Red Auerbach for a recommendation. Talk to John Thompson, Johnny Orr was told. He did, but Thompson again politely declined, telling Orr he was happy at St. Anthony's and did not want to leave.

Soon, however, another prestigious university would come calling, inquring about his interest and his availability. This time, John Thompson could not say no.

5

Some alumni would like to see a racially balanced team. I know there are trade-offs. If we are going to limit the basketball program to the same [academic] standards, we'd eliminate a lot of players who would benefit from coming to Georgetown. I understand that. But I do have some concerns."

—*Tom Coleman, a Washington attorney and member of the committee that selected Thompson*

AT THE SAME TIME JOHN THOMPSON'S ST. ANTHONY'S HIGH
School team was becoming the scourge of Washington schoolboy
basketball, over on the other side of town Georgetown University was
becoming a laughingstock on the local college basketball scene.

Not that Georgetown had ever been much of a national power. In
its previous sixty-four years, the team had only been invited to three
postseason basketball tournaments: It finished second to national champion Wyoming in 1943, when most of America's best young players
were off fighting World War II, and played in the NIT after the 1969–
70 season, losing in the first round to Pete Maravich and the Louisiana
State University Tigers. But the coach, an affable Bronx-born Irishman
named Jack Magee, despised recruiting and had a difficult time attracting top players to a university that was difficult to get into and stay in.
Georgetown was known for its school of foreign service and its medical,
law and dental schools, not for its basketball team.

Georgetown had not admitted its first black player until 1966; in
previous years most of the players came from Catholic high schools in
the New York and New Jersey areas, with a smattering of Washington
athletes. Most of the great black Washington stars never even considered Georgetown—"We knew better," George Leftwich said—and
wound up fueling nationally ranked programs in far-flung corners of
America. Elgin Baylor had gone to Seattle, Dave Bing to Syracuse,
Tom Hoover and Leftwich to Villanova, Ollie Johnson to San Francisco,
Austin Carr to Notre Dame and John Thompson to Providence. Most
of the Catholic colleges had been among the leaders in integration and
had also used their basketball programs to gain national attention, not
to mention the extra money that poured in from grateful alumni when
the teams did well. Georgetown, with a healthy endowment and graduates at the tops of their chosen fields who often contributed generously,
had never felt the need to upgrade its basketball team.

Still, by 1971–72 the basketball program was in disarray, and an
embarrassment as well. Magee was a competent man with chalk and a
blackboard, a Boston College graduate who had once served as an

assistant to Bob Cousy at his alma mater and had a good head for X's and O's. But even the most savvy basketball mind can do nothing unless he has the talent to execute the plays and the presses, and Magee had no stomach for the recruiting process. For one, he never felt completely comfortable among the sons and daughters of America's power elite after he was hired in 1966, and he never could make himself sell the place to potential recruits.

"Growing up, Georgetown was always the Ivy League Catholic school," Magee said, "and being the son of Irish immigrants and never having too much money, it was just a different situation for me. I loved Boston College. I loved the fact that there were a lot of Jesuits around and I loved the place and I loved the city, too. Coming to Washington was a different experience. I was enthusiastic early on, but I became less enthusiastic. You have to like what you're selling. Good salesmen sell themselves, never their product. I don't know if I ever liked the product. And I became less and less enthusiastic about it.

"I really did not like to recruit. I remember going to one of those high school all-star games in Pittsburgh and walking into a gym and seeing this line of college coaches waiting to get in, just to kiss ass. Tom Gola, my hero when I played in college, was waiting in line to kiss some eighteen-year-old's butt. There was something very distasteful about that."

Magee had another problem. He had been hired by athletic director Jack Hagerty, who had eventually been replaced by a retired army colonel, Bob Sigholtz. Magee and Sigholtz did not get along. In fact, they despised each other and communicated mostly by memo; during the 1971–72 season, they were hardly on speaking terms. Under Hagerty, Magee had done his own scheduling. With Sigholtz, the military man, in command, Georgetown had 15 games on the road in the 1971–72 season, including a brutal early stretch of 6 straight at LSU, Texas, San Francisco, Pacific, Randolph-Macon and Seton Hall. The Hoyas lost all 6, giving them a 1–11 record, and Georgetown finished 3–23, the worst mark in the school's history. Long before Georgetown closed the season with a 9-point loss to Boston College, Magee had been told his contract would not be renewed, and Sigholtz was fired as well.

"I thought they were both spoiled brats," said Reverend R. J. Henle, S.J., the president of the school at the time, now a professor at St. Louis University. "So I fired both of 'em and appointed a search committee to find a new coach."

Father Henle had come to Georgetown in June of 1969 at a time when the school was making its first strides toward catching up with the social consciousness of the 1960s. The Washington race riots of 1968 had destroyed block upon block of the inner city and had also been a kick in the pants to a university that began aiming some initiatives toward a black community it had ignored for generations. A program called Community Scholars had been implemented, aimed at attracting the best and brightest black students from the city's public high schools. If students' grades and College Board scores didn't measure up to the normal admission standards, the school accepted them anyway, then helped them get up to speed if necessary so that they could keep up in a highly competitive academic setting. Scholarship money paid the way, and tutors and remedial courses were available for anyone who needed the help.

When it became known that Magee would not be returning, several black students met with Father Henle and urged him to consider a black coach for the basketball vacancy. One of them was Alexander Hampshire, a twenty-six-year-old freshman football player who had worked as a community activist for several years in Washington before saving enough money to attend the school. "I told him athletics is the key to community relations," Hampshire told the student newspaper, *The Hoya*, that year. "All city kids relate to athletics. I suggested that Georgetown run a summer basketball clinic with the District Recreation Department. . . . But the big idea is getting a black coach here."

Father Henle was getting the same message from his new director of admissions, Charles Deacon, who had gone to Gonzaga High School in Washington and had played basketball there himself. He had seen Thompson play in high school and had followed his career closely through the days at Providence College, the Celtics and now St. Anthony's, where the young coach had built a widely respected program.

"It was my opinion that one of the ways to increase visibility to the university was through athletics," Deacon said. "At Georgetown, basketball was our only option financially. Even though we were only in the beginning stages of television, it seemed to me that one of the things that got you visibility was sports. We were into the Community Scholars program and basketball was a sport, even at that time, where it was clear that black athletes were really the leaders.

"Also, many Washington-area black athletes had become very successful in basketball but had left the city. It didn't take a genius to figure out that finding a coach who would be appealing to the Washington community and who would be able to bring black athletes to

Georgetown would not only help the Community Scholars program but also might help the basketball program to get visibility in the national limelight."

Deacon made his opinions known to Father Henle, and he was asked to head a search committee made up of professors, students and alumni to find a new coach to replace Magee. Deacon agreed to chair the search committee, but he also wanted Father Henle to know right from the start that John Thompson ought to be strongly considered for the job. Henle told him that he had no problems hiring a black coach and that if Thompson was among the three final candidates recommended by the committee, he would take a long, hard look and would be favorably inclined toward hiring him. "My feeling," said Deacon, "was that Father Henle's attitude was 'If we can get him in the final three, he'll be our man.' "

Thompson wasn't so sure. In fact, he wasn't certain he wanted to leave St. Anthony's for a school that had not always been in the forefront of affirmative action for blacks at any level—in the classroom, the locker room or the administration building. But an old friend from high school, Maurice Lancaster, was working in the Georgetown admissions office and urged him to apply for the job. Lancaster, who was black, told his friend that the university was genuinely committed to changing its image and that the school was ready for a black coach.

Thompson also made some other phone calls. He spoke with Dean Smith at North Carolina and asked his opinion. Smith, who also offered a formal recommendation to Georgetown on Thompson's behalf, told him he was ready to move up. He called Dave Gavitt, at that time the head coach at Providence College, and was warned that there was more to coaching on the college level than just practice and playing the games. Gavitt told Thompson he'd better be prepared for everything else that went with the job, the pressure to win, to produce, to sign the best players. Thompson also talked to Red Auerbach, who encouraged him to apply for the job. They all did. You can make a difference, you can coach at that level, his friends told him.

He also had a conversation with Jack Magee. "He asked me for advice about who to talk to on campus to get real answers," Magee said. "I remember telling him, 'John, you're never going to own the alumni association, so my advice to you is ignore them because they don't have much influence anyway.' I also told him, 'If you go, make sure you have one boss,' which is something I had problems with. I was dealing with a whole bunch of different people. He saw all of my failures and the reasons for those failures, and then he took appropriate action."

Shortly after the committee was formed, Deacon made the first formal approach to Thompson. They met for more than five hours at Thompson's home, and the questions from the young coach were nonstop and cut to the quick.

"He grilled me, oh yeah," Deacon said. "He was very concerned about applying because he didn't think he'd have a chance at getting the job. He said he didn't want to get involved if he felt the cards were stacked against him. He also wanted to know why Georgetown in 1972 would accept a guy like him, a black man from the city, if the school was not a welcoming place for him to go and play basketball not that many years before."

Deacon assuaged Thompson's fears that he would be just a token coach. He also talked about the school's plans to increase minority enrollment, told him he would work closely with him on admissions and assured him that Georgetown was prepared to accept athletes who might not otherwise qualify if they had the motivation and potential to handle the work load of sports and school. Thompson, he said, would have to make that determination, with Deacon having the option to overrule him. The coach also would have the major responsibility for seeing to it that the athletes went to class and stayed on top of their schoolwork. When the meeting ended, Thompson agreed to apply for the job.

Deacon had been thoroughly impressed. Thompson, he thought, clearly was an educator; much of the talk had centered that night on each man's general philosophy. His record at St. Anthony's—Thompson's teams won 128 and lost only 22 in his six years as their coach—spoke for itself. The fact that he was a lifelong Catholic with a master's degree in guidance and counseling and administrative experience running the 4-H program was an added bonus.

Still, there were other candidates. More than fifty coaches had applied for the position, and two members of the selection committee, James T. "Miggs" Reilly and Francis T. "Tommy" Coleman, both Washington lawyers and both former Georgetown basketball players, were pushing for the hiring of Thompson's bitter rival, DeMatha coach Morgan Wootten, a finalist for the job when Magee was hired in 1966. Wootten, in fact, was offered the job back then but turned it down when the school could not meet his demands on salary, budget and support staff.

Father Henle introduces John Thompson, Georgetown's new bas-ketball coach, in a 1972 press conference. (The Washington Post)

"We felt Morgan had been around a little more than John," Coleman said. "He'd been coaching fifteen years by then, and John had only a couple years of experience. I'd known Morgan for a number of years and I always felt he would have made a great college coach. He had developed a network of kids he'd sent to good schools, and we could have had a lot of those kids at Georgetown. The timing just seemed right to me for Morgan to come to college, and had the job been offered, I believe he would have taken it."

But the job never was offered. In fact, Wootten still insists he never even applied for it. He simply agreed to meet with the search committee as "a favor to my friend Miggs Reilly" and let it be known that he would prefer to be both the coach and the athletic director. When he met with the search committee, he also listed specific requirements—commitments on scholarships, assistants, recruiting budget and a summer camp—before he would formally apply. It never came to that.

Wootten was told by some of his friends on campus that the hiring of Thompson was a *fait accompli*. Shortly after his interview, the search committee recommended three candidates to Father Henle—Thompson, Wootten and George Raveling, the young black assistant coach at the University of Maryland. Raveling had impressed the committee with his poise and confident demeanor, but no one expected him to get the job. The committee members were asked to rank their candidates one-two-three in order of preference. Thompson had four first-place votes, Wootten two. Bob Reese, the former Catholic University coach, had the other vote, but Raveling had more second- and third-place votes, making him a finalist. The interviewing process with the school president and his top assistant, Dan Altobello, would soon begin.

Altobello was a university vice-president who also was a good friend of Deacon's and was aware that he favored Thompson. Still, he knew that Father Henle would make the final decision, and so he called Wootten to arrange a meeting between the DeMatha coach and the Georgetown president. "He said, 'Coach, you're one of the three finalists from the committee but we notice you don't have a résumé or anything,'" Wootten said of his conversation with Altobello. "And I started chuckling. I said, 'The other two are Thompson and Raveling, aren't they?' He said yes. I told him, 'You're not going to get my résumé because you only send a résumé when you apply for a job, and I never applied for the Georgetown job, past or present, so you'll have to find a third person to put up there by your search committee.' The next day it came out in the papers that I had withdrawn, but I had never applied. Hey, the job was locked up. There wasn't any question about it."

Altobello had another recollection of the conversation. "Morgan wanted an assurance that he was the first choice of the committee," he said. "He asked me, 'Am I going to be offered the job?' I said, 'I can't tell you that. You'll be interviewed by the president.' He said, 'Then let's just say I never was interested.' And he declined to be interviewed. It was characteristic of Morgan. He doesn't want to compete. He wants to win."

With Deacon and Altobello both leaning heavily toward Thompson and the search committee giving him a majority of its votes, there was almost no question about the next head basketball coach at Georgetown. Still, there was the matter of Thompson's final interview with Father Henle, and a grueling set of negotiations with Altobello on a contract and his terms of employment.

The interview was a smash. "He came through absolutely superior to anyone else," Father Henle said. "I offered him the job and he said he wanted to add a new staff member, an academic adviser to the team to ride herd on the players. I said, 'You've got it.' He said, 'I want to be an educator, I want them all to get a Georgetown degree,' and I told him that's exactly what I wanted, too. I told him I wanted a team that would get a national reputation. I asked him how many scholarships he needed, and whatever it was I gave it to him.

"Hiring John Thompson was one of the best things I ever did there. When I came to Georgetown, I definitely was trying to increase the number of black students. The school of nursing, for example, had no blacks. Can you imagine that? The excuse was that the black students were weak in things like chemistry and math. So we recruited black nursing students, had them live on campus in the summer and gave them basic courses in those subjects so they could keep up. That ended that. I got criticism before for my moves to get blacks. I wanted criticism. When I got a nasty letter, I'd write a nice letter back."

Altobello was responsible for the final details, and he said money was not at the heart of the discussions with Thompson. "What characterized the process was that he negotiated things in his contract for the benefit of students and players, not for himself," Altobello said. "The last thing we discussed was money. I think we paid him about twenty thousand dollars that first year, which was more than Magee was making.

"We discussed at length the role of the academic coordinator. He wanted there to be long beds in the players' dormitory rooms. We went through all of the things he described as 'the tools.' He kept saying, 'If I don't have the tools, I can't do the job.' After [the contract] was signed, John said to me, 'If we ever have to look at it again, we have a problem.'

"He wanted it all spelled out right from the start. One of his biggest concerns was that the president would back him on admissions as long as the kid had a reasonable chance to graduate, that with reasonable effort the kid could do the work. If the dean of admissions could make the determination that the kid could not make it, John would have to accept it. As long as I was there [until 1978, when Altobello left to join the Marriott Corporation], that's how it worked.

"There were people back then who were grumbling that we couldn't have a black coach. Father Brian McGrath, a senior vice-president who'd been there quite a while, would always say that 'the only answer is that we are doing today for minority students what we had done in the 1930s for Italian and Polish students. We're not changing a thing. We were taking a first-generation guy and working with him. These are the same immigrants we always took. Now they're black.' "

Thompson signed a four-year contract to coach the Georgetown basketball team, and on Monday, March 13, 1972, the school called a press conference to introduce its new coach to the Washington media.

In *The Washington Post*, a picture of Thompson in the background towering over Father Henle speaking into a bank of microphones appeared on the front page of the sports section. The picture caption directed readers to the story of the hiring on page D2. At the time, Georgetown basketball was hardly a high-priority item; the two papers in town never even staffed the team's road games, getting reports and box scores from Georgetown's sports information director. The story of Thompson's new job was headlined "Thompson Takes Over" and went on to say that "in a campus faculty lounge crowded with newsmen, students and athletes, Thompson . . . said his ambition was to lead the Hoyas to a post-season tournament but that a lot of work has to be put into the program to get to that level."

Father Henle praised Thompson for his "proven ability as a coach, manager, inspirer and leader of young people" and as "a man of high personal ideals any young man would be proud to work with." The *Post* also noted that Thompson would be the sixth black coach of a predominantly white college, and Thompson was asked almost immediately if he planned to bring more black athletes onto the campus and into the locker room.

"I would hope so," he said, "just as I hope white players would want to experiment with a black coach. . . . I don't believe I will have any trouble recruiting white players. I've coached white players at St. Anthony's. This is a new day and age and I think the kids are open-minded. I want to be judged as a person."

Describing his coaching philosophy, Thompson said, "I like to run and do a lot of things defensively," but what style of play he would use ultimately would depend on the type of players he could bring to Georgetown. That led to an immediate question about whether he was interested in any of the stars on his current St. Anthony's team, particularly all-metropolitans like Merlin Wilson, Greg Brooks and Jonathan Smith.

At the time of the announcement, in fact, St. Anthony's season had not ended; the team, with Thompson still on the sideline, would soon be finishing in the Knights of Columbus tournament at Georgetown's McDonough Gymnasium. "The Georgetown coach talked to the St. Anthony's coach about it," Thompson joked, "and was told that would have to wait until after the season. . . . We're still discussing it."

Reaction on the Georgetown campus to Thompson's hiring, particularly among black students and administrators, was predictably euphoric.

Dr. Roy T. Cogdell, the director of student community programs and one of the few blacks in the university's administration, was ecstatic. "Georgetown is moving from the talking stage to the acting stage by bringing John Thompson aboard as basketball coach," Cogdell said. "This will have a decided impact on community relations, specifically young people who will see Georgetown moving in the direction of providing equal opportunity to people for employment without regard to race, creed, color or nationality."

The student newspaper also jumped on the bandwagon. "With the naming of John Thompson as Head Basketball Coach, Georgetown has taken a bold step to remedy one of the many problems of the past few months," said an article in *The Hoya*. ". . . Thompson will almost certainly bring a new dimension to Georgetown basketball. He is a strict disciplinarian who will not tolerate anyone who does not give his all. Discipline is one of the things many found lacking in the team this year and in the past. Usually, the team could be found spending more time at Chadwick's or the Scoreboard [two local bars] than in the gym. Judging by Thompson's reputation at St. Anthony's, the Hoya hoopsters better do their boozing this summer because Thompson maintains that 'they'll never last through practice if they go drinking the night before.' This seems to be just what the doctor ordered, since the Hoyas were anything but disciplined this year."

Still, not everyone was enamored with Thompson's selection. "I'm sure some of their alumni were probably a little upset," George Leftwich said. "They'd broken from tradition—I mean they had really broken from tradition."

Yet Father Henle said he had only one complaint in the days and weeks after Thompson's hiring—an anonymous telephone call to the university's public-relations office. "They called and said, 'Now that Father Henle has turned the campus over to blacks, he'd better issue a statement condemning rape,' " Father Henle said. "Quite frankly, I was surprised that was the only complaint. I expected more."

"There was one time the first year when a white lady phoned," Thompson said a few years later. "She obviously didn't know anything about me, but she was very hot. The day before there had been a photo in the paper of a couple of my big kids standing on each side of a little white kid. They looked like they were going to mash him. The lady said her father, maybe her brothers, had gone to Georgetown, and if I was the coach I ought to stop what was happening there—abnormal niggers bullying white students. I told her things were worse than she thought and that I was going to send her two tickets to our next game so she could come see for herself, and what she would see would make her blood run cold. I was very sorry that lady couldn't use those tickets. They were for seats right behind where I sit on the bench. I wanted her to get a look at the most abnormal nigger of them all."

A few years later, Father Henle's replacement as school president, Rev. Timothy S. Healy, S.J., offered his own unique theory as to why Georgetown had decided to select Thompson.

"There is something about Washington, D.C., that has always reminded me of a cuckoo's nest," Father Healy told a writer from *Sports Illustrated*. "The local people make the nest. The cuckoos—the federal people and all their hangers-on—move into the nest. They fly in and out, but their main interests are elsewhere. They don't really care a lot about what they do in, or to, the nest. I think Georgetown has been, to an extent, one of the cuckoos. After the 1968 riots it became obvious that the university's position wasn't very smart or defensible—socially, intellectually, morally or empirically. We began making some changes, some statements to the local community that we were going to try to be at least more responsible and useful. I think it's fair to say that hiring

John Thompson was one of those statements. . . . I think it's taking too much credit to claim that what happened came about because of a farsighted policy. What I think happened is that an intelligent black man, with a clear idea of what he wanted, has weaved in and out between a lot of confused honkies and has accomplished things that have benefited both parties."

Thompson insisted on the day he was hired that Father Henle had not "said I have to win X number of games or anything like that." In fact, the school president talked vaguely about being satisfied with a respectable team the alumni could be proud of, one that might advance occasionally to the NIT. A few years later Thompson said, "I thought to myself that I'd eat my hat if I couldn't do better than that, but I didn't say anything except 'Yes sir, I'll try,' because you don't want to set yourself up."

A few weeks after Thompson's hiring, Father Henle accepted the advice of still another search committee appointed to find a new athletic director. Frank Rienzo, the track coach who had been serving as acting athletic director ever since Sigholtz had been fired, was a unanimous choice, and a popular one as well.

Rienzo had come to Georgetown in 1969 from Archbishop Molloy High School in New York, where he'd been a track coach and an assistant principal. "I came to Georgetown to position myself into a full-time coaching position and not to be involved in administration," Rienzo said. "I was the acting A.D. during the search period for a basketball coach. I was consulted, kept abreast, but I had requested not to be intimately involved because I didn't expect to be the athletic director when the decision was finally made."

Still, when the job was offered, Rienzo decided to accept. He had also spoken to Thompson during the selection process and had been impressed with his vision for the program. More important, they both had similar philosophical views on the role of education and athletics. "He knew what he wanted to do right from the start," Rienzo said. "From day one."

Now that he had the job, Thompson once again turned to his friends for advice. There were more telephone calls to Dean Smith. At one point, Thompson spent a couple of days with Smith and his staff in Chapel Hill. They discussed a myriad of subjects—the proper role of athletics on campus, the coach as educator. They talked about the exploitation of athletes by coaches only concerned with winning, about dealing with boosters and alumni. And they also talked basketball, picks and presses, traps and time-outs, rebounding and referees.

"I'll never forget or have enough gratitude for what he did," Thompson said of his discussions with Smith. "The most meaningful gift a man can give another man is his knowledge. So much insecurity exists among people in this business that they don't reveal, as honestly and as openly as he did, the things he felt I should know. It is a very difficult thing to sit down with anybody and be as candid as he was with me about why he felt the way he did. I was able to learn from his experiences and his failures."

Thompson also paid a visit to another coaching icon—at least he was one to Thompson when he was a young boy growing up in Washington, D.C. Dave Brown had been the coach at Spingarn High School when Thompson was in junior high school, and if Brown had stayed at the school a few blocks from Thompson's home, Thompson almost certainly would have played for him there. Brown had never met Thompson back then, though he knew all about him from his own players.

"I'd see this tall boy out there on the playground; I'd see him with a basketball or a baseball glove," Brown said. "He socialized with the kids on my team. They gave him the information about me; he knew who I was."

Years later, in fact, Thompson always said that Dave Brown had been an inspiration to him. He'd heard about him from his playmates, knew that he emphasized discipline and teamwork, that his basketball teams were tightly knit and well mannered, that the coach insisted that his players do their schoolwork, and if they did not they would not be allowed to play.

"He came to see me about the time he was going to take that job," Dave Brown said. "He asked me what I thought about it. I told him it was a great move, that he ought to do it. It's the only time we ever talked about basketball."

A few weeks after he took the Georgetown job, John Thompson got a note from Dave Brown. In the envelope the old coach had also sent him a three-by-five card with a poem by Henry Wadsworth Longfellow. Thompson still keeps that poem, the ink now faded and the paper yellowing, in his Georgetown basketball office.

The heights by great men reached and kept
Were not attained by sudden flight.
But they, while their companions slept,
Were toiling upward in the night.

The next year, when John Thompson's team played its first home game, Dave Brown went to the arena. He bought a ticket and sat quietly in a corner of the McDonough Gymnasium, just as he would do for several years thereafter.

"He was not a person who wants to walk out in front and do a lot of things," Thompson said years later. "That meant a lot to me. It meant as much to me that he came to see my teams play because even to this day I don't think he knows how much of an influence the man had on me, even though he never coached me for one day."

Nor could Thompson have known what it meant to Dave Brown to have a black man named as head coach at Georgetown University up on the hill across town. "We were so proud," Dave Brown said. "Just so proud."

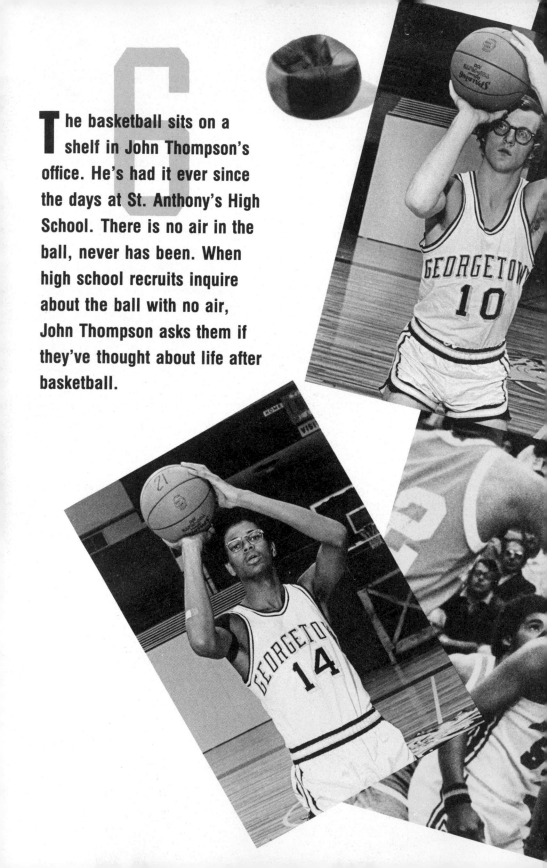

6

The basketball sits on a shelf in John Thompson's office. He's had it ever since the days at St. Anthony's High School. There is no air in the ball, never has been. When high school recruits inquire about the ball with no air, John Thompson asks them if they've thought about life after basketball.

WHEN HIS PLAYERS AT ST. ANTHONY'S HEARD JOHN THOMPson would be leaving them to become the head coach at Georgetown University, they were not quite sure what to make of it. His seniors were being recruited by a number of colleges, but none had any reason to even think about attending a university that had never shown much interest in attracting black athletes from inner-city Washington.

"Coach Thompson told us that he was going to talk to the people at Georgetown about the job," said Aaron Long, a senior on Thompson's last St. Anthony's team. "But he told us he just wanted to listen to what they had to say. We had no idea he would get it. And none of us looked at Georgetown seriously. We never thought of it like a big-time program. They had gone through some very hard times.

"I was looking to go to either Manhattan College or Catholic University. Even Manhattan was beating up on Georgetown back then. I think Jon Smith and Merlin Wilson were high on North Carolina State. Greg Brooks was a good student; he was talking about Brown or Boston College. But when John took the Georgetown job, it was case closed. We respected him enough that if he wanted us to go to Georgetown, we would have pretty much followed him anywhere he said."

Thompson talked to all of his players individually. Several told him they were concerned about attending a school with such rigid admission requirements and a strong academic reputation. Could they do the work? Would they fit in? How would the predominantly white campus adjust to a group of black athletes from the other side of town? Thompson tried to assuage their fears, telling them they had a chance to get in on the ground floor of the program, that it would be a struggle but that he would be there with them every step of the way.

Thompson also had another pitch, courtesy of the National Collegiate Athletic Association, which had voted that very same year to allow freshmen to compete in varsity sports for the 1972–73 season. With Georgetown coming off a 3–23 record, no one on the current varsity was considered an automatic starter. Playing time would be plentiful for any freshman, and particularly Wilson, Brooks and Smith. Aaron Long had started on the St. Anthony's varsity, and Thompson wanted him to come along as well.

"The fact that this was an Ivy League, white crowd didn't really bother us that much," Long said, "for the simple fact that we could always get back on that D.C. Transit bus and ride back home. And we knew we'd have each other. We were all a security blanket for each other."

Still, not everyone was completely convinced. Brooks, for one, wasn't even sure he wanted to go to college. Though he had done well academically at St. Anthony's, school was not particularly appealing to him, especially a university that would demand so much.

"I was going to get a job," Brooks said. "But then John Thompson was hired at Georgetown, and he was really strong on me coming there with him. I had very mixed emotions. I wondered if I could make it. I remember him telling me, 'The kids are not any smarter than you are. If you apply yourself, if you study and do the work, you'll get through.' My parents were all for it. My father worked at the post office, and I finally made the decision to stay close to home and go to Georgetown. I can't speak for the others, but John Thompson can be a very persuasive man."

Soon after, Smith, Wilson and Long had come to the same conclusion, and they would form the nucleus of a freshman class that would forever change the fortunes of the Georgetown basketball program. There also would be two other incoming freshmen that first season, including the first white player Thompson signed. Actually, there was not much arm-twisting to do: Mike Stokes, a bespectacled all–Catholic League guard from nearby St. John's High School in Washington, would be attending Georgetown because his father was on the faculty.

The other freshman recruit had a far more intriguing story. Thompson, in fact, called a reporter to tell him about William Lynn, a 6-foot-9 senior at Spingarn High School in Washington, because his background had been so unusual. Back then, Thompson was always on the telephone with reporters, called back almost immediately and always had an interesting perspective that could fill a man's notebook in no time at all. The Billy Lynn story was no exception.

Lynn had lived alone his entire senior high school season, occupying a small room above a barbershop in the neighborhood near Spingarn. Lynn was originally from the Bronx; his mother had died and his father, an auto mechanic, had sent him to Washington to live with an aunt, mailing him a few dollars on a fairly regular basis. In the summer between his junior and senior years at Spingarn, Lynn had moved out of his aunt's house and into a boardinghouse owned by another friend of the family's. One day in March, a few days after his final basketball season had ended, Billy Lynn went home after school and discovered the woman's body on the floor. She had apparently become ill, collapsed and died. A few days later, Lynn gathered his meager possessions and moved to the furnished apartment over the barbershop owned by Jim Wiggins. The barber knew about Lynn's situation—in fact, he had befriended Spingarn athletes for years—and he had known John Thompson as a young boy. They were still friends, and together the barber and the St. Anthony's coach had helped to start a summer high school basketball league in 1969 known as the Urban Coalition League.

Though Billy Lynn had been living on his own for almost two months, few people at Spingarn knew of his situation. One who did was Angela Corley, his guidance counselor, who described Lynn's case as "the most unusual situation I've ever come across in six years at this school. William seemed so well adjusted—there was no hint of drugs or any of those other problems. He does well in school, his grades have come up. He never cut class. Of course I know now that there was so much more we could have done for him."

Almost every day, Lynn wore the same faded T-shirt, the same weathered jacket, the same battered high-top basketball shoes. He told Wiggins that his father sent him money whenever he asked, but it was quite evident to everyone at the school that the boy was surviving on a minuscule budget.

"The thing that really shook me up," said Wiggins, "was when he told me he made his own pants." Indeed, unable to find anything off the rack to fit his 6-9 frame, with no money to afford slacks at a big and tall man's specialty shop, Lynn went out and bought a pants pattern and material by the yard, sewing his trousers by hand. What few friends he had called him Iceberg or, after seeing him leave a local laundromat with a sack full of clothes, Housewife.

"I prefer it this way," Lynn said at the time. "It's like I'm getting a head start on life. Nobody gets out of high school and gets luxury. And I don't have any problems. . . . When my father sends me money, I'll go out and buy a four-dollar steak and cut it into four pieces. That lasts awhile. I can boil a chicken. I have bacon and eggs or cereal and milk for breakfast, and I eat lunch in school."

Wiggins said he tried to watch out for Lynn as best he could. The rent for the room upstairs was minimal, and the barber lent him a television set and occasionally invited him to his home for dinner. "But he's refused food I've offered him," Wiggins said, "and I know he was hungry as hell. He's too proud to accept things. I don't press him because he's my friend."

Since Wiggins also was John Thompson's friend, he let the coach know about the skinny man-child living upstairs. But Thompson was not the only college coach recruiting Lynn. Several Washington-area schools were aware of his potential, but they had seen his high school transcript and felt he would be inadmissible to their schools.

In fact, one coach said he was stunned to read in the newspaper that Lynn would be graduating in the top 20 percent of his high school class at Spingarn. "Not with the transcript I saw when I went over there," he said.

Joe Boylan, at the time an assistant coach at American University in Washington and now an assistant athletic director at Rutgers, was very much involved in the recruiting of Billy Lynn. "We got his transcript and talked to a counselor at his school who told us it was doubtful that he could do college work," Boylan said. "Then we pick up this story about the kid going to Georgetown, this great sleeper, and we're saying, 'No way.'"

Boylan said that Thompson even called American University head coach Tom Young to talk about Lynn. "Thompson says, 'I hear you're going to turn us in on this,'" Boylan said. "Tom told him we had the transcript and we could not get him in here. So John said he wanted to send Mary Fenlon, the academic coordinator, over to look at the transcript we had. I showed it to her. She says, 'There's something not right here.' I told her someone had altered the kid's transcript, changed the grades. I didn't know who, but it was right there on paper. She left, and not long after that Tom Young gets another call from John, and now he's telling him, 'If you turn us in, we'll turn you in for something else.' Tom decided not to pursue it because the kid wasn't going to come to AU anyway. Thompson had just gotten there and there were some politics involved. Our old athletic director, Bob Frailey, always kids us about that now. He says if we'd turned Thompson in seventeen years ago, Georgetown might never have happened."

Tom Young declined to comment on the incident. "Ancient history," he said.

Lynn did wind up at Georgetown, and four years later would graduate with a degree and a double major in sociology and fine arts. Lynn had become an artist whose paintings Thompson hung on the walls of the basketball office. That graduation day, Thompson had a message for anyone who doubted Lynn's ability in the classroom. "I heard a lot of that four years ago," Thompson said. "Well, Billy destroyed that myth. I hope all those people who were bitching and griping back then can say their kids got as much out of college as Billy Lynn got out of Georgetown."

Georgetown got a lot out of Lynn and his fellow freshmen that first season under Thompson. The new head coach knew he had to count heavily on his freshmen because Magee had not left much to work with. "Plus, we were all a little shell-shocked from the year before," said Mark Edwards, a starter during that 3–23 season who was named a team captain by Thompson because he was the only returning senior.

"None of the holdover guys knew what to expect, and I was a little leery because I had gone to DeMatha and I knew all about his problems with Morgan Wootten," Edwards said. "But I also knew John. I'd gone over to St. Anthony's a couple of times to play ball with some of their kids. I thought they should have given the job to Morgan, but as a black man I was happy for John when he got it. There were just not that many black coaches around that I knew about. When we had our first little meeting, though, he said something that bothered me. He said he wasn't going to hold it against me that I'd gone to DeMatha. At first I thought he was kidding. I was dumbfounded. Then I sat down and talked to him and I realized there was still a tremendous amount of hate in him, which was out of his generation. But I understood where he was coming from. This was a guy they said was retarded in grade school. Look how far he'd come. I just thought to myself, Wow, this is gonna be one hell of a year."

Edwards was exactly right. Thompson and his two new assistants, Billy Stein, his old Providence College teammate, and George Leftwich, his Carroll High School pal, had joined the staff a few months after Thompson had been hired. Together they would be in charge of the basketball operation. Mary Fenlon, meanwhile, had been Thompson's first appointment, named to the position of academic coordinator and administrative assistant not long after Thompson had signed his own contract. Everywhere John Thompson went, Mary Fenlon was sure to follow, a practice that continues to this day.

In the beginning, there also was some talk that perhaps this was more than just a working relationship. "When I hired Mary and she started working closely with the kids and being visible all the time, you know how it is," Thompson told *Sports Illustrated* a few years ago. "You'd hear whispering, 'Thompson's going around with a white woman.' Dumb stuff. Ugly stuff."

And apparently untrue stuff as well. Leftwich said he had heard the rumors, too. "But let me tell you something," he said. "Mary Fenlon was safer with John Thompson than she would have been with the pope. In fact, she used to kid, if a woman of the streets ever approached John, he'd run the other way. I was there. I know. Yes, she was devoted to him. Still is. But there's nothing else going on there."

Fenlon took her job deadly seriously, establishing strict guidelines for the players, particularly the incoming freshmen. There was "Mary's book," in which players were required to log their progress in every course, on a weekly basis. They were asked to write down their test scores, what they thought their grades would be at that point, what upcoming assignments they had to complete. If there was a problem, Mary Fenlon wanted to know about it. If a player needed extra help, Mary Fenlon would arrange for a tutor. If a player cut class, Mary Fenlon wanted to hear from the professor. If the excuse was unacceptable, the player was not allowed to practice or play in the next game, and maybe longer.

At first, some players wondered about Fenlon. They thought she was nothing more than an academic nag, but before long they began to appreciate what she was doing for them. They also knew that "Miss Fenlon" was always there for advice, for a talk, for information. "She really had our best interests at heart," said Aaron Long. "Some people resented her and objected to signing the book, but I didn't have any problem with it."

"Miss Fenlon had a role," said Greg Brooks. "I didn't feel like I had to rely on her. I did the work on my own. I was responsible, but some guys definitely needed it. Nobody gave the basketball players anything in the classroom. If anything, some of them made it tougher on you because you were a basketball player. There was no free ride at Georgetown."

Fenlon has always preferred to stay in the background, declining interviews with very few exceptions. Over the years, she also developed a well-deserved reputation as a dragon lady among the media. She became a stern, uptight presence who seemed to go out of her way to be distant, aloof and often just plain rude. After games, she took it upon herself to shoo reporters out of the locker room in midsentence, and once she had a female reporter forcibly removed. She became fiercely protective of the players and particularly of Thompson, screening his phone calls and tightly controlling his schedule. According to the team's 1990 media guide, "this not only entails reminding the coach of appointments but also of determining when interviews, appearances and engagements are going to be possible. Since this may mean disappointing people who desire Coach Thompson's time, it is not the easiest or most popular position in the basketball office."

That first year, Fenlon told the *Catholic Standard* newspaper, "I really don't do anything that unusual. My job is to coordinate the team's academic schedule with their travel schedule and their game schedule. I say things like 'You'll be on the road next week and exams are coming soon, so make sure you get your studying in.' . . . I love to travel with the team. I'm so much a part of them when they're here, I'd really feel bad about it if I couldn't go."

Now she is everywhere. She sits on the bench with the team, home and away. She will often sit in on interviews between Thompson and members of the media. Thompson appointed her an assistant coach when he became the head coach of the U.S. Olympic basketball team for the 1988 Games. She has traveled abroad with Thompson, and she frequently accompanies him when he heads for his favorite vacation spot—Las Vegas, where he particularly enjoys playing the slot machines. When Denver beckoned Thompson in 1990, Mary Fenlon was part of his deal.

A few years ago, in an interview published in a team media guide, Fenlon described her job at Georgetown in great detail. "I'm here to assist Coach Thompson by running the office and by keeping him advised of the day-to-day academic responsibilities of the program." She also detailed the very hectic life of a college basketball player. "People don't understand the amount of time involved in school and practice, not to mention setting aside free time for socializing," she said. "These kids go to school until three or four in the afternoon, they practice until seven thirty or eight at night, they rush to eat their dinner at nine at night. . . . Then they have to get their schoolwork done, so they do a little studying but they have some time for themselves. . . . On Saturdays we try to give them some time off from practice, but that doesn't always work because some Saturdays we are playing or traveling. Then we practice every Sunday night so Sunday is time to see family, girlfriends, fulfill religious obligations. It's also the time to get to the library if papers are due, and we don't have any magic hampers, so that's when they do their laundry."

From left: *Merlin Wilson, Greg Brooks and Mark
Edwards with Thompson in 1973.* (Georgetown
University)

*Mary Fenlon, academic coordinator and strong right
arm.* (Georgetown University)

Thompson has described Fenlon as "my academic conscience. I'm a basketball coach, and if it were up to me, I'd spend all our time on basketball. Mary won't allow me to do that. She'll shoo the players out of the gym if she has to."

Thompson's hiring of Fenlon was hailed from the start, and no one has ever questioned her dedication to the task of guiding the players through the swirl of academia and basketball as best she can.

Few also can question Thompson's success. His graduation rate is among the best in the business; sixty-one of sixty-three players who have completed their eligibility at Georgetown have left school with a degree. Still, it also must be said that the percentage drops considerably when the number of graduates is compared with the total number of freshmen who have entered the program. Some of those freshmen eventually drop out of school or transfer, for either academic or athletic reasons. After the 1989–90 season, three Georgetown players—freshmen Michael Tate and David Edwards and sophomore Milton Bell—left school and transferred. All three struggled in the classroom and on the court; none will count against Thompson's ballyhooed graduation rate.

Just like every other big-time basketball coach in America, Thompson is recruiting many players who would not otherwise qualify for admission at his university. Thompson and the university maintain that the school has a responsibility to educate students from all strata of society, and as long as the tools are provided to help marginal students do the work and keep pace, their presence on campus can be justified.

Yes, Mary Fenlon serves as Thompson's conscience, as well as the university's, but no one should believe that she or any other academic coordinator working in a big-time collegiate sports program is there to produce brilliant scholar-athletes. She is helping most of her charges get through school balancing basketball and the books, any way she can.

That first year, Fenlon also answered the telephone, served as Thompson's secretary and ran the basketball office. Georgetown was a no-frills operation in those days; there was not even enough money to put out a basketball brochure for the media. Leftwich recalled sleeping in his car at the Cleveland airport on one recruiting trip because he could not afford to spend the night in a hotel. On another recruiting trip to Connecticut, Thompson spent one night in the home of the parents of his sports information director, Fran Connors, to save a few dollars. At the end of the season, Leftwich and Stein couldn't go to the annual coaches' convention in St. Louis because the budget couldn't spare the airfare and the hotel rooms. "John wanted to rent a car and drive us all out," Leftwich said. "We just decided to spend the money getting better players."

Still, when the team opened that first season against St. Francis of Loretto, Pennsylvania, there were plenty of changes. The locker room, once a dingy little space with cold concrete floors, had been enlarged and new carpet had been put on the floor. The basketball court had been reconditioned, with a picture of the school mascot, a bulldog, painted at midcourt. The local media turned out in full force, along with many of Thompson's pals from around the city, including a sizable contingent from Police Boys Club No. 2. Jabbo Kenner was there, along with Julius Wyatt and Bill Butler, who came to every home game in those years and occasionally hit the road to watch the Hoyas. So was Gwen Thompson, always a fixture at all the games. The students were home on Thanksgiving break, leaving more than a few empty seats, so Connors hired a rock band for a little extra noise.

Thompson started four freshmen against St. Francis—Smith, Wilson, Brooks and Stokes—along with junior holdover Tim Lambour, a 5-foot-8 playmaking guard who ran the offense. The coach was sweating all night, and he had a white towel draped around his broad shoulders to mop his brow.

"WHAT A BEGINNING!" trumpeted the headline in the *Washington Star* the next day after the Hoyas had held on for a 61–60 victory that was not assured until the visiting team missed a shot in the last twenty seconds. Stokes, who could not see three feet in front of him when he took off his thick glasses, had given St. Francis the ball at the end with a bad pass in the backcourt. "Had they made the shot," he said, "I'd have been some kind of goat."

Instead, he was a hero after leading his team in scoring with 16 points and handing out a bunch of assists. Merlin Wilson added 15 points and had 19 rebounds.

"Playing for a black coach was something that didn't even enter my mind, at least not seriously, when I was approached by John Thompson to play at Georgetown," Stokes said when it was over. "He impressed me then, he impresses me even more now."

Thompson said his biggest concern was to keep the team's older players satisfied with their roles. The second- and third-leading scorers from the previous year, Vince Fletcher, a guard, and Mark Edwards, had played only briefly and did not score a point, but no one was complaining, at least not publicly. "I can't say how extremely pleased I was to hear Mark Edwards praising Brooks at halftime," Thompson said. "He really pumped the kid up, told him how great a job he was doing. That was hard for him to do because Brooks is the one who took his job."

In a word, though, Thompson was ecstatic. "If only my heart weren't beating so wildly, I think I could really enjoy this," he said. "I'll take twenty-five more just like it."

The euphoria of that first victory soon was replaced by the hard reality of big-time college basketball. Thompson and anyone else who followed the Hoyas quickly learned that teams starting four or five freshmen can hardly compete at the elite level of the sport, no matter how good those players were in high school. Though the team managed to win 3 of its first 4 games, including a thrilling 73–70 upset of St. Bonaventure in overtime, there were losses in 6 of the next 7 games, including a 41-point pasting by St. John's and a 26-point loss to Maryland. Still, with Wilson becoming a forceful rebounder and Smith showing flashes of offensive brilliance, the Hoyas managed to close out the season by winning 6 of their last 8 games for a 12–14 record. Smith would lead the team in scoring, averaging 13 points a game; Wilson added 12.7 and averaged 14 rebounds a game, a rebound total that ranked him fourteenth in the nation.

"It was tough on all of us," said Aaron Long, who sat on the bench most of that first season. "Academically, you were more on your own than in high school, and it seemed like some of the professors were being hard on us because we were players. People on campus expected us to lose because of what happened the year before. The student body felt like 'Well, yeah, they might win a few games.' But we had come from a program at St. Anthony's that won all the time. We didn't like to hear that. Maryland killed us, but we had stayed close until the final seven or eight minutes. The faculty and students thought we played great, but we hated losing like that. It hurt us badly. We just weren't as good as we thought we were coming out of high school. We had no experience, and that cost us in a lot of close ball games."

Edwards, the team captain, also was frustrated. Though he played in all 26 games, he only scored 3.2 points a game and was asked to man several positions, all as a reserve. Like Thompson, Edwards was strong-willed and opinionated, an inquisitive student who had written and directed his own play on campus and wrote short stories in his spare time. The captain often clashed with the coach, over a variety of issues.

Once, Thompson berated him in front of the team for not calling a time-out when Thompson had ordered him to do so in the St. Bonaventure game, then benched him for several games afterward. Another time, Edwards complained about not getting enough money to eat over Thanksgiving and Christmas breaks. At midseason, Thompson once left Edwards behind in a rest room at the Providence airport while the team bus headed to Worcester, Massachusetts, to play Holy Cross.

"I went to the bathroom, told a couple of guys I'd be right back, and I walk out the door and they're gone," Edwards said. "I wound up taking a cab from Providence to Worcester, and I got there. John came out and I said, 'Pay this guy, will you? I don't want to go to jail.' He paid the guy but afterward he told everyone on the team they were getting two dollars for dinner because he had to pay for my cab ride and the meal money was gone. I told him that was okay with me because I'd stopped and had dinner with the driver anyway. But we were always doing little things like that to each other, tit-for-tat stuff.

"What I will say about John, though, is that he took some players who really did need his guidance, people like Smith and Wilson, and changed their lives. I'd come from a little more middle-class background. I didn't need this guy to be on top of me day in and day out. I didn't need this authoritarian 'you can't think for yourself or you might screw up so therefore I'll be on top of your ass.' Some of those kids did need that, and I understood what he was trying to do. Man, we would have practices at six thirty in the morning, five thirty sometimes. He'd call meetings at one A.M., and you better be there. He wanted to give them discipline, and I understood that.

"The practices lasted two and a half, sometimes three and a half hours. We did calisthenics first, fifteen-twenty minutes. And push-ups, sit-ups, jumping jacks. We'd do footwork drills—sometimes he'd have us rolling on the floor. It seemed like these things would go on forever. It was a big difference from the first three years, no question."

Thompson handled most of the workouts himself. Leftwich, in fact, once fell asleep during one session as he sat underneath the basket watching practice. "John was in total control," he said. "There wasn't that much to do. One day, must have been one of those early-morning deals, I just nodded off. Luckily, nobody noticed."

Stein was in charge of coordinating the recruiting, and as the years wore on, he became the main point man in Georgetown's quest for talent. He identified prospects, scouted high school players, made the initial contact through the mail and stayed in touch with each youngster until he had made his decision. Thompson also was actively involved in recruiting early on, though over the years his disdain for the process became more obvious and he simply allowed his assistants to handle the brunt of the work.

Leftwich left the program after that first season, somewhat frustrated over his role as a teacher of basketball. He took a job with the Converse shoe company and was replaced in the 1973–74 season by Frank Fuqua, a 1955 Maryland graduate who had extensive high school coaching experience and a reputation as an excellent teacher of big men. But Fuqua also lasted only a year, and he left when it became clear to him that only one big man counted in the Georgetown basketball program—John Thompson.

A few weeks before the Hoyas would begin their second season under the new man, Thompson's elderly father died after a short illness. There was no obituary in the local papers, simply a paid death notice in *The Washington Post*: "On Tuesday, October 23, 1973, Mr. John R. Thompson, Sr., of 766 19th St. NE, beloved husband of Mrs. Anna L. Thompson. He also leaves to mourn his passing one son, John R. Thompson, Jr.; three daughters, Mrs. Mary Barnes, Mrs. Barbara A. Murphy and Mrs. Roberta M. Montgomery; two brothers, Arthur and William Thompson; three sisters, Mrs. Susie Young, Mrs. Bessie Somerville and Mrs. Mame Evans; eleven grandchildren, seven great-grandchildren, a host of other relatives and friends."

He also left behind a legacy to his son—a rock-solid work ethic, a belief in the importance of education, of religion, of family. John Thompson, Sr., had been so proud of his son. The illiterate factory worker fussed and fumed when the newspaper wasn't on the doorstep at 6:00 A.M. so he could have someone—his wife, a daughter, a grandchild, a neighbor—read him the exploits of his son the player, and later his son the coach, over breakfast.

"I heard about Mr. Thompson's death a few months after it happened, and I was really saddened by it," said Jim Stone, Thompson's old Providence teammate. "That old man was so proud of his son. I would come down there and we'd start talking about John, and he'd get tears in his eyes. John felt the same way about his father. He knew what he'd done for him. It took him a long while to get over that."

Still, Thompson was back on the bench for Georgetown's season opener that year, and there were three new players close by—a 6-3 white guard from Saratoga Springs, New York, named Mike McDermott and two all-metropolitan selections from Washington, Alonzo Holloway, a 5-5 point guard from St. Anthony's, and Larry Long, a 6-6 forward from Mackin High School. Stokes, the first white player Thompson had recruited, dropped out of school and did not play his sophomore season. "He just told us he did not like school," Aaron Long said of Stokes, who now tends bar at a Georgetown club. But even without their third-leading scorer from the previous season, the team managed to improve slightly to 13–13 in Thompson's second year, losing the last 4 games down the stretch.

Nevertheless, Thompson was attracting some attention in the national media. The novelty of a 6-10 black coach and former professional athlete who emphasized education over athletics was the focus of most stories, particularly when reporters found out about the deflated basketball Thompson kept in his office as a symbol of his life-after-sports philosophy.

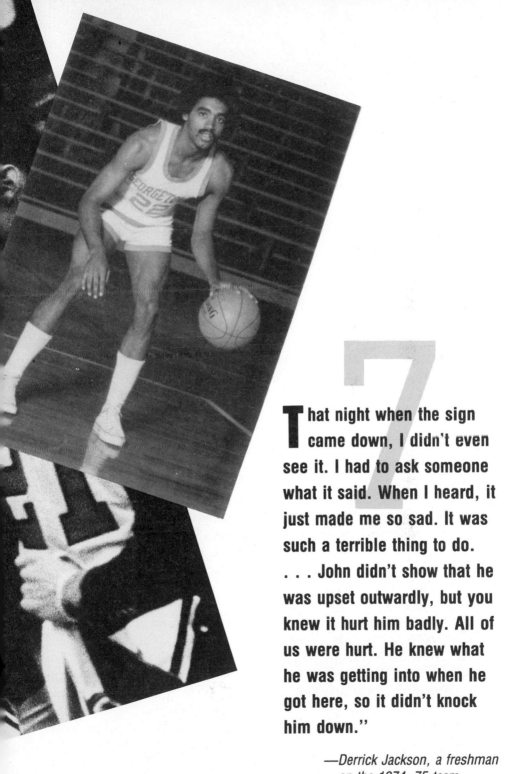

7

That night when the sign came down, I didn't even see it. I had to ask someone what it said. When I heard, it just made me so sad. It was such a terrible thing to do. . . . John didn't show that he was upset outwardly, but you knew it hurt him badly. All of us were hurt. He knew what he was getting into when he got here, so it didn't knock him down.''

—*Derrick Jackson, a freshman on the 1974–75 team*

AS JOHN THOMPSON ENTERED HIS THIRD SEASON AT GEORGE-town, expectations for a big year were running high on campus, and when the Hoyas won 7 of their first 9 games, including a tense 71–70 decision over an outstanding Syracuse team in the Kodak Classic in Rochester, New York, over Christmas break, there was every reason to believe something special was in store for the 1974–75 team. But the events on the night of February 5, 1975, were not exactly what Thompson, his players or the Georgetown University community quite had in mind when the coach had been hired three years earlier.

Georgetown's quick start had been deceiving. Five of those wins were accomplished at home in McDonough, a gym that was developing a reputation as a snake pit for visiting teams. And worse, Merlin Wilson, now a junior and one of the leading rebounders in the country, was having difficulty with his back and upper extremities, suffering from a mysterious neurological problem that did not allow him to fully extend his arms in the air and was baffling some of the finest medical minds in the country at the Georgetown University Hospital. Wilson was able to practice and play, but it was obvious that something was wrong.

Soon after their opening spurt, the Hoyas were jolted back to the real world of big-time college basketball. They lost by 10 on the road at Randolph-Macon, and Thompson wasn't around to watch. He'd been ejected for picking up three technical fouls fussing and feuding with officials, a tactic he has used mostly to his advantage over the years, just the way Red Auerbach taught him in the Celtic days. "But you couldn't blame John on this one," said former sports information director Fran Connors, who was there that night. "We were flat-out getting screwed down there. It was so obvious it was almost funny."

But there was nothing comical about the tailspin Georgetown found itself in over the next month, losing by 11 at Fairfield, by 17 at home against Seton Hall, by a point in double overtime to local rival American University, by 22 at Holy Cross, by 2 at home to St. Peter's—6 straight losses in all. And there were other problems. Jonathan Smith had cut a few classes and was held out of the St. Peter's game as punishment. Thompson told everyone that sophomore Larry Long had a foot injury that limited his mobility. In truth, Long had been sitting on the bench because of academic problems. But up in the stands no one wanted excuses, and there were some rumblings of discontent, even occasional cries of "Go back to St. Anthony's" and "Bring back Magee."

The team did manage to right itself and break its losing streak on the road with a come-from-behind victory at Penn State, but by the time Georgetown returned home to face Dickinson College, the record stood at 8–8, and the Hoyas seemed headed for a third straight mediocre year. Instead, the season quickly turned extraordinary.

As the band began playing the national anthem that night, a bed-sheet banner was thrown through an open window in the gymnasium, not far from a crucifix and an American flag that hung from the stage at the far end of the basketball court. The spray-painted message read:

"THOMPSON, THE NIGGER FLOP, MUST GO."

The banner stayed in place for only a matter of seconds before someone pulled it down, and few people in the crowd could actually read it. Down on the floor, neither Thompson nor his players were quite certain what had taken place, though Thompson was told almost immediately about the incident. If the team was upset about it that night, it hardly showed in their play. The Hoyas routed Dickinson College, 102–60, their most lopsided victory of the year.

Immediately after the game, Connors said there was some discussion about simply ignoring the banner, not even making an issue of it. In fact, several reporters left the building that night not even knowing about the banner and its message. But Thompson knew, and when he emerged from his office for a brief postgame interview, George Minot of *The Washington Post* wrote that "he was sad, almost subdued."

"Things like that bother me," Thompson said. "I still can't get used to them."

Thompson had another concern. At every home game, the coach had set aside an area behind his team's bench for groups of youngsters from around the city, usually black children from public schools, recreation centers and Boys Clubs. He called it the Coach's Corner, and many of the youngsters had also seen the bedsheet that night.

"I can't even articulate how stunning that was, to see that," said Rev. Ed Glynn, S.J., then a Georgetown administrator and now president of St. Peter's College in Jersey City. "And after the game, John was still hurt. But his first reaction told me a lot. He said, 'Those little kids that saw that—it'll be in their memory banks forever.' "

By the next morning, the university was in an uproar. No one knew who had been responsible for the banner; though several campus security men were dispatched during the game to find the culprits, they had come back empty-handed. Father Henle, the school president, was furious. "At seven o'clock this morning," he said the next day, "I would have been willing to slug somebody."

That day, he first met for about ten minutes with the basketball team and the coaching staff in athletic director Frank Rienzo's office, telling them he was deeply disappointed and disturbed by the incident. He referred to the perpetrators as "bigoted idiots" and said that the message on the banner in no way reflected the attitude of the faculty, the staff or the students of Georgetown University.

"The kind of people who do these things do not have the guts to come out in the open," he told the players. "The attitude of the bigots does not represent an evaluation of you or your coach. . . . I hope you discount it personally and do not let it interfere with your devotion to Georgetown. . . . I was happy when I appointed John Thompson, and I am not less happy today. I have no complaints about what John Thompson has done here, nothing but pride. . . . He's my man, and I'm happy to have him with us as the coach and as a human being."

Later, Father Henle appeared at a press conference that actually had been called by the basketball team. Several players, in fact, had spent the morning informing newspapers and radio and television stations that they would be available to talk about the sign later that afternoon. Father Henle, in high dither, described the act as "despicable," the work of a "bigoted kook, a stupid fellow . . . the person was cowardly, without the guts to stand up and be counted."

He also offered a strong endorsement of Thompson. "I have the greatest respect for John Thompson as a coach, an educator and as a human being," he said. "His philosophy is the same as mine. He looks at athletes as students. I support him one hundred percent." And he backed that up with a short written statement, declaring, "I regret that it happened and, as president, will continue to do everything in my power to prevent any display of bigotry at this university. When I appointed John Thompson coach nearly three years ago, I had full confidence and respect for him both as a coach and person, and nothing has happened to change my opinion of him."

The players, meanwhile, brought the bedsheet to the session. Felix Yeoman, a freshman who had played for Thompson at St. Anthony's, was appointed the spokesman because he was the youngest man on the team. "The sign," said Yeoman, reading from a prepared statement,

> was a personal affront to every man on this team—white and black.
> We came to Georgetown to play basketball because Mr. Thomp-

son is the coach. I guess he's a flop—a nigger flop—because rather than sacrifice his principles he's dealt with us as people, not things to be used for his own ambitious desires. He told each of us before we signed a grant-in-aid to GU that he would only promise us one thing—an education. In fact, he told us, "If you don't want to work hard, don't come here." Does that make him a flop—a nigger flop?

Let me give you some more specific examples of his flops—his nigger flops. Larry Long, a starter, missed three crucial games. Now it's true he does have a foot injury. However, only last night at a meeting did we find out from Larry that he had been unable to play because of serious academic problems. Mr. Thompson never told us this because he didn't want Larry to be publicly humiliated. . . . Making this known would have taken the monkey off Mr. Thompson's back. Once again, Mr. Thompson was a flop—a nigger flop.

Jonathan Smith didn't start for the St. Peter's game, which we lost. The reasons weren't that Jonny was loafing, or cut practice, or came late. Because Jonny didn't satisfy a class requirement, Mr. Thompson wouldn't permit him to start. The reason was academic, but again, he didn't publicly humiliate Jonathan. For refusing to start Jonathan, Mr. Thompson received numerous criticisms. You guessed it. A flop—a nigger flop.

At the end of Mike McDermott's first semester, though he was nowhere near failing, Mr. Thompson knew that Mike was not working to capacity and selling himself short. He told Mike that he was going to send him back to Saratoga Springs if he didn't put some mileage on his books. Just one more instance of a flop—a nigger flop.

Merlin Wilson's illness has just been revealed publicly this past week. Mr. Thompson has been aware for well over a year that something was wrong with Merlin. It would have been easy for him to say that Merlin was having difficulty rebounding, but that would have affected Merlin's future. Mr. Thompson, though searching relentlessly for a medical solution, kept the issue private. Yes, you're right! A flop—a nigger flop!

All of us on the team know of personal instances when Mr. Thompson has protected us from public criticism and shouldered the blame himself. That's why we've decided it's time that we speak up. We have no intention of boycotting. GU is our school. We will continue to play for Mr. Thompson, the flop—the nigger flop. But let us caution a certain element that our patience is growing short. Let me say that all of us have only one regret—that our names weren't listed under Mr. Thompson's on that sign.

Felix Yeoman that day did not elaborate on what he meant by a "certain element," but he didn't have to. Thompson, the black coach, and Georgetown, the predominantly white university, had been going through a somewhat strained adjustment, and his support among some academicians and alumni—particularly after he began bringing in a majority of black athletes, many of whom would ordinarily not qualify academically, was hardly overwhelming.

Still, this was a school that prided itself on its academic integrity, its rich tradition of scholarship, and the fact that such a thing could happen in 1975 was abhorrent to the entire university community.

"It was one of the lowest points of my time at Georgetown," said Dan Altobello. "But after it happened there was a great deal of support for John. Father Henle acted immediately to assure John this was an isolated incident—we all did. We tried to reassure John of his place in the university community. We tried to emphasize that it was just a few fools, not the sentiment of the university. John was not emoting anger, he was emoting hurt. If they had attacked his performance, he said it wouldn't have bothered him. But they attacked his race. At no time was there ever any thought of him quitting. I told him I hoped he didn't judge the university by the acts of a few. I told him there were some racists among the alums and the students, just like there were in society. But never once did he think about walking away. I think it strengthened his resolve. I think he said to himself, 'I'll show the bastards.' "

Altobello and Rienzo also said the question of Thompson's job security had never been an issue before the bedsheet incident, despite the six-game losing streak. Though his team had been struggling and there was only one year left on his original contract, the administration at no time was considering a change, despite the grumbling in the stands and some newspaper talk that Georgetown's patience was wearing thin.

"The only suggestion I had ever heard about that [Thompson's job security] came from a newspaper writer from the *Washington Star*," Rienzo said. "I told him, 'That's the most ridiculous, absurd suggestion I've ever heard.' I guess some people who might not have been offended by that sign maybe were hoping that would be the case. Is that what you call wishful thinking? Absolutely, unequivocally, undeniably, his continuance at the university was never an issue during that period."

Now the issue was racism on the Georgetown campus, and support continued to grow for Thompson and his team. Petey Green, an ex-convict who had become a well-known leader in Washington's black community through his weekly television talk show, met with Thompson and school officials and tried to spread the word around the city that this was an isolated act. In university classrooms, professors encouraged their students to talk about the bedsheet and the larger issue it raised.

The Hoya, the student newspaper, was full of righteous indignation. In an editorial headlined "Bigots Go Home," the team was praised "for reacting so intelligently and rationally to the bigotry. Instead of rashly boycotting the rest of the games [as some had feared], the players backed their coach and declared that 'GU is our school.' They proved themselves to be above the deplorables. . . . *The Hoya* wishes to apologize to Coach Thompson and his team for the banner. We can only say that the people involved should be pitied and not held as representative of the university."

Another student columnist wrote, "There's no denying that sentiments such as these are heard every so often, in the cafeteria, at the games . . . and now on banners . . . . What the episode does not demonstrate is just how pervasive racist feeling is at Georgetown. Our thinking is that the vast majority deplore this sort of attack upon Thompson."

Clearly, as Rienzo said, "it provided the university an opportunity to examine itself and for each one of us to examine ourselves in terms of racism in athletics, racism in higher education and racism in America. That's one of the good things about being an institution of higher learning: You can take a rotten experience and learn from it."

They never did find "the bigoted kooks" who had dropped the bedsheet into McDonough that night, and over the years the incident has been described as a turning point in John Thompson's career at Georgetown. Was it a sick practical joke, a student prank that got out of hand? The work of an outraged alumnus or faculty member? Or, as one rather farfetched theory goes, was it a calculated effort by some of Thompson's friends in the black community, without his knowledge, to take the heat off a young coach going through a disastrous losing streak?

"I've heard that said around town," said one Washington-area college coach, "that maybe some of his buddies were behind it just to get the people off his back. Maybe they did it to get the fans fired up and take some of the pressure off him so he'd have the time to get the players he needed to turn it around. I'm not saying it's true, but it happened that way, didn't it?"

Something else happened to the Georgetown basketball team that season. A team that had been flirting with disaster before the bedsheet incident suddenly was transformed, winning its next 5 games, including a 90–82 double-overtime decision against Boston College, and 7 of its last 8 in the regular season. Whether the Hoyas had rallied behind their wounded coach, or whether they had been the beneficiary of some savvy scheduling that included only one road game down the stretch—and that against neighboring George Washington in a game five minutes from campus—is only a matter of speculation. But their transformation definitely involved a little of both.

"To tell you the truth, we knew we had a good chance to win a lot of those games," said Aaron Long. "After the press conference, we pretty much put it behind us. We were concerned about the business at hand. We figured we could win a lot of games and still maybe get into the ECAC [Eastern College Athletic Conference] tournament. We knew everything was pretty much at home, and we knew we were better than almost everyone we were gonna be playing."

That year, in addition to Felix Yeoman, the Hoyas had added four other freshmen who would go on to make significant contributions to the program, either right away or down the road. There was Ed Hopkins, a 6-9 center from Baltimore who had played in high school for another up-and-coming young black coach, a former Washington Redskin named Bob Wade. Hopkins took some of the pressure off the ailing Wilson and averaged 10 points a game, starting all season. There was Derrick Jackson of Wheaton, Illinois, a 6-foot guard who had been drafted out of high school by the Texas Rangers to play baseball but had decided he wanted to go to college. He, too, would average 10 a game as a freshman, and before his career ended he would become a player Thompson would refer to for years afterward as an example of the model Georgetown student-athlete.

Though he could hardly have known it at the time, Thompson also signed two future assistant coaches who became valuable additions to his staff in the 1980s. He plucked little Mike Riley out of the Navy, recalling that the 5-8 guard had been a defensive star at Cardozo High School in Washington who had impressed the coach with his play in a

Anthony Jones against Villanova in 1981–82. (The Washington Post)

Sleepy Floyd scores against Missouri in 1982. (The Washington Post)

Ewing goaltends a shot against North Carolina in 1982 NCAA title game.
(AP/Wide World Photos)

Ewing blocks a shot in first half of 1982 title game. (The Washington Post)

Eric Smith plays belly-to-belly defense against James Worthy of North Carolina in 1982 NCAA title game. (AP/Wide World Photos)

Billy Martin fouls Sampson in 1982 game.
(The Washington Post)

Typical Georgetown defense as Gene Smith and Bill Martin harass Jeff Allen of St. John's. (Cameron, The Washington Post)

All-Americans Patrick Ewing and Chris Mullin collide in 1985.
(Cameron, The Washington Post)

Patrick Ewing in 1985 NCAA semifinal game against St. John's; (below) *blocking out Walter Berry.* (Cameron, The Washington Post)

Ewing hooks one past Ed Pinckney of Villanova in 1985 NCAA title game.
(Cameron, The Washington Post)

Ewing against Villanova's Harold Pressley in 1985 title game. (Cameron, The Washington Post)

Villanova's Ed Pinckney, game's MVP, shoots over Ewing in second half. (Cameron, The Washington Post)

Charles Smith, Georgetown all-American guard in 1988. (Herndon, The Washington Post)

Alonzo Mourning in action, 1989. (Guzy, The Washington Post)

Dwayne Bryant plays typical head-over-heels defense in 1990. (Cameron, The Washington Post)

Thompson during 1989 season, towel in its usual place. (Brooks, The Washington Post)

game against DeMatha. "He was the first high school guard I saw who dominated a game defensively," Thompson said. "I turned to my players and said, 'That little boy will never play in college because coaches will say he's too small.' Then I got here and I remembered him. Somebody said he was in the service."

Thompson tracked Riley down on the USS *Holland*, where he was handling Polaris missiles and nuclear warheads—in basketball vernacular, the ultimate defensive weapons. When the ship returned to port in Charleston, South Carolina, a slightly startled Riley had a message to call John Thompson as soon as possible. They talked, and when Riley was discharged after his three-year hitch in the Navy, the young veteran enrolled as a freshman at Georgetown University.

From Springbrook High School in suburban Maryland came Craig Esherick, a second-team all-metropolitan selection with a fine outside shooting touch. Never would that be more apparent than on the night in 1978 when he hit a forty-footer at the buzzer against George Washington University to send the game into overtime. Georgetown eventually won, though Esherick also would be remembered for another achievement that made his coach proud—he became the first Thompson-era Georgetown basketball player to graduate from law school and pass the bar.

But in 1975 there was really only one shot most basketball fans in Washington were talking about. It came in the final of the postseason ECAC tournament against West Virginia and was taken by Derrick Jackson, a twenty-footer from the left corner with two seconds left for a 61–60 victory and a spot in the NCAA tournament. Father Henle had said he'd be satisfied with an occasional NIT bid; now Georgetown had its first berth in the NCAA tournament since 1943.

When the season started, no one really expected that Jackson would emerge as a hero on this team. In fact, Thompson only recruited him in the first place because of the persistence of a Georgetown alumnus, Mike Foster, who lived in Jackson's Illinois hometown and had seen him play.

Jackson had not been a widely sought-after recruit, mainly because he was in an automobile accident his junior year that slowed his development and scared the recruiters away. But Jackson had a productive senior season, and Foster kept calling the Georgetown basketball office, telling the coaches about a prospect at Wheaton Central who kept hitting clutch shots in big games.

"To get Mr. Foster off his back, Coach Thompson came out here,"

Jackson said. "I don't really think he was that interested—he'd been recruiting mostly in the East—but I guess he was curious. He and Miss Fenlon came out one day and they went to the school to see if I was academically okay. My first impression of Coach Thompson was that I had never seen anyone so big. I talked to him at the school, and then I went to Georgetown for a visit. The only other big school interested in me was Boston College, and it wasn't a hard choice.

"As soon as I began talking with him, it became apparent to me Georgetown is where I wanted to go. In all the time he recruited me, I don't ever remember talking about basketball. It was all academics, academics. When I visited the school, he wanted to make sure I went out and saw Washington, D.C. That impressed me, too. He was interested in my personal life, not just what I could do in basketball."

When Jackson arrived in Washington, he was not particularly confident about his basketball skills. At the time, the University of Maryland had three outstanding guards, all future pros—John Lucas, Brad Davis and Mo Howard—and Jackson at first was hesitant to play against them in summer pickup games around town. "I had never gotten to play against anybody of that caliber," he said. "But I was holding my own against these guys, so I told myself I must be able to play. At first I was saying, 'I can't handle them.' Mr. Thompson told me I shouldn't be saying that. He said, 'You should be saying, "I can handle them."' I began to realize that was true, and that I could play with anyone in the country."

Jackson demonstrated that constantly during his freshman season, and never was that more evident than in critical games. Georgetown had qualified for the ECAC tournament by winning 9 of its last 10 games, then avenged an early-season defeat by beating local rival George Washington, 66–59, in the first round of the tournament. Jackson had 18 points against GW, and 18 more against West Virginia, including the game-winner.

Of his famous shot to beat the Mountaineers, Jackson said, "I just knew time was running out and I better put it up. It's something you never forget."

Georgetown's players were in the midst of a raucous celebration in the locker room when their big coach walked through the door with a stern look on his face. "I told them to be quiet," Thompson said. "I wanted to tell them something. I said it was a great win, mostly for me, that I was going to get a lot of publicity, maybe I'd get a raise, even a better job offer. Then I said, 'What are you guys getting out of it?' and I walked out. I didn't want them ever to forget the bargain they'd made, the real reason they were at Georgetown."

The Hoyas would also never forget what happened in their final game of the season, an NCAA Mideast regional game against Central Michigan in Tuscaloosa, Alabama. With the score tied at 75-all and the clock winding down, Jonathan Smith went up for a long jump shot that bounced off the back of the rim. As he came down, he made contact with Central Michigan's Leonard Drake after he had released the ball. Both players fell to the floor, and while it looked as if Drake had undercut Smith, the referee, Big Ten official Ed Maracich, called Smith for an offensive foul. Central Michigan was in the bonus situation, and Drake made both free throws at the other end with no time remaining on the clock for a stunningly controversial 77–75 victory over a Georgetown team that could not believe what had just happened.

"It's just not fair to go that far and then have your whole season decided on one judgment call," Thompson said that day, arguing that no whistle should have been blown, or at the very least that Drake should have been charged with the foul, not Smith. The bad call cost Georgetown a chance to face Kentucky in the next round, not to mention almost $30,000 dollars in lost revenue.

"I remember walking into the locker room and seeing John standing there," Fran Connors said. "I could tell he was just heartbroken, given the ups and downs of that season, and here was the opportunity to go one step further in what had turned out to be a Cinderella season. But the official just took us right out of it. What a way to end a crazy year."

Thompson, who years later would be severely criticized for his media relations, took his case to the newspapers the next week, inviting several reporters over to his office to watch a film of the final play. They all concluded that Thompson had been exactly right, but when the Mideast regional opened the following week in Dayton, Ohio, it was Central Michigan playing Kentucky, not the Hoyas.

A few weeks later, at Georgetown's annual athletic banquet, John Thompson presented the Francis "Reds" Daley Memorial Trophy for the most valuable player to the fourteen young men on the Georgetown basketball team. "Team Award" is the way it's listed on the shiny silver trophy that is on permanent display at McDonough Gymnasium, where a bigoted bedsheet banner once dropped through an open window during a basketball game in 1975 and changed John Thompson's life forever.

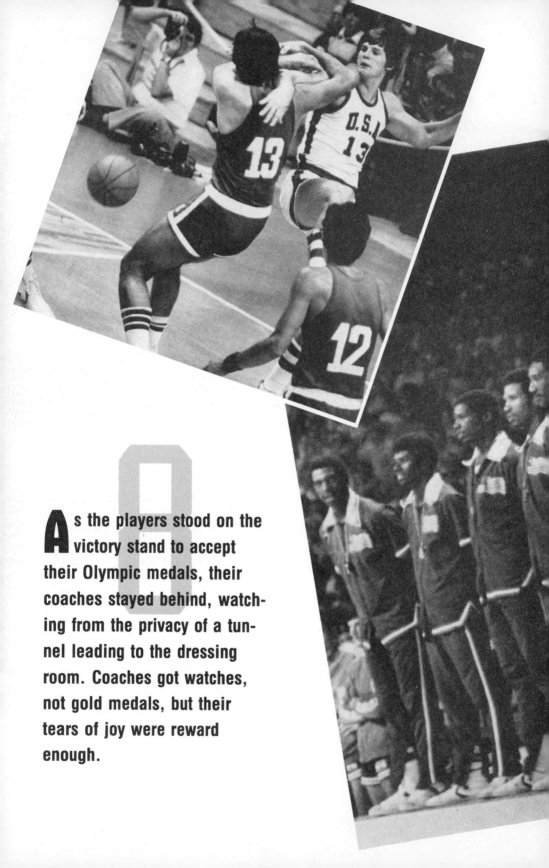

As the players stood on the victory stand to accept their Olympic medals, their coaches stayed behind, watching from the privacy of a tunnel leading to the dressing room. Coaches got watches, not gold medals, but their tears of joy were reward enough.

DESPITE THE DISAPPOINTMENT OF THAT CONTROVERSIAL LOSS to Central Michigan, by advancing to the NCAA tournament the Georgetown program had climbed to a new level, with the summit of college basketball still on the horizon. John Thompson, the so-called coach with a conscience, was attracting more coverage in the local and national media. Elite athletes were starting to pay attention when Thompson or his chief recruiter, Bill Stein, showed up to watch them play. No longer was Georgetown mail tossed unopened into the trash. Prospects and their coaches were actually returning telephone calls.

Thompson was making a name for himself and for his program. He also was learning the fine art of making friends in all the right places, the better to enhance his chances of landing better players. He'd become a regular at the Five Star basketball camp in the Pocono Mountains, where the nation's elite players spent two weeks every summer in an open-air meat market run by New Yorker Howard Garfinkel. "Garf," as he was known to coaches coast to coast, made his living by rating high school athletes and selling his service to colleges around the country. Georgetown was a very good customer, with four subscriptions to Garfinkel's newsletter when one would have been more than sufficient. But Thompson also knew that a kind word from Garf to a camper about the Georgetown program might just influence his decision on a choice of schools.

Thompson also was getting close to Joe Dean Davidson, the new coach at Washington's Dunbar High, a man who had revitalized that school's basketball program and was attracting some of the city's finest players, convincing them to stay in the public school system that had been bleeding athletes to the parochial schools for years. Two stars on Davidson's Dunbar team, Craig Shelton and John Duren, had expressed some interest in Georgetown, and Thompson was definitely interested in them. If his schedule allowed it, he occasionally would come to Dunbar's games, causing a stir in the stands whenever he walked in. The players on the court knew he was there too, and that's exactly what Thompson wanted them to know, especially when it came time to choose a college.

Thompson's childhood friend, Bob Grier, was now coaching the basketball team at St. Anthony's, still a city power in the mid-1970s after Thompson had left. And an old high school teammate, Billy Barnes, was the head coach at Archbishop Carroll, where all-American Al Dutch was about to graduate in the spring of 1975.

Dutch was a genuine blue-chipper, a 6-7 forward who had averaged 25 points and 15 rebounds a game in his senior season, the best schoolboy player in Washington and one of the top ten prospects in the country. Georgetown was on his final list of three schools, along with Maryland and Notre Dame. And Thompson had another friend who could help Al Dutch make up his mind.

George Leftwich had coached Dutch at Carroll and had followed his career closely ever since. "I really did think Alfred needed what John could offer him," Leftwich said. "He needed structure and somebody to kick him in the butt. Al was not a muscle player—he was more finesse. He could shoot, he could drive, but he didn't want to get beat on. I thought John could make him a complete player. I told him he'd be making a mistake not to go there."

Dutch listened to his old coach. He also was intrigued about playing for a program that clearly was on the rise, and just a few minutes from home. "I had been watching them on and off for the last two years of high school," Dutch said. "John Thompson never really directly recruited me; Bill Stein did most of the work. But they told me I'd be in on the ground floor of something great, and I liked that idea."

The signing of Dutch that spring was Thompson's first significant recruiting coup. And while Dutch never developed into an outstanding college basketball player because of injuries and some personal problems that caused him to take a year off from basketball, his initial decision to attend Georgetown marked yet another turning point in Thompson's mission to build a national power. It was the first time a local superstar sought after by more than one hundred schools had decided to stay home. And the fact that Thompson had won a recruiting battle with Lefty Driesell at Maryland made it that much sweeter.

Driesell had been king of the Washington-area basketball hill ever since he arrived from Davidson College in 1969 and pledged to make Maryland "the UCLA of the East." Driesell was a flashy showman, with a down-home drawl and a reputation as one of the shrewdest recruiters in the country. In 1972 he'd won a nasty recruiting war to convince Moses Malone to matriculate at Maryland, only to lose him to the professional ranks before he ever attended a class. But Driesell's rebuilding of the Maryland program also had a ripple effect in Washington, forcing other local schools to upgrade their teams or be left behind. Now, with the signing of Al Dutch, Thompson had sent a message to College Park, Maryland, as well.

Two other Washington players came to Georgetown that year without much of a recruiting struggle. The St. Anthony's pipeline had produced Tom Scates, a huge 6-foot-11, 250-pound center, and Gary Wilson, a 6-8 forward. Thompson had known both for years. He had recruited Scates out of an Alexandria, Virginia, junior high school across the river while he was still coaching at St. Anthony's. Wilson was the younger brother of Thompson's starting center, Merlin Wilson.

The fourth and final member of that incoming freshman class was almost heaven-sent. Steve Martin, a 6-5 guard from St. Augustine's High School in New Orleans, had never heard of Georgetown until one of the Jesuit faculty members mentioned the school to him. Brother Fox had been reading about Thompson and recommended to Martin, a good student, that he might want to consider the school. Through another coaching friend, Thompson had also heard about Martin. Always on the prowl for a big guard, Thompson was interested, and so were a slew of other Louisiana schools, including LSU, Tulane and Southern University, which had recently hired Martin's high school coach to take over the program.

When Martin came north for a visit, Thompson took him on a tour of the campus. More important, he took him all over the city, stopping for dinner at a well-known soul food restaurant, the Rib Pit, in the heart of Washington's black community. "That still sticks in my mind as one of the reasons I decided to come to Georgetown," Martin said. "On my other recruiting trips, I was wined and dined. He took me to a place that a kid like me really felt comfortable in. That impressed me more than any fancy dinner could. I was impressed because I felt like it was all genuine.

"When I first met him, he said to me, 'Welcome to D.C., young man,' in this big, deep voice. I could see where he might intimidate some people. But when I started talking to him on the visit, I was very impressed, and he really put me at ease. He told me he wanted me to come there, but that he couldn't promise that I'd start in any year. Nobody had told me that before. Most of them said, 'You'll come in right away and play.'

"He also said he'd work hard to get me a degree. That was very important to me. My mother was a stickler for academics. So when he talked about the academic part, I was impressed. He said, 'If you work hard, you'll play.' That's really what sold me. Every other recruiter told me how great I was, what they would do for me. John Thompson told me what I could do for myself. There was no question that's where I wanted to go."

Thompson had also been impressed. "I asked Steve what he wanted to be," Thompson once said, "and he said, 'I'm going to be an accountant.' There were no maybes, no I hopes, no I don't knows. I like that."

Still, that first year was difficult for Martin. He didn't play much. He was homesick and lonely. He'd been a solid B+ student in high school, but the rigors of basketball and adjusting to college left him struggling at times. He had never played against the high caliber of competition he was facing every day in practice, and he also was beginning to doubt his own talent.

"It seemed like Mr. Thompson could tell when I was down," Martin said. "He always stayed in touch. He wanted to make sure I wasn't discouraged. There were times when I was second-guessing my decision. At one point, I almost left. But one day we had a long conversation. He called me into the office and he talked me into not leaving. It was the best decision I ever made."

Martin did not play that much during the 1975–76 season, a year that saw the Hoyas finish 21–7, win the ECAC tournament again and advance to a first-round NCAA game, an 83–76 loss to Arizona in Tempe, Arizona.

Instead, Derrick Jackson once again was the leader: He earned a starting position after the 5th game of the season and averaged 17 points. Dutch was the second-leading scorer, with an 11.6 mark, and little Mike Riley continued to dazzle opponents with his defense, leading the Hoyas in both steals and assists.

The season also marked the end of the line for Thompson's first recruiting class, though only three of the six players who had joined Thompson that first year were still on the roster. Mike Stokes had dropped out of school during this sophomore season. Aaron Long stayed on scholarship but a series of nagging injuries left him unable to play. And Greg Brooks had what he now describes as "a disagreement" with Thompson, and did not play his senior season.

In fact, it was a disagreement about Brooks's girlfriend. He had become involved with another student, and eventually they were married. But Thompson did not want Brooks spending so much time with the girl, and told him he had to make a choice between the team and his social life. "He defied Thompson," one of Brooks's friends said, "so he just cut him from the team."

Merlin Wilson, mostly recovered from the physical problems of the previous year, averaged 11 points and 10 rebounds for the Hoyas and set a school record for career rebounds. Doctors finally diagnosed his injury as a disorder of the lower back and shoulder muscles, and he was given a series of stretching exercises to alleviate the pain. And while he never became the all-American everyone had predicted four years before, he was finishing off a solid career. Jonathan Smith came back from a broken toe and was named MVP of the ECAC tournament, scoring 22 points against Villanova and 16 in the championship game against George Washington. But Smith had gone from leading scorer as a freshman to part-time player as a senior, another testament to Thompson's recruiting prowess, and another reason the coach always emphasized his deflated basketball as well.

And Billy Lynn finished his career as the team's second-leading rebounder and third-leading scorer. More important, the Iceberg had melted. He had become immersed in his art, painting, sculpting, drawing, working at the Smithsonian in the summertime, making silk-screen posters and setting up art exhibitions.

That spring, Thompson was in the bleachers of McDonough Gymnasium as his first players got their Georgetown degrees.

"Sometimes these things become too mushy," Thompson said that day. "It's like an ending, and I don't like endings. But these kids are something special. They were the first. They came with me when we had nothing, and they took a hell of a chance. No one in this whole class at Georgetown is coming out of Georgetown with more than these kids got from it. And the Iceberg walking around with a Georgetown degree. That's what it's all about."

None of those players in Thompson's first recruiting class made it to the NBA. Wilson played in Europe for a number of years; Brooks works for the Social Security Administration as a caseworker in Boston; Lynn moved back to New York to work as a commercial artist; Smith had a pro football tryout but never made it and has a construction business in suburban Maryland. Smith's friends say he is somewhat bitter about his experiences at Georgetown. He scheduled six different interviews to talk about them, but he never showed up for any of them.

Wilson said he would be happy to talk about John Thompson, for a fee. "Why should I talk to you?" he said one day. "Thompson is making all this money. I'm tired of promoting things for people and not getting paid for it. All I know is a lot of us helped make him the number-one team in the country. Hell, in high school we were number one in the country and that helped him get the job at Georgetown. A lot of guys from those years are very upset with him. I'm not saying why, but you figure it out. I don't ask him for nothing. I know he can be a very vindictive person, but there's nothing he can do to me. I just don't want to talk about him. You're gonna make money from this book. Maybe I'll write my own book. When they pay me, that's when I'll talk."

Brooks also was reluctant to elaborate on his problems with his old high school and college coach. "I haven't talked to John Thompson since I graduated," he said. "I don't want to get into why. Let's just say the people who pay their money to see a basketball game don't always see the other side of it, they don't know what goes on behind the scenes. I just disagreed with the way some things happened there, and I expressed my feelings by staying away. I'll just say that success can change a person in more ways than one. It can change you for the best, or the worst."

For John Thompson, success meant other significant changes in his life. That year, Georgetown signed the coach to a new five-year contract with a considerable raise. He also was very much in demand for speeches and clinics, locally and around the country. And he was making an impression on many of his colleagues.

Only four years before, John Thompson had come as a neophyte to the annual coaches' convention held in conjunction with the NCAA Final Four in St. Louis. He knew a few people in the hotel lobby crowded with gossiping coaches, and he asked a reporter to introduce him to a few more. He also wanted to know about the National Association of Basketball Coaches. Who runs it? he asked. How do you sign up for committees?

It did not take long for John Thompson to find out. By 1976, he was among the movers and shakers of his profession, elected to the NABC board of directors, the youngest coach in that group. And in March of that same year another one of his friends came calling. This time it was Dean Smith, asking Thompson to serve as an assistant coach for the 1976 U.S. Olympic basketball team.

At the time, Thompson said he was gratified by the selection because he was tired of people talking about him as a superior recruiter and a mediocre bench coach. "I can't deal with knocks," he said. "I've been to the NCAA tournament two years in a row. If I can go to the NCAA tournament two times without knowing how to coach, then when I learn how to coach I might be real good.

"It's an honor for me to be recognized by those who know the game. The sport is full of critics. The lobby at the coaches' convention is full of them. . . . You grit your teeth. People want to throw things in your way rather than go forward. The only good coaches are the losers; they sit down and tell you how to win. So when my peers select me for something, that's why it means so much to me personally."

Thompson had always dreamed about being involved in the Olympics. He had tried out for the 1964 team but had been cut early. "It was one of the most frustrating times of my life," Thompson once said. "I felt so many spots were given to segments of the basketball community and I'm sure the selections were not the fairest. Let me tell you who didn't make it: Willis Reed, Rick Barry, Billy Cunningham, Jerry Sloan, Wally Jones, to name a few."

Thompson has also said he would never have taken the assistant's job for any other coach but Smith. "Too many black coaches in the past became symbols of the U.S. assistant," he said a few years later. "I would like to be head coach, but I've been an assistant once and the only man I'd ever do it for again is Dean Smith. I don't want to be another symbol."

But in 1976 he was more than that, according to Smith. "He did a great job for us, just a great job," the North Carolina coach said. "And the kids just loved him."

The kids and their coaches—Smith, Thompson and North Carolina assistant coach Bill Guthridge—also were on a mission, hoping to avenge the most shocking upset in Olympic history, a 51–50 defeat to the Soviet Union in Munich in 1972. None of the players on this team had been there, but most had seen the game and its controversial finish, when the Russians were given new life at the end and Alexander Belov scored with no time left for the disputed victory. Belov and several other Russians would be back in Munich, and the Americans wanted them badly.

But not all the Americans. Before the start of the trials to pick a team, a number of the top collegiate players had decided not to try out, fearful that injury or a poor performance in the trials or the Games might hurt their stock in the pros. Notably absent were some of the best big men in the country—6-10 Leon Douglas of Alabama, 7-1 Robert Parish of Centenary and 6-10 Richard Washington of UCLA—all of them advised by agents or pro teams not to try out. And another large body, 6-10 center Kent Benson of Indiana, was missing because of recent surgery on his wrist.

Jesse Owens, President Ford and Thompson at a White House Olympic reception in 1976. (AP/Wide World Photos)

"I blame the times more than I blame the players," Thompson said. "If somebody had been waving a million dollars in front of me at the time, I might not have tried out for the Olympics either. It shows the hypocrisy under which we're operating. In 1972, everyone screamed when there was talk of a black boycott in the Olympics. But now, when the concern is the almighty dollar, nobody is screaming at the agents for telling players to boycott the Olympics. Now it's looked upon with grace."

When the selection committee picked the final squad, it had a decided Atlantic Coast Conference look with a heavy emphasis on North Carolina. Seven of the 12 players on the final roster played in the ACC, including four of Smith's Tar Heel stars—6-10 centers Mitch Kupchak and Tom LaGarde, forward Walter Davis and guard Phil Ford. Smith had a vote in the initial process to cut the squad to fifteen players, but not the final say, though he did have the right to make the final three cuts down to the twelve-man Olympic roster. In fact, Smith wanted 7-1 Tree Rollins of Clemson and big guard Bobby Wilkerson of Indiana, but was outvoted by the committee. There were only four college seniors on the team, making this the youngest U.S. squad in Olympic history. And perhaps the most heavily criticized.

Bill Russell, Thompson's pal, was quoted as saying the selection process was political. Dave Anderson, the highly regarded sports columnist for *The New York Times*, wrote that there had been a racial quota for making up a team that had eight black players and four whites. Red Auerbach said the team was weak down the middle. And everyone was pointing to the Carolina connection.

"There would have been criticism whoever was selected," Smith said at the time. "And it would increase if we don't win, no matter where it is aimed. If everyone who was eligible attended the tryouts, maybe we wouldn't have all this to scream about. But I'm not going to worry about it. We had our selection process and I didn't politick among the committee."

Kupchak said he was stunned and somewhat disturbed by all the carping. He had gone through a crisis of conscience himself about trying out. He had undergone a back operation as an undergraduate, and also was getting pressure from the pros not to risk playing in Montreal. "The criticism began the day after the team was selected in June," Kupchak said, "and we didn't stop hearing it until we won the gold medal at the end of July."

Still, in retrospect, Kupchak said, all the negative talk may actually have pulled the team closer together and worked as an incentive. And the Americans did have some talent. Quinn Buckner, the all-American guard from Indiana, would team with Ford, a ball-handling wizard, in the backcourt, backed up by Tate Armstrong of Duke. The forwards were Adrian Dantley of Notre Dame, Kenny Carr of North Carolina State, Phil Hubbard of Michigan, Scott May of Indiana and Ernie Grunfeld of Tennessee, with LaGarde and Kupchak manning the center spot. Maryland's Steve Sheppard, a 6-6 swingman and the biggest surprise of the selection committee, played several positions, though he would see limited action during the Games. In fact, a number of players on the team would be used in both the frontcourt and the backcourt.

Most of the players on that team also would go on to long and distinguished careers in the NBA, "but at the time, we kept reading and hearing that there wasn't enough talent," Phil Ford said. "It just made us play harder."

Smith ran a tough, physical training camp for his team, which only had about two months to prepare for the Games and learn the nuances of international basketball. Thompson worked closely with the two big men, Kupchak and LaGarde, and also paid particular attention to Smith's handling of the team. Smith was a superb teacher, and Thompson was taking notes on his principles of pressure, his use of run-and-jump traps, his disguising defenses, his four corners offense. As much as the players were learning, Thompson also was getting the benefit of a two-month, twenty-four-hour-a-day coaching clinic from a master of the game. When Thompson returned to Georgetown, in fact, many of Smith's drills were incorporated into his practice sessions, and he would take Smith's philosophy and blend it with his own to the point that some would say Georgetown became "the Carolina of the North."

By the time the Olympic players arrived in Montreal, they were ready to play. An exhibition tour against professional all-star teams had toughened them up and built their confidence, despite all the complaining about the roster. The players also had become good friends and teammates in every sense of the word, and their close quarters in the Olympic Village helped solidify the process. The coaching staff and team manager Joe Vancisin roomed together in a cramped apartment. Thompson and Guthridge spent their off-hours trading souvenir pins in an Olympic Village surrounded by massive security. The massacre of Israeli athletes by terrorists at the Munich Games four years earlier was still fresh in the memory of Olympic officials, and every precaution was taken to avoid another tragic disaster.

Everywhere Thompson went, the big man commanded attention. Some people could not believe he was actually a coach and team administrator. "Several times people asked me if I was the manager of the U.S. team," he said later. "They could not conceive, from what they heard of America, that a black could be in an administrative position."

The Americans opened the competition with an easy 106–86 victory over what was supposed to have been a strong Italian team. That night, they went back to the village and watched Yugoslavia easily handle Puerto Rico, their next opponent two nights later. The Americans were not so fortunate.

They struggled against the Puerto Ricans from the opening tip-off, and no one could handle Butch Lee, an all-American guard at Marquette who had been born in Puerto Rico but had learned his basketball on the playgrounds of New York. Lee scored 35 points that night, but one of his few misses in the final seconds allowed the Americans to escape with a 95–94 victory. It would be their closest call during the Games. They followed that victory with a 112–93 rout of Yugoslavia, won on a forfeit against Egypt and finished the preliminary round with a lackluster 81–66 decision over Czechoslovakia in a game played at nine in the morning.

With a 5–0 record in their part of the draw, the U.S. team advanced to the semifinals and crushed the home-team Canadians, opening a 13-point lead at the half on the way to a 95–77 victory despite the presence of seventeen thousand fans in the Montreal Forum, most of them pulling for the undersized and overmatched Canadian team. That same day, however, another underdog did prevail. The Yugoslavs upset the favored Russians, ending the possibility of a U.S.-Soviet grudge match for the gold in the final game. The American players insisted it didn't matter to them, even if they had been pointing toward the Russians. "None of us was in Munich four years ago," Buckner said. "We just came to play as a team. It didn't matter at all if it was Russia or not."

Still, Smith was concerned enough about a possible letdown that he brought the team together a few hours before game time and asked John Thompson to say a few words. Thompson did better than that. He talked for five minutes.

"I told them I was sick of hearing people run them down," Thompson said. "I told them, 'Don't say anything to those people when you get home, just smile and walk on by.' " He also talked a lot about opportunity. He told the players it was "an opportunity to shove the words of your critics down their own throats . . . an opportunity to walk past all your critics with your heads high . . . an opportunity you are only going to get this one time in your whole lives." Several players said they saw tears running down Thompson's face as he finished up, telling the team, "God, I wish I could have it."

"It was very emotional," Kupchak said years later. "It definitely got us going."

Said Smith, "Coach Thompson spoke for four or five minutes and said more than most people say in a lifetime. He reminded the team of all the hard work and said, 'Wouldn't it be nice to go back and visit some of the people who said this wasn't a good team?' "

Early on, it became quite obvious this would be no contest. The Americans quickly took a 10–2 advantage over Yugoslavia, opened a 20-point lead at halftime and never looked back. The only tense moments came with four minutes gone in the second half. Adrian Dantley, who would score 30 points for the night, got an elbow in the eye and had to leave the floor for three and a half minutes while doctors closed the wound with seven stitches. When Dantley returned, the American lead was down to 10. Dantley came back with 12:41 left in the game, stole the ball once, fed Phil Hubbard for a few easy baskets and scored one himself on a neat baseline move. Within six minutes the U.S. was back up by 17, and the celebrating was about to start.

The Americans eventually prevailed, 96–74, and as the team mounted the victory stand to receive their medals from IOC President Lord Killanin, Smith, Thompson and Guthridge watched the ceremony from a tunnel leading to the locker room. Only the players got the medals; the coaches had to settle for a different reward—sweet vindication. "We had some tears when the kids stood up there," Smith said. "We were over in a dark corner. It was a very special time for us."

Kupchak said he knew his teammates were ready to play when the whole squad was dressed and waiting for the bus twenty minutes before it was time to leave for the game. "Like a lot of other guys," Kupchak said, "I had to think seriously about whether or not I would try out for this team. . . . In the week before the trials began, I went to bed every night saying 'I won't go' and got up every morning saying 'Yes I will.' I didn't really make up my mind until the Friday before they began. But standing on that platform out there tonight, I was thinking what a fool I must have been to even consider missing this.

"I think everyone will have to agree that it was a pretty good feat, the U.S. winning this thing with only four players."

What did he mean by four players? a reporter asked.

"Well," he said, a sly smile on his face, "we didn't have a center, did we?"

The next day the team scattered forever, but to this day, Kupchak said, "there will always be a special feeling between all of us." In fact, when Kupchak was recovering from serious knee surgery a few years later, Thompson allowed him to rehab at Georgetown. "I was a pro," Kupchak said. "He treated me like one of his own." For Thompson there would always be a special feeling for the Olympics and U.S. participation in international basketball. A few weeks after he returned from Montreal, he was back on the road again, this time taking his own Georgetown team to Taiwan for a series of games. The Olympic experience, and his memory of a tour of the Soviet Union he took while at Providence College, had convinced him that he wanted his own players to broaden their horizons.

"I went to Montreal with an air of sophistication, feeling that I'd done just about everything in basketball either with Carroll, Providence, the Boston Celtics or at Georgetown," he said at the time. "But I felt like a kid. I called home every night to say I'd never seen anything like this in my life."

Thompson chose Taiwan in part because he had been disturbed when Canada refused to let that country participate in the Games as the Republic of China, a move that would have offended Communist China, which had full diplomatic relations with the Canadian government but did not compete. Taiwan went home.

"If you withdraw from the Olympics or begin to ban countries because of their political beliefs, then what do you start withdrawing from next?" Thompson said. "If the Olympics die, I will see it as a symbol of worldwide giving up on each other. That feeling came home to me one day when an Arab came up and wanted to have his picture taken with me. He wanted a picture with his arm around a great big guy. And I wanted a snapshot of him just as much. The next day we learned that particular contingent had pulled out of the Games because of politics. That depressed me. I still remember the way we talked to each other with hand gestures and smiles and laughs. The Arab never got to compete. He just has a picture of me giving him a bear hug."

Thompson said he wanted his own players to have similar experiences. "I want my players to learn to give importance to how other people live, whether it's the Italian Olympic team having wine bottles all over their locker room or the Ethiopians doing pull-ups on each other's belts because they don't know what a Universal machine is."

So it was off to Taiwan for more than two weeks, in towns like T'ai-nan, Taipei and T'ai-chung, with stopovers in Hawaii and at the Georgetown branch campus in Tokyo. Of course, Mary Fenlon went, and so did Jim Wiggins, the barber from the old neighborhood near Spingarn High School. The twenty-four-person entourage was treated royally almost everywhere they went, though accommodations occasionally left a bit to be desired.

"We weren't in a lot of luxury hotels," said Fran Connors, the sports information director who went on the trip and also kept a diary.

At an overnight stop in a town in southern Taiwan, Connors wrote, "Fear didn't begin to set in until we entered the billets where we were supposed to sleep. They were alive with ants, mosquitos, spiders and lizards that slithered along the ceilings and walls. For protection, nets were suspended over the beds. Yao-Yuan Chao, our faithful guide, suggested to Coach Thompson that we seek accommodations elsewhere if we didn't find the living quarters suitable. Thompson decided that we would remain. He told Chao, 'My players will learn tonight and rest tomorrow. Some of them are too spoiled.' . . . Sunrise couldn't come soon enough for the Hoyas. Some of the players forced themselves to stay awake through the night by shooting pool, studying or playing cards. As we were leaving, sophomore Tom Scates was asked how he slept.

" 'With my eyes open,' he said."

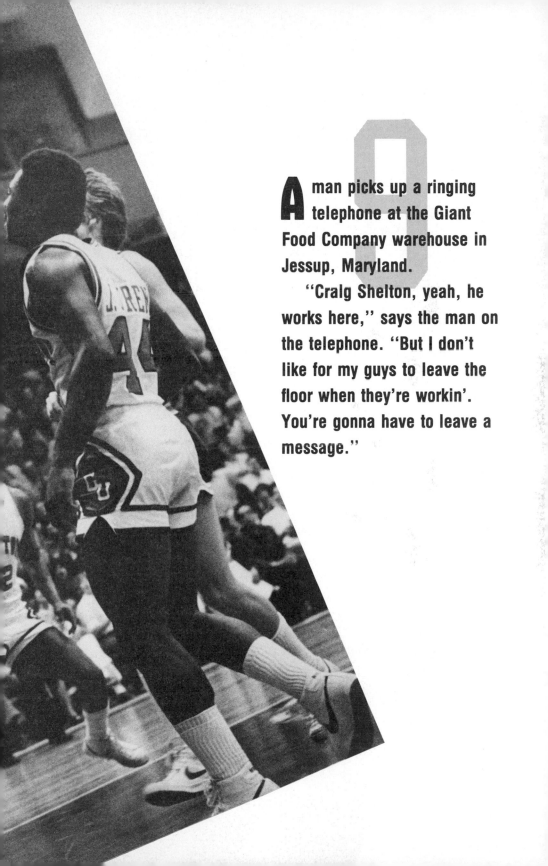

9

A man picks up a ringing telephone at the Giant Food Company warehouse in Jessup, Maryland.

"Cralg Shelton, yeah, he works here," says the man on the telephone. "But I don't like for my guys to leave the floor when they're workin'. You're gonna have to leave a message."

HE WAS KNOWN AS BIG SKY, A YOUNG MAN JOHN THOMPSON once described as the most intense basketball player he had ever seen. Craig Shelton could run all day and leap to the stars, and when he set his mind on grabbing a rebound or going strong to the basket, pity the poor fool who tried to get in his way. He practiced and played in only one gear—warp speed—and helped carry Georgetown to the brink of the Final Four in 1980, his senior season.

Craig Shelton did everything John Thompson ever asked of him on the basketball court. Though he was barely 6-foot-6, he usually guarded the tallest and most powerful men in the game, often jumping center despite the presence of two 7-footers on his own team. As a freshman, working to rehabilitate a wounded knee, he turned to the weight room to build his upper body. When his knee began to come around he started running long distances, and in practice sessions he drove himself to win every sprint before the team was excused for the day. Some nights he came home so exhausted he was too tired to eat, let alone crack a book. Still, he tried to go to class and do the work because he knew that was the only way he could keep playing basketball, the only way he'd have a chance at the big money of the pros. Everyone told him he'd be a first-round draft choice, and he had no reason not to believe them.

But now, ten years later, Craig Shelton knows better. There is no air left in his basketball, just as John Thompson had always warned him. Shelton used to hear that speech all the time from the man his players used to call Pipehead behind his back because Thompson enjoyed puffing tobacco, and all the other admonitions as well. If you need help, we'll find you help. If you've got problems, we'll help you solve them.

Craig Shelton had a problem when he returned to the United States after six years of playing pro basketball in Europe. He had no Georgetown degree and he wanted to talk to John Thompson about coming back to school to finish what he had started so long ago. But Shelton says John Thompson never returned his repeated telephone calls, turned his back on a player who had carried Georgetown to new heights in the late 1970s and had helped set the stage for a national championship contender of the early 1980s.

When Shelton left school as the second-round draft choice of the Atlanta Hawks in June of 1980, he was forty credits short of a diploma. He hadn't even declared a major, but at the time it didn't seem to matter much. Big Sky once told interviewers that he enjoyed the academic life at Georgetown, that he was particularly enamored with the works of Plato and Aristotle. But mostly he was majoring in basketball, and all John Thompson and Mary Fenlon, the academic coordinator, could do was insist he go to class and do the work.

"I took good courses," Shelton said. "I just didn't graduate. I'm one of the few guys who didn't, and he told me back then to tell people that I had graduated, so I went along. When I came back [from Europe], I thought the school at least owed me a degree—that's all I wanted. But he never responded to my calls."

That surprised Shelton, and saddened him, too. He knew Thompson had a lot on his mind at the time—he was preparing for the 1988 Olympics—but surely he could have picked up the telephone and talked to Shelton. It never happened.

So Shelton did not go back to school, never even went to see his old coach. He had too much pride for that, he said. Most of the money he had earned in one and a half seasons with the Hawks and six years abroad is gone now. There were some bad investments, he admitted. The company that represented him, ProServ of Washington, "had bigger fish to fry."

In Europe, he said, laughing into the telephone, "half the time I was chasing the guys to pay me. When I left Georgetown, Thompson steered me to the people at ProServ. He had some personal deals going with them, and he felt I should go with them too. Financially, they were terrible with me. They didn't give me the respect I felt I should've gotten. When I was in Atlanta, I didn't even have a car. It just seemed like they were always more concerned about other guys. I signed for about ninety thousand dollars. . . . But I got into some bad investments. I had no tax shelters, no house, nothing. Everything I ever made in basketball I earned myself. In Europe, those people were always trying to cheat me, but I usually got my money. I'm a happier man now. I cut my losses, got away from all the problems."

Big Sky Shelton works these days for an hourly wage in a huge warehouse owned by Washington's largest supermarket chain, selecting the food that will go on the shelves for the consumption of many people who used to pay good money to watch him play basketball. He's on his feet most of the day and his boss doesn't like him to take calls at the warehouse. The work is hard, but that never bothered Shelton as a basketball player, and it does not concern him now. He has a seven-year-old son and "I'm going to teach him about his history, his heritage, his people," he said. If the boy should decide he wants to play sports, Shelton will teach him about that as well. He will tell him about college basketball as a bottom-line business, even at a place like Georgetown under a man like John Thompson.

"Thompson's main concern is to keep his job and to win," said Shelton, who lives in Glenarden, Maryland, not far from the District of Columbia. "It's about money. The bottom line is the dollar, keep the job, keep it going. How can you be a father figure when you have the pressure to win? And everything they've got now, I helped them get it.

"I don't blame John Thompson for the situation he's in. I don't blame him for my situation. But he is not a schoolteacher. His job is to win. Could he have done it without me? I don't think so. I was six-six and I played like a seven-footer. We had a couple of seven-footers who played like they were five-eight. Basically, I had to perform athletically, not academically. He tried to do the best he could, but most of the time I was too damn tired to do the homework. Craig 'Big Sky' Shelton had to play for John Thompson to succeed."

Shelton says he does not watch much basketball on television anymore, though he will occasionally tune in a Georgetown game. He's never gone back to campus, never knocked on Thompson's door since the coach ignored his phone calls. "For me to be a fan of his, he has to be a fan of mine," he said.

A man who once lived for the competition stays away from the basketball court as well. His friends are always asking him to join them in recreation-department or summer-league games, "but I can't do it. I can't run down the floor for free anymore. I gave too much to the game. So I'll just leave it alone and go on with my life. I can deal with it.

"John Thompson always said, 'To err is human, to forgive is not my policy.' But I don't blame John—I'm really not a bitter person. I blame the system. We're supposed to be student-athletes, but it's more than that. You're on TV, you're traveling, reporters want to talk to you, the fans want to see you. There's so much money involved. I learned that the hard way, but life goes on. I just hope John Thompson knows that it was people like me who got him where he is today. I hope he appreciates that."

Through a spokesman, John Thompson declined to be interviewed.

Certainly the people who watched Shelton and his Dunbar High School teammate, John "BaBa" Duren, appreciated what they helped accomplish at Georgetown, leading the Hoyas to four postseason tournaments between 1976, when they entered as freshmen, and 1980, when they left as professional draft choices.

The two had gone to Georgetown mostly because of their high school coach, Joe Dean Davidson, who directed Dunbar to a 29–0 record in 1976 and the number-one ranking in the Washington area. Thompson and Davidson met when Davidson was coaching junior high school basketball in Washington and Thompson was recruiting one of his players for St. Anthony's. "We got to be friends," Davidson said a few months before his death in May 1990 of a heart attack. "And John sometimes cultivated friendships to suit his purposes."

Davidson began building a power at Dunbar at the same time Thompson was starting at Georgetown. The two coaches spent a good bit of time together; Thompson had even prevailed upon Dean Smith to allow Davidson to work as a coach during the Olympic trials in 1976. Davidson, in turn, would ask Thompson to put in a good word with a youngster or his parents for the Dunbar program as he tried to corral the best inner-city athletes.

Shelton had been heavily recruited by a number of schools before his decision came down to Georgetown or Villanova. "At the last minute, I picked Georgetown," Shelton said. "You're a black kid, he's a black man in that position, and that was a big part of it. Joe Dean steered me towards John, too, and I respected his advice. Joe Dean was great with kids, a wonderful man. He could have sold us all to other schools and gotten his pockets filled up, but he was looking out for our interests. He thought we'd do well at Georgetown. John was his friend and he thought we'd be treated right there."

Duren, meanwhile, had known about Thompson for as long as he could remember. He lived down the street from the Boys Club and "I could look out the front door and see the court over there," he said. "I knew about Thompson since I was eight years old. I'd seen him play pickup games there. I played for Jabbo Kenner at the Boys Club, and he and John were good friends. Mr. Jabbo was always telling me I ought to go to Georgetown. He helped convince me. So did Joe Dean Davidson. I knew the program, I knew a lot of the guys there and I thought I could play right away."

Duren had narrowed his choices to Howard, Clemson, Villanova and Georgetown, and in May of their senior year, Duren and Shelton held a press conference to announce that Georgetown would be their destination. "We were walking around shaking our heads and thinking, Where are we going to go?" Shelton said. "We didn't plan on going together. It just happened that way."

At the time of the announcement, Shelton was on crutches. He had broken his kneecap jumping for a rebound in an all-star game in March, and the injury would eventually force him to miss all but 7 games late in his freshman season at Georgetown. Duren, meanwhile, moved into the starting backcourt with Derrick Jackson as a freshman and averaged 10 points a game that year. Shelton became a starter as a sophomore during the 1977–78 season, and for the second straight year the Hoyas accepted a bid to the NIT tournament after losing to Virginia Commonwealth in the first round of the ECAC Southern Division tournament.

The Hoyas had been prohibitive favorites to beat VCU, but the night before the game Derrick Jackson, the team's senior captain and leading scorer, had a flare-up of a bleeding ulcer that had bothered him occasionally in the past and had been discovered in several other family members as well.

"I was a worrier," Jackson said. "I was worried about graduating, I was worried about my career, whether I'd keep playing basketball. The night before the game, I started feeling real bad, spitting up blood. I wanted to play so badly I told my roommate, Craig Esherick, not to say anything. I was hoping they wouldn't notice it and I'd be better with some sleep. At breakfast the next morning I tried to hide it, but I was having trouble standing up. I couldn't even sit up straight. I couldn't eat. We had a little shootaround, and I got through that okay, but Craig knew something was wrong. He told Coach Thompson about it."

Thompson went to Jackson's dormitory room on campus and found Jackson lying on the bed in agony, an open Bible on the floor. "That's when I really got scared," Thompson said a few days later. "The problem with Derrick is that he will never, never tell you when anything is wrong with him. He has very strong religious beliefs and he earnestly believes that he can cure himself with prayer.

"We're dealing here with things a lot more important than taking a player in and out of a ball game. It upsets me that a kid I love could hide this from me. We confuse the gung ho, win-win-win thing with common sense. Sometimes these kids can't tell the difference. When Derrick gets better, I'm going to cuss him out good for not telling me. I thought he had things in better perspective than this."

Jackson would never again play for the Hoyas, undergoing surgery two weeks later to remove the ulcer. For years afterward, Thompson would invoke Jackson's name countless times when he talked to his players about the importance of basketball and putting the game in its proper place. Jackson's picture occupies a place of honor in Thompson's office, and the two still talk frequently. "He asks me how the collection is going," Jackson said from the church in Wheaton, Illinois, where he is an assistant pastor. "I consider him a great man and a great friend."

But not everyone would agree. As Thompson climbed the ladder to the pinnacle of his profession, some people were left behind, and others invoked his considerable wrath. Joe Dean Davidson, the man who helped steer Shelton and Duren to Georgetown, was one. Bob Dwyer, his high school coach at Carroll who had recommended him for his first coaching job, was another. He feuded with Lefty Driesell for several years. There was even a bitter rift with Jim Wiggins, the neighborhood barber who had been a constant companion and one of his most loyal supporters in the early days of the program. "If you got nothing nice to say, don't say it," Wiggins said. "A lot of what you see with John is not what you get. That's all I'll say about it."

Joe Dean Davidson and Thompson began growing apart in the late 1970s. Davidson said Thompson was upset with him when another one of his talented players, shooting guard Kenny Matthews, decided to attend North Carolina State instead of Georgetown. "Kids didn't go to Georgetown because I shoved them in that direction," Davidson said a few weeks before his death. "I had kids talk to other schools, too. To him, that was treason. And as time passes, he's been known to retaliate."

Davidson also got upset with Thompson because he felt Thompson hurt his chances to get a job as the head basketball coach at Drake University in 1981. "I asked him if I could use his name as a reference," Davidson said. "He said he was happy to do it. Then I found out he got in an argument with the Drake athletic director about the selection process. John told me they asked him how he thought I'd adjust to a Midwestern environment. His answer was 'It's not how he'll adjust to you, it's how will you adjust to him?' It made it sound like I was inflexible. His statements added up to a nonreference and created a shadow of a doubt. I can't say that's what killed my chances, but a friend of mine out there told me that after their conversation with John they pretty much shut it down as far as I was concerned.

"I called John after that. I told him I had supported him for years because I always said positive things about him to my players. I told him, 'I never asked you for anything, but when it was time for you to reciprocate, you cut my throat.' We talked about it. He told me I was crazy and we needed to sit down and talk some more. I called him back a few days later to set it up. He never called me back.

"For a long time, there was the conception that John Thompson was a saint. A lot of people, including me, had a great deal of respect and admiration for him. After a while, people started to see the real person, and they didn't like him as much."

Thompson's split with his own high school coach, Bob Dwyer, also occurred in the mid-1970s, and the two have not spoken since. By then, Dwyer was coaching the basketball team at St. Anselms, a small, exclusive Catholic high school in Washington. One of his players, Steve Castellan, a white 6-10 center, was being heavily recruited during the 1975 season, and college coaches were constantly coming around to see the team play or practice. St. Anselms always hosted an annual postseason tournament, and that year Dwyer had invited Calvert High from southern Maryland to participate. Calvert had a promising player as well in Rick Weber, a white 6-7 forward who had played with the Georgetown team in the summer league before his senior season and was being wooed by Thompson.

A number of scouts had come to the tournament to watch the two players, and Dwyer asked a few of his friends what they thought of Weber. "They all told me the same thing," Dwyer said. "They said he's too slow, he can't play big-time basketball. He was an awfully good shooter, but he didn't have enough movement.

"Anyway, the season ended and this kid calls me on the phone. 'Mr. Dwyer,' he says, 'will you give me some advice?' I told him I'd do the best I could. He said he'd been offered a scholarship by Roanoke, Randolph-Macon and Georgetown and he didn't know what to do. I told him if I was him, I'd go to either Roanoke or Randolph-Macon if he wanted to play. I told him if he went to Georgetown, I didn't think he'd play much.

"So he said to me, 'What do you mean? Why are they recruiting me?' And I said, 'Primarily because you're white.' I said they might want a couple sitting around the place. Well, unfortunately, his coach told that to Thompson, and of course Thompson got pissed off, and I guess he had a reason to be. I maybe should not have said that, but I always told it like it was. That's the only reason they were recruiting him, and sometimes the truth hurts."

Weber, now an assistant basketball coach at Old Dominion University, does not recall talking to Dwyer himself and says that his high school coach, Frank Moore, made the phone call. "I do remember he [Moore] told me that Dwyer said I'd be better off at a smaller school," said Weber, who would end up going to Roanoke and playing regularly for four years.

"From that time on," said Dwyer, "I've never seen John Thompson or spoken to him and he's never spoken to me. I sent him a letter, and he sent me a Christmas card back. I made the first move. But that's all there's been. I wrote him that I thought it was time to settle it, as adults. I told him I don't have much time left and I'd like to face up to the facts with him and let him know I had nothing to hide."

Some people thought that Thompson and Dwyer would finally bury the hatchet in 1987 when the players from the undefeated 1959-60 Carroll team gathered in Washington for a reunion dinner, prompted by the recent elevation of Monk Malloy to the presidency of Notre Dame. All the old gang was there: George Leftwich and Tom Hoover, Walt Skinner and Billy Barnes. But Thompson chose not to attend.

"John sent me a note telling me he didn't feel comfortable in coming, but that it had nothing to do with me or the other players," Malloy said. "I just felt badly because whatever feelings John had either directly toward Bob Dwyer or whatever, well, he didn't say it explicitly, but that was the implication of it. I guess I always felt that whatever it was that strained the relationship could be healed over time. Maybe the reunion could have been the chance for some of that to take place. But it didn't, and it's really too bad."

Thompson's problems with Driesell eventually did heal. In the 1970s, Thompson had been the upstart threatening Driesell's stranglehold on Washington-area basketball interest. Still, he was careful not to offend the big state university down the road, and at one point he even paid a visit to College Park to learn about the marketing tools former Maryland promotions director Russ Potts had used to help sell out Cole Field House, where Maryland played its home games.

But in 1977, a bit of bad blood spilled. Maryland was trying to put some pressure on the NIT committee to schedule Georgetown at Cole Field House in a first-round game. When the NIT declined, Maryland decided not to accept a tournament bid. The resulting brouhaha did not sit well with Thompson. "We do something positive and we still play second fiddle to Maryland," Thompson fumed at the time. "I have no anger toward Maryland. . . . I'm upset that something positive is going on here at Georgetown—we've been in postseason play three years in a row, how many schools can say that?—and it goes unnoticed. People tell me, 'Just stick to sports,' but it seems like maybe I need to do something controversial to get my players the attention they've earned."

Relations simmered between the two schools until an incident early in the 1979–80 season. The year before, Georgetown had finally ended a streak of 5 straight losses to Driesell under Thompson, and the Hoyas were beginning to be on an almost equal footing with their neighbors from College Park for players, publicity and postseason consideration.

Midway through the first half of their December 1979 game, Thompson vehemently protested when a referee awarded Maryland a free throw after one of his players had dunked the ball and momentarily hung onto the rim, a technical foul. While Thompson ranted at the officials, Maryland's Ernest Graham, a notorious on-court hot dog, patted Thompson on the head. "I was just telling him that he was too big to get that mad," Graham said.

Thompson was not amused, and his temper tantrum increased in pitch and profanity. Driesell, a notable foot-stomper himself, walked over to Thompson on the sideline and suggested that perhaps it was time to stop arguing and take a seat back on the bench. The two exchanged heated words.

"He called me a motherfucking son of a bitch, or something like that," Driesell recalled years later. "I didn't shake his hand after the game. The thing that really irked me was that if it had been me and I'd flown off the handle, I would have called him the next day or that night and apologized. He didn't apologize to me until the Final Four that year, which I thought was real late in coming."

Relations between the two men were strained, and that game marked the last time Maryland has played Georgetown during the regular season. The teams did meet once more that same season, in the 1980 NCAA tournament, with Georgetown prevailing again. Before that game, in fact, Thompson publicly apologized to Driesell for the incident months earlier. "Because I was rude in the first game . . . there are those people who would like to think that there is some form of belligerence or some form of hate out of proportion to the competitive aspect of it," Thompson said. "I've contributed to that myself by my actions in the last game, which I said publicly that I was wrong. Even in the church now, you don't have to give public penance. Lefty was not in error. That was a one-way street. John Thompson was wrong at that time."

John Thompson was also now moving ahead of Driesell and his program. In fact, that victory over Maryland during the regular season, and the second a few months later in the NCAA tournament, clearly marked a turning point for Georgetown. No longer were the Hoyas the plucky underdogs to the Atlantic Coast Conference power, no longer was Driesell the dominant personality on the local college basketball scene, no longer would Maryland's games get the banner headlines while Georgetown would appear below the fold.

Georgetown was now the big story in Washington basketball, and when the Hoyas advanced to the Final Eight that same 1979–80 season, the transformation was complete. Thompson was even in a position to end the longtime rivalry between the two schools the following year. Georgetown has not played Maryland since, and over the 1980s Thompson also ended longtime local rivalries against George Washington University and American University. His rationale was simple enough: He had nothing to prove by beating them, and everything to lose if his team was upset by a clearly inferior program. Still, in 1986, when Driesell was under siege in the wake of the cocaine-induced death of his star player, Len Bias, Thompson publicly defended him and criticized the school for firing him. "I bled for Lefty," Thompson said.

These days, in fact, Driesell describes Thompson as "a friend." When one of Thompson's players, Michael Tate, decided to leave Georgetown in 1990 after his freshman season, Thompson recommended Driesell's program at James Madison University, and Tate enrolled at the Harrisonburg, Virginia, school. But Thompson still won't schedule Driesell's team. "We could fill up the Capital Centre," Driesell moaned, "but he just doesn't want to play. Hell, it'd be an easy win for him. I don't know what he's so worried about."

Back in the Shelton-Duren era, it was Driesell who did not want to play Thompson. But the Georgetown coach wasn't about to let that snub slow his program's progress. His team was on the verge of becoming a national contender, a perennial top-twenty power, and his recruiting efforts intensified and spread geographically. He maintained his interest in signing the best players in the nation's capital, and he still had some rather unorthodox sources for talent, but as the success continued, he was able to broaden his base.

In 1978, for example, he was looking for a shooting guard to replace

Derrick Jackson. Thompson was on the telephone with Clarence "Big House" Gaines, the legendary coach at Winston-Salem State, who told Thompson about a guard from Gastonia, North Carolina, named Eric "Sleepy" Floyd. He'd gotten his nickname when a youth-league baseball coach teased him about dropping a pop fly, yelling, "Are you asleep out there?" But there was nothing wrong with his basketball skills years later, though not too many people were paying attention to Floyd in his senior year of high school.

Most recruiters were showing up at Hunter Huss High to watch one of Floyd's teammates, Jon Robinson, who eventually signed with Maryland and had an injury-plagued career. Across town, James Worthy, now an all-star with the Los Angeles Lakers, was playing at Gastonia Ashbrook and attracting the attention of most college scouts. Floyd's grades also were said to be suspect, and some complained that he was a bit of a show-off on the court. Thompson was not among them. He thought the youngster was a major talent, and might even have had something to prove, so he signed him. Four years later, Floyd would be the senior captain of Thompson's first Final Four team and also the first all-American in the school's history, a number-one draft choice of the New Jersey Nets who went on to a productive career in the NBA.

Another recruit that year also had a fascinating route to the college game. When Ed Spriggs had graduated from Northwestern High School in Hyattsville, Maryland, basketball was the last thing on his mind. He'd been a skinny kid who couldn't even make his high school team as a senior. College was of little interest to him, so he went to work, driving a truck for the post office at $14,000 a year. The slightly built 6-7 boy soon grew to be a muscular 6-9 man, and his friends convinced him to join a recreation-league team. One summer, a Georgetown assistant spotted Spriggs on the court, and before long Thompson was on the telephone asking if he might be interested in going to Georgetown. At first Spriggs thought Thompson was joking. Then he declined, unwilling to give up a steady job and a secure future. But Thompson stayed on him, and Spriggs eventually signed a letter of intent.

"I was impressed," Thompson said of Spriggs's initial reluctance to go to school. "It showed me he was a mature, thoughtful individual. Quitting his job and going to college was a gamble. He gave up security. He was about to get an apartment, but he gave that up to room in a dorm with a bunch of kids. He had a car. It was a big step."

The Hoyas, meanwhile, were taking giant steps. The 1978–79 team won 24 games, a school record, including its first victory over Maryland and, the following week, a 60–54 decision over Bobby Knight's Indiana team. Floyd had immediately stepped in and led the Hoyas in scoring as a freshman, serving notice that he was a force to be reckoned with by scoring 28 against Maryland and 20 against Indiana. A loss to Rutgers in the NCAA tournament ended the season on a somewhat sour note, but in 1979–80 Georgetown set another school record with 26 victories, and just missed making the Final Four.

This was the first season of the newly created Big East Conference, formed in May of 1979 with seven eastern schools—Georgetown, Syracuse, Providence, St. John's, Connecticut, Boston College and Seton Hall, with Villanova added the following year and Pittsburgh joining for the 1982–83 season. The Hoyas won the first Big East tournament in Providence, Rhode Island, with an 87–81 victory over Syracuse, then advanced to the finals of the Eastern Regional against Iowa by winning their first two NCAA tournament games under Thompson, against Iona and Maryland, stretching their winning streak to 15 games.

The Iowa game was yet another heartbreaker for the Hoyas and their faithful fans who journeyed to Philadelphia to watch it. It began splendidly, with Georgetown holding a 10-point lead at the half, a 14-point advantage early in the second half and another 10-point bulge with less than eleven minutes to play. But Iowa managed to get back in the game with torrid 71-percent shooting in the second half, making all 15 of its free throws and committing only 1 turnover in the last twenty minutes.

The Hawkeyes had actually scored on 15 of their last 16 possessions and killed almost two minutes down the stretch setting up for a last shot with the game tied at 78–78. Iowa center Kevin Waite scored the winning points on a three-point play when he faked Spriggs out of position and headed down the lane. Craig Shelton came over to help out, but it was too late. Waite hit the short shot, was fouled by Shelton, and added the free throw for an 81–78 lead. The Hoyas tried to set up a three-point play of their own at the other end, but could only get a field goal with no foul as time expired.

"You feel bad," Thompson said when it was over, "but you feel proud of what the kids have done. We gave it our shot. It wasn't intended to be for us this year. But we'll be back." Indeed, for John Thompson and his Georgetown basketball team, the best was very definitely yet to come.

Lou Carnesecca,
St. John's University Head Coach

Paul Evans,
University of Pittsburgh Head Coach

Jim Boeheim,
Syracuse University Head Coach

Rollie Massimino,
Villanova University Head Coach

10

If you think that I am up here
because our kids graduate
from school, you're foolish. I
am up here because I win. I
have one question to ask regarding revenue sharing. Am I
the only capitalist in the
room?''

—*John Thompson addressing*
the 1988 NCAA convention

HIS TEAM HAD JUST BEEN ELIMINATED FROM THE NCAA BAS-ketball tournament, but John Thompson had little time to mope about that disheartening loss to the University of Iowa. Suddenly, as he told one interviewer three days after that depressing defeat in the East Regional title game, "I'm in demand now."

In fact, earlier in the season Thompson had been contacted about the vacant head coaching position at the University of Florida and had met with school officials before calling back and asking that his name be withdrawn from consideration. Florida basketball had fallen on hard times, and an almost total rebuilding job was in order. Still, that contact had also given rise to some speculation that Thompson was not entirely pleased with the commitment of Georgetown to his nationally ranked basketball program.

Washington Post sports columnist Dave Kindred wrote that "what a college basketball coach does when he sees his job become a dead end is the same thing a mechanic, a newspaperman or truck driver does. He looks for another job. . . . That's why John Thompson, the Georgetown University coach, is talking to the University of Florida athletic director. . . . Florida's basketball job is open and Thompson is at a dead end. . . . His friends will tell you that Thompson is tired of being promised a new basketball arena that is never delivered. He is tired of seeing blueprints for this mirage arena. And it gets worse every time he drives up in front of McDonough Arena."

A few days after that column appeared, Thompson dropped out of the running at Florida, and the job was eventually taken by North Carolina State's Norm Sloan. "I don't feel it's advantageous to me in general," Thompson said. "Florida is a great opportunity, but not for me." But for the first time Thompson also expressed publicly his concern about keeping up with the elite schools in college basketball if his own team continued to play in a tiny on-campus gymnasium.

"I don't feel the administration has misled me," he said. "I don't feel the administration has been unfair to me. But if John Thompson were at the University of Kentucky, with twenty-three thousand seats,

I'd walk around there every day trying to figure out something else I'd ask the university to do. . . . Somebody at Syracuse wasn't satisfied with a nine-thousand-seat gym either, so they got twenty-three thousand. That's why they win. People who get satisfied don't win. Certainly I'd love to see a large, big, beautiful gym. If we made a cost analysis with the people we're competing with and beating and being in the top twenty with, we'd probably say we've done a doggone good job. So I'm sort of curious what we'd do if we had a few more things."

Thompson got more curious a few days after the Iowa game. Officials from the University of Pittsburgh and the University of Oklahoma also called him about their vacant head coaching positions. Though he initially said he was not interested in either school, the people at Oklahoma were particularly persistent. While he was in Indianapolis attending a meeting of the National Association of Basketball Coaches, five representatives of the university, including the chairman of the Oklahoma Board of Regents and the president of Phillips Petroleum Company, paid Thompson a surprise visit. Over breakfast one morning, they beseeched him to at least come out and look at the campus before turning them down.

Thompson agreed. He passed up the NCAA final to fly to Norman with Mary Fenlon, and soon they were being escorted around Oklahoma by none other than Barry Switzer, the school's flamboyant football coach. At the time, Thompson's compensation package at Georgetown was estimated at about $50,000 a year. Oklahoma was offering a deal that would pay him $120,000, and Thompson was getting all the right answers to his typically blunt questions.

Concerned about Oklahoma's location, so far from urban centers of basketball talent like Washington, New York and Los Angeles, Thompson asked Switzer if he might have access to a private plane to go recruiting.

"Yes," Switzer said, "about sixty."

While touring the basketball arena, Thompson casually mentioned that he did not particularly care for the rubbery Tartan court surface Oklahoma was playing and practicing on. "It'll be wood when school starts," one school official told him.

Mary Fenlon was not that impressed. "At the airport," Fenlon said, "they put us in separate cars, I suppose on purpose. The man riding with me—I didn't realize how important he was until later—asked me what it would take to get John to come there. I told him about John's feeling for Georgetown and how the academic program was truly important to his basketball program. The man was very polite. He said he could see that Georgetown had a lot to offer, but then he said, 'We have more oil wells.' "

Thompson's head was turned by his trip to the Southwest, and for several days back in Washington he agonized over his decision. Could he uproot Gwen and the two boys, fourteen-year-old John and Ronny, eleven, from their hometown and plunk them down in the middle of nowhere? What about his staff at Georgetown, the players he'd recruited and committed to? And what about his loyalty to Georgetown, a school that had taken a huge chance on him eight years before, supported him in the terrible times and allowed him to build a program his way, with virtually no interference?

And could John Thompson, a fiercely independent, outspoken black coach from the big city, find happiness in the conservative heartland of America?

"I have to analyze it," Thompson said after Richard Bell, the chairman of the Oklahoma Board of Regents, offered him the job. "I hadn't realized basketball was that big-time. There's no comparison between this deal and Florida from a financial standpoint. The money is very inviting, but I'm not looking for a job at all. . . . Georgetown has satisfied me. There are a few things I'd like changed and I've talked about them before. But they're not unlivable. It would be foolish with the kind of money they're talking about not to evaluate it."

In the meantime, Georgetown was hardly sitting on its thumbs. Thompson was being told that the university did not want him to leave, that while it had no desire or inclination to get into a bidding war to match the Oklahoma offer, certainly the school would be more than willing to discuss Thompson's contract, make adjustments and address his needs. There were no oil wells, but there was certainly no reason that John Thompson couldn't be made happy at Georgetown.

A few days later, Thompson announced his decision. He would stay, though he admitted "I'm sick as hell about giving up the money.

"I don't think I can pinpoint one reason. I think it's in the best interests of everybody that I stay where I am. . . . I have a good job, but I also feel it is my responsibility to listen to opportunities when they present themselves. I don't want to come across as some pious person who gave up a lot of money. You can be just as much a family man, just as religious, with money. I'm not ready to say the rich are damned. . . . The only people who tell you the money is not a factor are the people who have it."

"It was very attractive," Thompson said a few months later. "The facilities, all the advantages that a big school has for a coach and, let's face it, the money. But I decided that, at least for now, Georgetown was a better place for me and for what I wanted to do. That doesn't mean things won't change and I won't change."

How much of a role Gwen Thompson played in her husband's decision can only be a matter of speculation, though a longtime friend of the family said she was not particularly excited about relocating so far from home. The same friend also said that Thompson would never have made the move without her blessing. While Thompson made every effort to keep his private life and his family out of the public eye, their friends knew that Gwen Thompson could be just as strong-willed as her husband.

In fact, Gwen Thompson occasionally sat in on John Thompson's contract talks with the university. One source involved during one particularly difficult negotiation in the early 1980s said that Gwen Thompson, not John, was letting his representative know what she did and did not want in the contract simply by rubbing her nose a certain way. "John would do all the talking," the source said, "but it was Gwen who negotiated that contract."

Friends say their marriage seems rock-solid, though slightly unorthodox. When Thompson was considering a job offer from the Denver Nuggets in the summer of 1990, he was prepared to keep his wife and family in Washington and commute west, much the same way his mentor, Red Auerbach, had done for years with the Boston Celtics. Whatever John Thompson wanted—long hours at the office, out-of-town trips, many with Mary Fenlon, even separate vacations—apparently was fine with Gwen Thompson.

"Actually, it's more of a problem when he's home," she said in a rare interview in 1980. "He has all this nervous energy. If he's not doing something, he's just itchy. So the kids give him their schedules, I give him my schedule, and if he can make it, fine. If not, that's fine, too."

Willie Leftwich, the older brother of John's high school teammate George, helped Thompson negotiate the basic contract he still works under, a five-year pact that is renewed every three years, meaning that at any point Georgetown is committed to Thompson for at least three more years. "The contract is forever," said Leftwich, who declined to provide any specifics or talk about Gwen Thompson's role. "It never has to be renegotiated. It has cost of living, bonuses, incentive clauses built in. There is no situation short of his death that he won't be at Georgetown. Even if it's not basketball, he's slotted in a tenured position at the school."

Leftwich no longer has any dealings with Thompson. They split in the early 1980s, because Thompson did not want Leftwich representing any of his players. At one point he asked Leftwich, a man he had known since he was a teenager and one of the most highly respected attorneys—black or white—in Washington, to provide him with a résumé of his qualifications. Incensed, Leftwich declined, and the two have not done business ever since.

Thompson also was getting legal and practical advice from another Washington attorney with a far more public profile. Donald Dell, whose primary interest in the 1970s involved tennis, was beginning to attract clients from other professional sports. A native Washingtonian himself, Dell had been a world-class tennis player as a younger man. He went on to Yale and the University of Virginia law school and opened up a small practice with three of his classmates in 1969. Within a decade, the firm had a number of top-ranked tennis players under contract, and Dell started a marketing and investment firm known as ProServ in 1971 that now has more than two hundred clients in every major sport. Thompson and Dell became friendly in the 1970s, and the relationship paid off for both when Thompson began steering all of his players toward ProServ after they graduated and headed into professional basketball.

"Even after they leave his program, his players stay under John's control," said another agent. "A couple of years ago, John brought a couple of his kids over to hear ProServ's presentation. When it was over, he looked at both of them and said, 'Well, you are going to sign with ProServ, right?' Of course they did. There was almost no question about it. I'm sure he's got an arrangement with them. Normally, they would get twenty percent of anything they could get a client in endorsements or speaking fees. With John, I'm sure he gets a very reduced rate. Maybe he pays them nothing. It's definitely a relationship that helps ProServ get his players. Signing Patrick Ewing was very important to them, but they had to give him a special deal. I've been told they get three percent of Ewing's contract. But that's still a lot of money."

Thompson, who earns a twenty-thousand-dollar personal appearance fee, remains the only college basketball coach on ProServ's roster of clients, represented by David Falk, a George Washington University law school graduate who handles almost all of Thompson's affairs these days, including his contract talks with the Denver Nuggets. Falk has a reputation as a skillful negotiator and a shrewd businessman.

"The people he represents usually love him, and the people who he goes up against probably hate his guts," said another agent. "That's how it is in this business. I don't know many agents who will say nice things about one of their competitors."

One Washington attorney who has known Falk since his days in law school also described him as "a guy with a very arrogant personality. My father always told me there are no important lawyers, only important clients. David believes just the opposite. He's also done some rotten things. He'll trash the competition and tell these kids that ProServ is the only firm that can get them a good contract and endorsements. Dell has a little more class."

Another longtime Washington agent said much of Thompson's outlook, and particularly his ambition to make a lot of money, comes from Dell. "He's learned a lot from Donald," the agent said. "Donald has always operated from the principle that you should let people see that you are rich, and they'll respect you more. Other people think money should never be discussed publicly. Dell doesn't believe that. And when you listen to John talk, he's always saying the same thing. Money is power. That's Donald Dell talking, too."

While Georgetown was hardly in a position to make Thompson a rich man in 1980, the university made all the right moves to keep him. A few months after Thompson announced that he would not be taking the Oklahoma job, an anonymous group of Georgetown alumni purchased a house for $350,000 and essentially gave it to Thompson. The house, at 4881 Colorado Avenue, Northwest, in a posh and elegant neighborhood, had been owned previously by two well-known Washington hairdressers, Charles Stinson and Roi Bernard, owners of Charles the First, a high-profile establishment that prided itself on coiffing only the finest heads in Washington society. The place also came complete with a $35,000 swimming pool with a tile mosaic of Marilyn Monroe on the bottom, detailed right down to the black beauty mark on her face. At the time, one Georgetown official said the purchase of the house was "evidence of the esteem in which Coach Thompson is held."

A few years later, Father Healy, the Georgetown president, confirmed that the house had been transferred to Thompson in 1982 in lieu of a pay raise, a transaction that had been recommended by Frank Rienzo, the athletic director. "Frank said to me, 'Look, we're going to have to buy the next guy a house, so why not do it for the guy we like?' " Father Healy said. "The real feeling was if John left and we were recruiting a new coach, given the housing situation in Washington, we'd have to offer him a new house. So the alumni and everybody pitched in and we decided to do it."

That house is now valued in the $1 million range, and Thompson owns it with no strings attached. The decision to take care of their coach paid off handsomely for both Thompson and Georgetown over the next decade, and so did another decision Rienzo played a significant role in—the start of the Big East Conference, with Georgetown a charter member and its athletic director one of the key players in its formation.

The central figure was Dave Gavitt, the highly successful coach and athletic director at Providence College, who had been contemplating the possibility of a new league made up of the East's better independent teams for several years. Gavitt and other eastern coaches had watched some of the region's best players spurn their schools for more glamorous institutions in big-name leagues like the Big Ten and the Atlantic Coast Conference. Lew Alcindor had gone even further west, deserting the streets of New York City for the lush green Westwood, California, campus of UCLA, and many more followed him out of the Northeast Corridor.

In addition, the television networks also were far more likely to air critical conference games or intriguing intersectional rivalries like UCLA versus Notre Dame on their Saturday afternoon showcases. Providence College, in fact, was the only eastern school to appear on a national broadcast during the regular season for the entire 1970s, and then only twice.

The crowning blow came in 1978 when the NCAA, the governing body of collegiate athletics, issued a mandate: All members of a conference had to play the other members of that conference in a double-round-robin format. Providence, like Georgetown, was a member of the East Coast Athletic Conference, a jumble of 234 colleges divided up into regions for purposes of postseason play. Under the new NCAA mandate, Providence, by now playing a strong national schedule, would have been forced to retrench and schedule some of the smaller schools in its area—the Universities of New Hampshire, Maine and Vermont, among others—and play them twice a year. Gavitt was vehemently opposed after all his years of building Providence into a program of national prominence with games against many of the country's elite.

He also was concerned about the television situation. The ECAC had sold the rights to its Saturday package for $80,000 for 10 games, a

Eric "Sleepy" Floyd for two. (Cameron, The Washington Post)

paltry sum even in 1978. The teams would make almost nothing, and exposure would be limited as well. Meanwhile, potential recruits knew that if they went to the ACC, the SEC or the Big Ten they'd be on television all the time.

"Our schools had a tradition of good basketball," Gavitt told *Boston Business Magazine*. "We had that going for us. We just didn't have a very good vehicle for letting the rest of the country know it."

In the spring of 1978, the ECAC held its fall meeting in Hershey, Pennsylvania. One night, Dave Gavitt, Frank Rienzo, John Thompson, St. John's athletic director Jack Kaiser and Syracuse athletic director Jack Crouthamel met for dinner at Gavitt's suggestion to discuss the theoretical concept of a new league. Over the years, Gavitt, either through coaching or in his role as his school's athletic director, had become good friends with every man at the table. Crouthamel, at the time the new A.D. at Syracuse, had even been a Beta Theta Pi fraternity brother of Gavitt's at Dartmouth in the late 1950s. But this was no time to talk about the good old days. Gavitt had an agenda, and better yet, he had a plan to bring these four schools, and several more, into a conference that would be able to compete on an equal footing with anyone in the country for recruits, for fans and for television money and exposure.

"I don't think anyone at the table was intensely interested," Crouthamel said. "It was a good idea, but a lot of good ideas never get off the ground." This one did. Over the course of the next thirteen months, with Gavitt leading the way, the group continued to meet, often on weekends in a conference room at La Guardia Airport in New York.

"We flew in and we went into this room," Rienzo told *Boston Business*. "The rules were no coffee and no food until we hashed things out, until we finished business. It would go on for hours. It was a Gandhi starvation mentality. . . . We talked about the role of inter-collegiate athletics in the country, about the compatible attributes of our institutions and the realization of the concept that we could join together without losing our autonomy. The key issue was whether we were institutions that viewed athletics as an integral part of some larger ideals and therefore whether the administration of athletics would be compatible with goals and aims of educating young people. We tried to avoid the trap of some large institutions, where the athletic departments were independently incorporated."

At the La Guardia meetings and several other sessions at other locations, the group, according to Rienzo, "dealt one point at a time with what it would take to form a conference that could compete nationally both athletically and economically."

Thompson was enthusiastic about the idea. He and Gavitt went way back together, from the days when Gavitt was an assistant coach to Joe Mullaney at Providence and Thompson was still an undergraduate. They trusted each other. And Thompson and Rienzo definitely saw advantages for Georgetown—fighting Maryland and the ACC for players and attention in its own backyard—to get involved in a major conference.

The same could not be said for Lou Carnesecca, the feisty little head coach at St. John's. The Redmen owned college basketball in New York City, and it had been that way ever since NYU decided to deemphasize basketball in the early 1970s. Carnesecca was always able to attract top-flight city talent to his campus in Queens, and he seemed virtually assured of nothing but 20-win seasons as long as he could pick and choose the opposition. He had to be convinced, and in 1979 Gavitt had the perfect opportunity to do just that.

They were in Milan, Italy, of all places, waiting for a plane to take them to a basketball clinic, where both had been asked to teach. Gavitt had been scouting in Europe in his role as head coach of the 1980 Olympic basketball team; Carnesecca was mixing a little business with a vacation in the home country. When they were stuck in the Milan airport waiting for a plane, Gavitt had Carnesecca's attention for almost twenty solid hours, and before long Carnesecca was in the fold.

Thompson was a supporter from the start, and Rienzo said he never made a move without consulting his coach. "I had a particular advantage when we started," Gavitt told Bill Reynolds, author of *Big Hoops: A Season in the Big East Conference*. "John has an innate suspicion of people he doesn't know. He doesn't trust people easily. But we always had a good relationship the two years we were at Providence together in the early sixties."

Gavitt was more than just another basketball coach. He had a keen sense for marketing and a unique vision for the future of college basketball. He wanted a conference that would stretch from Washington in the south to Boston in the north, with representatives from as many big cities and major TV markets as possible. In the beginning, Holy Cross was offered a spot, but the administration turned it down, believing that its academic integrity might be compromised. Boston College had no such reservations, and jumped right in. So Boston and Providence were covered. Gavitt wanted a presence in Philadelphia, and Temple was his first choice. The school also declined, and Villanova was next on his list, though it could not play the first season because of a prior commitment to another new conference, the Eastern Eight.

Before long, Seton Hall of South Orange, New Jersey, a second college from the New York metropolitan area, was added, along with the University of Connecticut, a state school with eighty thousand alumni still living close by and only one professional team—hockey's Hartford Whalers—to compete for media attention.

Now there were teams in and around Boston, New York, Philadelphia and Washington, four of the eight largest television markets in America—and when Pittsburgh joined two years later, the conference had a stranglehold on 25 percent of the nation's television viewers.

Almost from day one, the Big East was a financial success. Each member kicked in $25,000 for operating expenses (every nickel was returned at the end of that first 1979–80 season) and Gavitt leased a small suite of offices in downtown Providence for league headquarters. He also hired a local advertising and public-relations firm, Duffy and Shanley, to promote the new conference.

Jim Duffy came up with the name. Suggestions had included the President's Conference, the Seaboard Conference and the Super Seven. But according to Bill Reynolds, Duffy "walked into a meeting, looked around at everyone scratching their heads and said, 'What's the big deal? It's going to be big, right? And it's going to be in the East, right? How about the Big East?' "

That hurdle leaped, the next step was television. Gavitt and his cohorts knew this was the key to success for any new sports venture. He and Mike Tranghese, the league's first full-time employee and a former sports information director at Providence, drafted a six-page letter of specifications that was sent out to all the major networks and syndicators. One network replied, "When you guys grow up, call us back." But there was a smattering of interest, and the new conference signed an agreement with the William B. Tanner Company of Memphis, Tennessee, to package and distribute its games. There was not much money involved; in fact, part of the deal involved a barter arrangement for production equipment. Tanner found stations that needed equipment and exchanged that for two hours of airtime. Big East games soon were being televised on top independent stations like WPIX in New York, WTTG in Washington and WLVI in Boston. The Big East would be on the air in its major markets that first year in a Monday night package that also featured announcer Len Berman handling the play-by-play and Gavitt as the color man on the telecasts. Tranghese was listed as the executive producer and the league even sold its own advertising. Over the years, Gavitt continued to work league telecasts even as he remained the conference commissioner and was rightfully criticized for this blatant conflict of interest. But he couldn't have cared less. The league was getting widespread exposure right from the start, and Gavitt and his fellow conference members could laugh all the way to the bank. And as the Big East grew, so too did the role of television in college basketball, particularly the involvement of cable and ESPN, the all-sports network that began in 1979, when the Big East also was just beginning to feel its way.

When Villanova joined the conference before the 1980–81 season, ESPN and another sports-oriented cable network, USA, wanted the Big East Monday night package. The contract went to USA the first year, then ESPN took over in the league's third season. In 1982, the Big East negotiated an exclusive deal with CBS, and over the years Gavitt has refined the televising of conference games and made it an art form. In addition to the network exposure, he developed his own in-house Big East network that feeds games only to the two home markets of the participating schools. Twelve years after its modest start with the ECAC's $80,000 contract, the league signed a four-year CBS contract extension in 1990 for $19.2 million. With additional revenues from its $3.6 million package with ESPN and the $1.5 million a year generated by the in-house network, as well as revenues from the sale of Big East tournament tickets at New York's Madison Square Garden, corporate sponsorships and sales of its own videos and Big East paraphernalia, the conference now takes in between $10 and $12 million a year in revenue; operating expenses are about $1.5 million a year, which includes the costs of administering league play and championships in a number of minor, non-revenue-producing sports. From television alone, each school makes about $600,000 a year from the Big East contracts, and no conference has more games on national TV. The move to take the Big East tournament to New York was another of Gavitt's brilliant ideas. The tournament signed a three-year, $1 million deal to begin play at the Garden in 1983, and while there was some skepticism initially, the annual tournament, a three-day event in early March, has been wildly successful, generating almost $2 million per year in ticket sales alone.

While none of the schools will offer specifics, it is safe to say that the Big East has been highly profitable for its members. Syracuse, with its thirty-two-thousand-seat Carrier Dome, was estimated to have earned about $5.8 million from basketball alone in 1987 before expenses, according to *Boston Business Magazine.*

Georgetown's basketball program is believed to earn approximately $1.5 million per year from ticket sales, general revenues from the Big East and television and radio rights fees, though that figure does not include NCAA tournament money, a significant sum considering that each of the Final Four participants earned $1.43 million in 1990 and could get $3 million this year. Of course, not all of that goes directly to the schools in the Big East. Conference members have a revenue-sharing formula that gives each school that qualifies for the tournament about half the NCAA money, and it is generally regarded as a rule of thumb in college sports that half the money you take in goes out in expenses. Georgetown, according to Rienzo, does not consider any NCAA money in its basketball budgeting. The funds go into the school's general endowment account "because we don't ever want to be in a position where the coach feels pressure from having to do well in the NCAA," Rienzo said. Still, there is no question that Georgetown has profited greatly from its Big East affiliation, in cold cash and in other intangibles like increased exposure and visibility. "The impact of the Big East on Georgetown athletics has been extremely dramatic and positive, not only in the area of basketball but in cross-country and indoor and outdoor track, women's sports, everything," Rienzo said. "When you are an independent, you are involved in individual games that seem to have no common thread other than the final score. Playing in a conference you are in a continuation of educational and athletic experiences. The mutual pride we have in one another, as institutions, in spite of the rivalries is one of the characteristics we worked very, very hard to foster and develop.

"I think it's critically important to know that the financial aspect of the Big East was never a primary goal or focus of the establishment of the conference. It's been a fringe benefit, icing on the cake, that has evolved. . . . I don't want you to put words in my mouth that we don't have any appreciation for the financial benefits that the conference develops. . . . But I don't want anybody to think that we place undue significance on the financial aspects of it because it's a benefit, not a goal. But we're not turning the money back, either."

Gavitt resigned as commissioner in May 1990 to take over as director of operations for the Boston Celtics. But the Big East is now an institution, operating these days out of a tastefully decorated suite of offices overlooking the Providence River, with nine full-time employees. Last October the University of Miami joined the fold, yet another large TV market. And the money just keeps rolling in. "It's the wheel of fortune," says Villanova coach Rollie Massimino. "You get players, you get on television, then you can recruit better. Then you get on TV more, then you have more money."

When Mike Tranghese, who replaced Gavitt as commissioner in June 1990, looks back over the dozen years he's been with the conference, from that first announcement on May 31, 1979, he says, "The single biggest reason for our success is Dave Gavitt. People believed in him. If Dave said the sky was green, people in the conference accepted it. There is no question he is the number-one reason for our success."

The number-two reason?

Tranghese has several. "In all sports you have standard-bearers— the New York Yankees, the Boston Celtics and the Lakers—and from the start I'd have to say Georgetown and Syracuse were the two teams from that standpoint that set the tone for the conference. John Thompson's style of play was so unique, he forced people to get better to play at his level, and that pulled everyone's program up. There is no question that Georgetown University had a lot to do with our success."

Georgetown University, but in particular a young athlete just finishing his sophomore season at a public high school in Cambridge, Massachusetts, when Dave Gavitt announced the formation of the Big East. His name was Patrick Ewing, and his role in elevating the conference to elite status in college basketball was about to begin.

11

Patrick tried to listen to every word you said, not only with his ears, but with his eyes. It was the same thing as when he played basketball. If he got knocked down, if he messed up, he didn't quit. He came right back at you. He was totally committed."

—Mike Jarvis, Patrick Ewing's
high school basketball coach

ONE DAY IN THE WINTER OF 1979, RED AUERBACH PICKED UP the telephone and called his friend John Thompson in Washington to tell him about the promising young player he'd been keeping his eye on over at a public high school called Cambridge Rindge and Latin just across the Charles River from Auerbach's office at the Boston Garden.

"I called him up and said, 'There's a kid up here with a great reputation.' I asked him if he'd heard about him. He said, 'Vaguely.' I just told him, 'John, you've got to get this kid.'"

A few weeks later Thompson made a trip to Boston, and together he and Auerbach watched a tall, skinny sophomore named Patrick Ewing tear up Boston Latin School in a state play-off game at Boston Garden. Thompson didn't say much that night, but he didn't have to. "Hell," said Auerbach, "it didn't take a genius to figure this one out. The kid was a player, and he wanted him."

Thompson was not alone in lusting after the sixteen-year-old sophomore who had come to the United States from Jamaica only five years before and still spoke with the island patois of his native land.

His mother, Dorothy, had come alone to Cambridge in 1971 in search of a better life, leaving behind her husband, Carl, and seven children for a job in the kitchen of Massachusetts General Hospital. She was a strong, religious woman—much like Anna Thompson—who believed in the value of education, and of hard work. So she saved her money diligently, working other odd jobs to supplement her income, and by 1975 her family was able to join her, moving into a five-room apartment on River Street in Cambridgetown, a working-class neighborhood less than a mile from Harvard Square.

From his second-story window, Patrick Ewing, by then 6 feet tall, would watch the boys across the street playing basketball on an outdoor court. One day he was invited to join in, and before long he was a playground regular, learning about this new game that seemed such fun but could also be so frustrating for a boy who was all arms and legs and awkward coordination.

In the classroom the shy youngster, somewhat embarrassed by the sound of his own voice, was also frustrated and struggling. He tested poorly and was placed in a special remedial program for seventh and eighth graders conducted at Rindge and Latin School. In his first year in the school, a friend convinced Ewing to try out for the junior high team, and in the summer between the seventh and eighth grades, young Patrick grew to 6-foot-6.

Steve Jenkins was a physical education teacher there, and though he was more of a football man, he had been asked to coach the basketball team as well. Jenkins's friend Mike Jarvis was teaching physical education at Rindge and Latin. Jarvis, like Jenkins a young black coach, had been an assistant basketball coach at Harvard a few years before, working under head coach Satch Sanders, Thompson's old Celtic teammate. When Sanders left Harvard and Jarvis didn't get the head job, he went back to teaching, hoping to land another coaching position before too long. In the interim, Jenkins asked his friend Jarvis to help him with his seventh-and-eighth-grade team, and in particular to work with Patrick Ewing. Jarvis set up special drills for the boy and tried to teach him a few fundamental moves. Progress at first was slow, because Ewing had virtually no skills.

"When I first met Patrick, he was timid, shy and unknowing about the game," Jenkins said. "At that time, he had been growing at such a rapid pace that he had a difficult time because of his size. In seventh grade he was six-one, and his coordination had not developed as quickly as his physique. He had never played the game, and he had difficulty jumping, dribbling, rebounding and shooting. He struggled. He really struggled."

By the eighth grade, Patrick Ewing was catching on. One day in a game at nearby Peabody Elementary School, he stole the ball and went in for an uncontested lay-up. But this was no ordinary shot. Patrick Ewing summoned up all his energy, leaped high in the air and dunked the ball, the first time an eighth grader had ever done that in Cambridge, Massachusetts.

By the time Ewing was a sophomore in high school he was 6-foot-9, and Mike Jarvis, his old tutor, was now the head basketball coach at Rindge and Latin. That year the school won the state championship, and John Thompson was not the only coach starting to pay attention.

The following summer, between his junior and senior years in high school, Ewing was invited to try out in Lexington, Kentucky, for the 1980 Olympic team, coached by Dave Gavitt. Though the team never did compete in Moscow because of Jimmy Carter's ill-conceived boycott, Ewing benefited greatly from the trials. He would be facing some extraordinary competition against college big men like Tom Chambers, Bill Laimbeer and Sam Bowie, and over the first few days of scrimmages he was constantly picking himself off the floor, the victim of a stray elbow here, a heavy-handed shove there, administered by his bigger, stronger foes, most of them three and four years older.

"About midweek, he finally decided he was not going to be pushed around anymore," Jarvis said. "One game in particular, he was going against Bill Laimbeer, who played then like he plays now, very rough, very physical, and Patrick said, 'I've had enough.' He turned around and punched Laimbeer right in the face. You don't like to see that happen normally, but for Patrick that was a good statement, a real turning point. I don't think anybody's really pushed him around ever since."

A few months before the Olympic trials, Jarvis also had decided to set up procedures he hoped would protect Ewing from the recruiting circus that seemed inevitable for yet another player already being described as "the next Bill Russell." Eventually that prediction would come true, but in 1980 Patrick Ewing was just another talented big man whose services would be sought by colleges from coast to coast. Jarvis, a former college coach himself, had seen the insane recruiting of players like Moses Malone, Sam Bowie and Ralph Sampson and wanted to protect his player as much as possible.

So he formulated a plan. Jarvis would head a committee made up of Ewing, his parents and his first basketball instructor, Steve Jenkins. Together, they drew up a seven-point program that began with letters to two hundred colleges in the spring of Ewing's junior year, telling them about Ewing, his basketball and academic background and his specific requirements on the court and in the classroom wherever he wound up going to school.

"In order for Pat to be successful in a regular college curriculum," the letter said,

> he will need the following:
> 1. Conscientious guidance in course selections.
> 2. Daily tutoring (the services of the tutor must include covering reading material with Pat, some level of explanation of new material, proofreading of papers and help with construction of papers).

3. Permission to use a tape recorder to tape lectures, and untimed testing. (Pat's slowness in writing does not give him ample opportunity to express himself.)
4. If there are basic Skills Development Programs, Pat should take these.
5. Constant monitoring of his program.

Pat is quite motivated to do well and is conscientious in getting his work done. He learns a great deal through listening, a skill that he has developed to compensate for his reading deficiency. The Ewing family, Pat, and all those concerned are interested in a positive educational experience, a diploma, and the necessary skills that are needed after graduation.

In the letter, The Committee also set up a timetable, asking interested coaches to write back by May 30 "a personal letter that addresses the educational and athletic opportunities that are available at your school (Basic Skills Program, Support Services, Tutoring, Minority Student Program, Academic Record of Former Players). In addition, please include a course catalogue, a basketball brochure and an application. . . ."

Over the next six weeks, approximately eighty coaches wrote back. Phil Berger, writing in *Inside Sports* in 1981, reported some of the responses.

Michigan State "would have no objections to allowing Patrick to use his own tape recorder to tape lectures in his classes."

Marquette "can arrange for untimed testing in many of the courses but we cannot guarantee it in each and every instance. However, other players of ours in the past were granted this concession in over half their courses. I cannot foresee any difficulty arranging for Pat to do likewise."

Boston College: "The direct link between the basketball program and the counseling office is provided through the graduate assistant. Basically he would talk with you each school night about your studies. He might also help with constructing a paper or proofread any of your work."

America's institutions of higher learning were lining up and taking a number for a basketball player Jarvis later said was a C to C+ student with relatively low College Board scores. Clearly, they would have to make concessions for a young athlete who had some difficulty with reading and writing, an athlete who had attended Upward Bound programs over the summer to improve his basic skills but was still hardly a candidate for academic excellence. But eighty schools, including Georgetown, were still very interested in pursuing Patrick Ewing, and most hadn't even seen his transcript or his College Board scores.

"Patrick had some problems because of the difference in cultures and in language, even if it was English," Jarvis said. "Something said in this country is not the way it is said in Jamaica. But Patrick was a good student because he was willing to work. Work did not scare him. Patrick would do things until he could do them well. It wasn't a question of him not being motivated, because he was. It was a question of making sure he had the resources to have a chance to make it and be successful."

From those eighty responses, The Committee narrowed Ewing's choices to sixteen schools—Boston College, Boston University, UCLA, Cincinnati, Georgetown, Kentucky, Maryland, Marquette, Massachusetts, Michigan State, North Carolina, Providence, Southern Cal, Syracuse, Villanova and Western Kentucky. Though Ewing's high school was only five minutes away from Harvard, that school chose not to get involved. Harvard coach Frank McLaughlin had contacted Jarvis early on and asked him if he thought a heavy load of tutoring might get Ewing in position to qualify for admission. When Jarvis was told Ewing would need at least 1,200 on the College Boards, he told Harvard he did not think that was feasible, and the school never pursued the hometown hero.

On June 15, each of the sixteen coaches was invited to visit Ewing the following fall, in a two-week period in early September. They were welcome to bring their assistants and any material that would help The Committee make a decision. Only Kentucky coach Joe B. Hall declined. He already had an outstanding big man, Sam Bowie, and was not interested.

The coaches were scheduled in alphabetical order of their schools. The Committee would meet two coaches a day in a conference room at the high school. Thompson was in the middle of the pack, and when he arrived for his session, of course Mary Fenlon was right by his side, as was Bill Stein, Georgetown's chief recruiter. Each head coach was allowed to make an opening statement, then asked to provide the answers to a series of eighteen questions posed by The Committee. Patrick Ewing, as usual, didn't say much. Jarvis's assistant coach, Vinnie Mili, took notes on each of the sessions for use later on in evaluating Ewing's final choice.

Thompson's pitch stressed academics, but touched on all aspects of

Billy Martin battles for a rebound. (The Washington Post)

his philosophy. "Education is about change—if you have the potential," he said, according to Mili's notes. "It is my job to make you reach that potential. Players travel in coat and ties in public because they have a responsibility to represent Georgetown. Mary Fenlon—academic co-ordinator. John's conscience, his own check system. Freshmen must talk to Mary every day. Must answer questions in John's book concerning academics: cutting classes, grades, class work. John tells them: 'Do not sign this book if there are any lies in it.' John feels that no one should take the place of your parents. He is not your father and Mary is not your mother. But they are there to help guide you and their development. John—'God help anybody who is black. I will not give you anything because you are black, or take away anything because you are white.' No athletic dormitory. Wants you to meet people and make contact with people (other than athletes) who will help you find human resources for the future. Georgetown's responsibility to protect your individuality and not let the public out there know everything that goes on concerning you as a person."

It was vintage Thompson, in a setting not unlike the grilling he had once put Dean Smith through when he was recruiting Donald Washington. Dorothy Ewing, a woman Thompson would later say reminded him of his own mother, was listening closely.

"This lady was watching me the whole time and I swear I don't think she ever blinked, not once," Thompson told *The National Sports Daily* a few years later. "I mean this lady was just staring at me—she was just glaring at me. And not once did she give me so much as one nonverbal clue to what she might be thinking. Well, after I was through, she finally asked me what social opportunities our educational environment might provide. I said, 'Mrs. Ewing, it is not a responsibility of mine to get involved with your son's social opportunities. But the city of Washington is seventy percent black, if that interests you. And if there are no social opportunities that Patrick can find there as a young black man, he has a problem, ma'am, that I frankly can't solve.' And she looked at me for a while, like maybe she sort of liked that. But she never smiled, never broke into a laugh to let me be sure. She just looked at me and said, 'Ha, funny man, funny man.' And that was it."

Stein, in fact, thought the exchange might have been fatal to Georgetown's chances of landing the nation's prize recruit. He was worried that Thompson had wisecracked himself out of contention. But when Ewing narrowed his final choices to six schools, Georgetown was right there, along with Boston College, Boston University, North Carolina, UCLA and Villanova.

Between October 17 and the last week in December of 1980, Ewing visited all six schools. Jarvis said UCLA was ruled out because it was too far from home. Ewing was not wild about Carolina either. In the end, it came down to the two Boston schools (Tom Davis was coaching at BC, Rick Pitino at BU) and Georgetown, with Villanova's Rollie Massimino also still in the hunt.

Thompson stayed in touch with Jarvis all fall, and Stein attended a number of Ewing's games that senior season as well. "John would call, I guess, about once a week," Jarvis said. Ewing's coach also got some other calls.

One alumnus of a major university offered to make Jarvis a millionaire if Ewing went to his school, promising him he would work it out so that Jarvis would represent Ewing in his contract negotiations with the pros and would get a piece of the action too. Another told Jarvis he was in a position to arrange for him to be an assistant coach, and then eventually head coach, if Ewing was steered toward his school. "I laughed at them," said Jarvis, who also knew he could arrange a nice package deal for Ewing and himself at a number of colleges around the country. It was done all the time. But he was not interested. "I was not in this for thirty pieces of silver—none of us were. This was a great kid, and we wanted to make sure it was done the right way."

On February 2, 1981, Mike Jarvis called a press conference to announce Patrick Ewing's final decision. More than a hundred reporters and photographers and camera crews from every Boston television station squeezed into a local restaurant owned by Satch Sanders. There were no college coaches in the room—NCAA rules prohibited them from attending such sessions. John Thompson had been in town earlier in the week, showing up along with several other coaches to watch one of Ewing's games just to let him know he was still very much concerned; but now he was back in Washington, waiting for a telephone call.

Patrick Ewing, a 7-footer sweating profusely in a dark, pin-striped three-piece suit, towered over a battery of microphones and read from a prepared statement. "After considering all the factors," he said softly, "my decision is to attend Georgetown." There were shrieks of joy at the back of the restaurant from several Georgetown alumni who had managed to get in, and Ewing, slightly flustered, quickly yielded the podium to Jarvis, who then listed the reasons for Ewing's final choice.

Ewing felt comfortable with the Georgetown campus and the community, Jarvis said. He liked the idea of playing in the growing Big East Conference and relished the chance to learn how to play center from a former Boston Celtic. And, of course, Jarvis mentioned Thompson's reputation for emphasizing academics, which was critical to Ewing's parents. "He will stay four years to get an education," Carl Ewing told reporters that day.

Thompson had one more nervous moment a few days later when he went to Ewing's home to have him sign the national letter of intent that would bind him to Georgetown and formally end the recruiting process. After all, when Ewing announced his decision, Maryland coach Lefty Driesell had warned that Thompson would not be able to rest until he signed on the dotted line. As long as Ewing stayed unsigned, every college coach in America still had the chance to talk him out of Georgetown, and many—Driesell included—definitely would have tried. But a signature on the letter of intent would ease that concern.

"After making the usual small talk," Thompson said years later, "I said, 'Well, ma'am, we're here today to sign the letter of intent, so we might as well get to it.' And Mrs. Ewing looked at me and said, 'Sign, sign?' Well, I looked at Jarvis and I looked back at her and . . . I explained that it was normal NCAA procedure. But when I was through she looked at me and said very firmly, 'Mr. Thompson, you sign for land. You do not sign for people.' Right about then I about near fainted. I thought the whole thing was off. But then Mrs. Ewing broke into a smile and said, 'Carl, sign the papers.' That was her way of saying to me, 'Mister, you had better understand that this is my son, a human being.' You'll never find a mother who loved her child more."

A few weeks after Ewing had announced his choice of schools, Thompson and Georgetown found themselves in the position of defending their decision to admit Ewing. *The Boston Globe* had obtained a copy of the original letter The Committee had sent out and ran a front-page story about it, listing the five prerequisites on untimed testing, tape recording of lectures and all the rest.

"Six of the more prestigious universities in America were prepared to accept Patrick Ewing . . . despite several extraordinary academic conditions demanded of the schools by his high school coach," began the story, written by *Globe* reporter Mike Madden. "Furthermore, these schools were ready to accept Ewing apparently with little or no documentation of his academic capability. As one coach put it, 'We were assured by the people in Cambridge that Patrick could do the work. We took their word.' "

The *Globe* also reported that coaches of at least three schools—Boston College, Boston University and Villanova—"were prepared to take Ewing even though they had no record he had applied to their schools or documentation of his academic record."

Villanova coach Rollie Massimino admitted, "To this day I don't know his grades or College Board scores. He didn't apply with us. It's never happened that way before with us. Usually we make them apply first."

The implication was obvious. Once again, in their lust to get the best athletes into their programs, some of the nation's finest institutions had made a mockery of the term *scholar-athlete*. And worse, Georgetown, a bastion of academic excellence, had just signed a player who would not have been remotely considered for admission unless he stood 7 feet tall. The public perception was clear: Another dumb jock was going to college when he should have been going to remedial reading classes. Sports columnists, op-ed writers and broadcasters coast to coast jumped in with all barrels blazing, and John Thompson and Georgetown were their main targets.

Jarvis took great offense. To this day, he insists that the *Globe* story was prompted by sheer spite in view of Ewing's decision to leave the city, that if he had attended Boston College or Boston University the issue never would have come up. *Globe* reporters and editors have always downplayed that criticism, as well they should have. It was a good story, meticulously reported and properly displayed in the newspaper, and clearly it struck a nerve.

Jarvis also believes that institutions like Georgetown and all the other schools on Ewing's list have a responsibility "not just to educate the elite kids. If you have a great university with great professors, if they're really that good, then they can take a person with lower grades and take a person who might need extra help and basically help that person get a degree. Patrick needed that help. If they did not want to provide it, they could have said so. We weren't hiding anything. It was all aboveboard."

Thompson agreed. A few weeks after the *Globe* story appeared, he strongly questioned the furor that followed Ewing's decision to attend Georgetown. Getting up on his very high horse, Thompson was outraged.

"I've never seen anything intended to help someone backfire as much as this," Thompson said. "It didn't work because of the present state of college athletics . . . and because of the way in which the letter was presented in the media. The guidelines were drawn up to help keep the youngster from being exploited. Jarvis and the family made no stipulations and there has never been a contractual agreement regarding Patrick Ewing's course of study at Georgetown. What Pat Ewing is getting at Georgetown is no different from what any other student who needs help at Georgetown would get. This kid has never asked us for one thing—not even a soda. I think he's a fine kid and a plugger who will work hard and progress steadily toward a degree at Georgetown.

"I will get credit for being a good recruiter because we signed Patrick, when in fact I did less with him than any player we've ever gone after because of the guidelines. The first time I ever called his house was two days before he signed the national letter of intent.

"It bothered me that some people thought he was going to Georgetown only because I am a black coach. I think some coaches used that to put him on the defensive. I like to think I'm more complicated than the pigment of my skin. If that was the case, it's about time. Still, how come no one said Ralph Sampson wanted to play for a white coach at Virginia, or Moses Malone wanted to play for a white coach at Maryland? Of course I have my selfish motives. I did not recruit him for what he can do for society. I did it for basketball, and he's a great player. People are always talking about making exceptions. Well, there are exceptions. I am astonished at people who are amazed that things are not equal. Patrick Ewing, because of who he is, can influence others. And good institutions have a responsibility to educate someone like that. Society is not equal; we know that. Specifically, more qualified blacks have not been admitted to college rather than the individual exceptions who do get in."

In fact, the Georgetown admissions office had been making exceptions for Thompson's program for years before Ewing and would do so for years after, funneling as many as half his players into the mainstream undergraduate curriculum through the school's Community Scholars program, according to director of admissions Charles Deacon. While Georgetown's average College Board scores for incoming freshmen were in the 1,200 range, many minority students had far lower scores and grades.

The Community Scholars program, first started in the late 1960s, allowed Georgetown to admit a number of minority students who did not ordinarily qualify. Originally it was set up to attract more inner-city students from Washington, but over the years it has expanded to a national scope. Participants attend an intense summer session before the start of their freshman year. "It involves academic, social and cultural training," Deacon said. "They become adjusted to the community, learn where things are, learn what it means to live in a dorm, learn how to interact with other college students. The program determines where these students are in reading and learning skills." During their freshman year, participants are given individual or team tutoring and take basic courses in philosophy, literature and theology taught by a special team of professors. Their progress is closely monitored, and tutorial help is provided whenever necessary. After the freshman year, the Community Scholars are integrated into the normal college program and must meet the same degree requirements and take the same mandatory courses for graduation as the rest of the student body. And basketball players also have to contend with Mary Fenlon.

Patrick Ewing's academic background was not much different from that of a number of other Community Scholars of that or any other year, Deacon said. "He was a student who had what I would call a learning disability. It came from his background and from another linguistic system. But he was so totally convincing, as was his family, in terms of motivation to do well and his desire for a degree. He had also taken a strong academic program in a good high school, not your typical inner-city high school classes. And so he was not a major problem for us to accept. I really think it was a lot of sour grapes more than anything else that caused a lot of coaches to go running around and saying all those things. Knowing we had support programs that were available and how successful they had been and knowing what kind of kid we had here, in hindsight, Patrick Ewing was one of the easiest people to deal with that we've ever had."

Father Timothy Healy, the school president, also found himself defending the admission of Ewing. In an interview with editors and reporters at *The Washington Post,* Father Healy was asked about a critical commentary on the ESPN sports cable network accusing the university of prostituting itself in signing Ewing.

"They went through the same old *Boston Globe* story," Father Healy said. "I do know the numbers [entrance exam scores and grades] and it's a crock. That's all. It's absolute nonsense. This much I can legally say: Had Patrick Ewing been a Washington resident and gone through our Upward Bound program, as he did in Boston, and been three feet high, we'd have taken him. If he were three feet high nobody would have fussed about it. . . . If you poke John Thompson about it, the first thing he said about that silly letter was 'Look, we're making no deals. About examinations, courses, tutors . . . All we'll do is lay on a good education. But you're not going to tell me how to do it. Don't ask me to educate your son and then tell me how.'

"All I ever knew about Patrick Ewing's recruiting—there is, you know, some doubt as to whether God knows who John Thompson is recruiting, he's so secretive—is that John was leaving one day when he turned back and said of Patrick, 'This man is going to be a leader in the black community. I'd like a chance to make sure he's got something to say.' "

Thompson got that chance for the obvious reasons. The fact that he was a large black man who could look Patrick Ewing in the eye certainly was critical. The fact that their backgrounds seemed so similar, right down to strong-willed mothers and problems in school at an early age, was another. Academics was important, too, but most of all, Mike Jarvis said, Patrick Ewing trusted John Thompson, felt he had a coach he could talk to and confide in, a man who would understand from firsthand experience what it was like to be 7 feet tall in a much smaller world.

Georgetown, meanwhile, had made a decision, and a statement as well. Despite Father Healy's protestations, the school was admitting yet another marginal student because of his basketball skills, and because he was 7 feet tall. Certainly it was the school's prerogative, and, as Jarvis and John Thompson argued, the school's responsibility. But this was a basketball decision, and Georgetown's basketball program was the main beneficiary of the school's largesse.

Thompson needed a player like Patrick Ewing to get to the next level of college basketball. That was never more obvious than in the 1980–81 season, as the Hoyas, playing without the departed Shelton and Duren, were clearly struggling. With no dominant big man, or any reasonable facsimile, the Hoyas finished with a 20–12 record, including an embarrassing 61–55 loss to an undersized and outmanned James Madison team making its first-ever appearance in the NCAA tournament.

Still, with Ewing in the fold and players like Sleepy Floyd, point guard Fred Brown and swingman Eric Smith coming back, Georgetown would almost surely be a top-ten contender in 1981–82. There also was more help on the way, for Ewing was the prize catch of a recruiting class that included three highly sought-after Washington area players— Anthony Jones, a smooth 6-6 forward from Dunbar High; Billy Martin, a 6-7 swingman from McKinley Tech; and Ralph Dalton, a 6-9 center from Oxon Hill, Maryland, who had played at Fishburne Military Academy in Virginia for two years, staying an extra season at Thompson's request to improve his academic and basketball skills.

Dalton had caused Thompson a bit of embarrassment the previous summer when *The Washington Post* reported that Dalton had played in several summer all-star games in Boston and New York under an assumed name, allegedly to avoid being hassled by other recruiters. At that point, Dalton had told Thompson he would be coming to Georgetown after another year of prep school. John Feinstein, then a reporter at the *Post*, had received a tip on the Dalton story, and he decided to check it out. "I drove out to their house, and he and his father were in their living room," recalled Feinstein. "We walked out back and I asked the kid, 'Why are you playing under the name Ralph Brown?' He said he didn't want recruiters bothering him. I asked him whose idea it was. He smiled and said, 'Let's just say it was mine.' I said to him, 'Why do I think it's Coach Thompson's idea?' He said, 'You said that, not me.'

"I got back to the office that night and John Thompson was on the telephone. 'How are you, John?' I asked him. 'Terrible,' he says. Then he starts screaming at me. 'Do you know that boy's momma has been sick in the hospital? How dare you go out there. If he was white, you'd never knock on a white kid's door.' We wrote the story. There was nothing illegal about it. There was no rule that said you couldn't play under an assumed name. Georgetown hadn't violated any rules; the kid hadn't signed anything. But I think it told people that John Thompson can get down in the dirt just like everyone else."

When Thompson eventually calmed down, he issued a nondenial denial to Feinstein. "I'm not going to tell you it would be beneath my dignity to tell Ralph to play under an assumed name because it wouldn't be," Thompson said. "There are fifty kids in the country who I would tell to play under an assumed name if I thought it would alleviate some of the problems and pressures that go with recruiting, as long as it broke no rules, which this did not."

Still, Thompson was widely criticized for the incident. "Big-time college recruiting sometimes turns good men into merchants of foolishness," wrote the *Post*'s Dave Kindred.

"This is just what our profession needs," said South Carolina coach Bill Foster. "Something else to create doubt about us in people's minds."

But Dalton stayed true to his word. He honored his commitment to Thompson, and in the fall of 1981 he joined Patrick Ewing, Billy Martin and Anthony Jones on the campus of Georgetown University. They represented the greatest recruiting class in the school's history, and the place would never be the same again.

Junior point guard Freddie Brown has the ball and heads up the court, looking quickly toward his coach on the sidelines shouting instructions. Down near the basket his teammates are jockeying for position, darting and weaving behind picks and screens, desperately trying to get open for a shot that will win the game.

Nine seconds . . . eight . . . seven . . .

Out of the corner of his eye, over near the right corner, Fred Brown sees a moving blur and hears a voice call his name . . . Freddie, FREDDIE.

Six . . . five . . . four . . .

Instinctively, just as he's done so many times before, he throws a pass toward the blur and the voice. But now, from nowhere, comes another large body. It is James Worthy, North Carolina's all-American forward.

AFEW MONTHS AFTER PATRICK EWING HAD ANNOUNCED HE would be attending Georgetown University in the fall of 1981, John Thompson and Frank Rienzo sat down for their annual meeting to review the previous season and to talk about the future. Then they took a short walk across the hall from Rienzo's office into the dark gymnasium, turned on the lights and started to look around the forty-four-hundred-seat McDonough Gymnasium that had provided so many memorable moments over the previous ten years.

They were looking for places to add more seats; a nook here, a cranny there might provide a few extra chairs, even if the view would be slightly obstructed. Before very long, it became obvious to both men that this was an exercise in futility. Patrick Ewing was on the way, five starters were returning from the 1980–81 team, including a genuine all-American candidate, Sleepy Floyd, and interest in the Hoyas was at an all-time high. Rienzo and Thompson looked at each other that day and made a decision: It was time to get a big-time arena for a very big-time basketball team.

"We knew we had to make the move," Rienzo said. "There was no other way."

Within months, Rienzo negotiated a deal for Georgetown to play a dozen games that season at the Capital Centre, a nineteen-thousand-seat arena in Landover, Maryland, that was twenty miles from the school geographically, and light years away philosophically from its basketball past and the cozy little gym no more than a five-minute walk from anywhere on campus.

The move was not well received in the Georgetown community. "When I heard about it, I was against it," said Charles Deacon, the school's admissions director. "I called John and Frank right away and told them so. I think ideally kids should be able to have a drink at the Pub and then walk down the hill to the games. But we also have a responsibility to the Washington community as a whole, and with forty-four hundred seats, we can't fill the responsibility in McDonough. That's why we had to do it."

William Stott, Georgetown's vice-president and dean of student affairs, admitted, "It's not the ideal situation, we know that. But remember, it is just an experiment. We're committed to providing transportation for the students to the Capital Centre. If it doesn't work out, we won't do it next year. It's natural at this point in time with all that has happened that people would be suspicious of athletics at an academic institution. But we think the way we've done it is compatible with our general philosophy. There is nothing inconsistent with what this university is in our having an excellent basketball team. We strive for excellence in everything we do, and athletics is certainly an important part of life here. In this year's freshman class, eight hundred of the twelve hundred entering students played a varsity sport in high school. We're an academic school, but there's also very much a jock orientation around here."

Though Georgetown would continue to play several games on campus against the growing number of cream puffs on its schedule, the move to the Capital Centre merely confirmed the team's ascension to the elite status of college basketball and all the trappings that went with it. The big time also meant big money, and while school officials have always insisted that was never their motive for upgrading the basketball program, no one was complaining, either.

Without a successful, high-profile basketball program, Georgetown then and now would have difficulty funding all its other sports. And despite the basketball program's visibility and profit, Georgetown, like most other American colleges, is probably near the break-even point on athletics. In his book *College Sports Inc.*, Indiana University professor Murray Sperber writes that "if profit and loss is defined according to ordinary business practices, of the 8,902 members of the NCAA, the 393 of the NAIA [National Association of Intercollegiate Athletes] and the 1,050 non-affiliated junior colleges, only 10 to 20 athletic programs make consistent, albeit small profit, and in any given year another 20 to 30 break even or do better. The rest—over 2,300 institutions—lose anywhere from a few dollars to millions annually."

Georgetown pays Thompson over $300,000 a year, making him the highest-paid man on campus. With all his other perks—television and radio shows, a free house, a free car, endorsement deals, speaking fees, and a summer basketball camp, he is in the $1-million-a-year range, ranking him with the elite of college basketball coaches. Rick Pitino's package at Kentucky is said to be worth $950,000 a year; Jim Valvano was making $750,000 a year at North Carolina State before he was forced to step down in the wake of recruiting and academic scandals during his tenure; most coaches at big-time programs are among the highest-paid people at their schools. Sperber, in fact, estimates there are more than a hundred Division I coaches earning at least $100,000 a year.

Georgetown clearly considers the investment in Thompson worth the money, even if some members of the faculty complain privately about the disparity between their salaries and that of a mere basketball coach. Those same professors also know it would be campus suicide to make too much noise about it, if only because they know Thompson is the darling of the school's administration, and particularly the school's longtime president during most of Thompson's tenure.

Father Healy, the school president who left Georgetown in 1989 to run the New York City public library system, was John Thompson's biggest booster, giving him virtually carte blanche to run the program as he saw fit. In 1977, Father Healy even made Thompson his personal urban affairs adviser, describing his role as "assisting me to fulfill my inaugural pledge to be of service, of use and of help to the city." If there had ever been any doubt about Father Healy's commitment to high-level college basketball, it was dispelled by a flowery philosophical piece that appeared under his byline on the op-ed page of *The Washington Post* shortly after Iowa had ended Georgetown's 1980 season.

"The house of intellect is rich, but it can also be a place of starvation," Father Healy wrote. "All too frequently missing in the coded chatter of learning is beauty, physical beauty. . . . I'm talking about the beauty that calls for contemplation, for awe—the kind that makes a man or woman proud to be human, proud to be that 'half-witted angel strapped to the back of a mule.' Starved as we are for this kind of physical beauty, the speed and skill and grace of a basketball team feed a hunger that most of us seldom stop to know we have."

And in the same soppy, syrupy piece, he also admitted that a winning basketball team "makes alumni and students proud and happy. For a private school like Georgetown to have its name on national telecasts and in national newspapers is good for recruiting future students. Other friends who care for the university have their generosity raised and their pleasure in giving heightened."

With Ewing in the fold, the giving began to get serious. Rienzo said he needed to sell only five thousand seats a game to break even at the Capital Centre that first year. Before the start of Ewing's freshman season, more than six thousand season tickets were sold, two thousand more than the professional team occupying the Capital Centre, the Washington Bullets, was selling two years after winning the NBA title.

Media attention also was getting intense, as Thompson discovered when he took Ewing with him to the National Sports Festival in Syracuse, New York, the summer before Ewing's freshman season. The NSF, sponsored by the U.S. Olympic Committee, was designed to provide high-level national competition in thirty-three sports, and Thompson would be coaching the Eastern Regional team in the basketball competition, with Ewing on his squad.

From day one, Thompson decided to close his practice sessions to the media and the public, just as he had always done at Georgetown. He also kept Ewing under wraps, declining to make him available at press conferences or interview sessions. At Georgetown, Thompson also had instituted another rule—freshmen were not allowed to speak with the media until January 1 of their first year in school—and though Ewing still had not even registered for classes, the gag order was definitely in effect.

One day, the Syracuse *Post-Standard* ran a story across the top of its sports page under the headline "Georgetown's Ewing in Hiding." The sports editor, Frank Brieaddy, wrote that Thompson "is doing his darndest to make sure the media gets as little information as possible about NSF basketball to pass on to sports hungry audiences. . . . Whatever his motives are, they are bad for college basketball, bad for the relationship between the media and coaches and bad for the National Sports Festival."

Thompson responded in kind.

"Before I came here, I made a request, not a demand, to have closed practices," he growled one day. "The request was granted. I have a different style of coaching. I'm not trying to be secretive and I'm not trying to shelter anybody. I have a tendency to be offensive in coaching but I do not want to offend my players in public. I feel my practices should be closed because I have a personal relationship with all my kids."

Ewing, he insisted, had told him he did not want to give interviews because he did not want to divert attention from his teammates and because, Thompson said, "he would rather be with the guys. . . . His mother sent him to me for some guidance. I am the director of the program. We are not running a democracy down there."

Ewing did show up at one press conference late in the competition and was mobbed by a media horde, an experience Thompson later said stiffened his resolve to protect Ewing. The session was held in a small room, and at one point the player and the coach literally were pinned up against a wall as the massed media closed in around them. It would be the last such meeting of the press for Ewing until the middle of his freshman season.

The education of Patrick Ewing on media matters continued a few weeks before the official start of basketball practice on October 15. Thompson arranged to meet one Sunday afternoon with the author, then an assistant sports editor at *The Washington Post*, for lunch and a tour of the newspaper. Thompson wanted Ewing to hear firsthand how reporters and editors did their jobs and, further, to understand what sort of demands they would be making of him as a star athlete in a prominent college basketball program.

The author told Ewing that most journalists covering his team were responsible professionals whose job it was to inform their readers about anything connected with the Georgetown program, good or bad. He tried to explain the difference between "on the record" and "off the record," the distinction between news stories and opinion columns, the way decisions were made on the placement of stories on the front page. No one was out to get him, Ewing was told, and he also was advised that honesty was always the best policy when dealing with the media. If he had nothing to say, that was certainly his prerogative. But don't blame the press for asking the questions—that's their job.

Ewing devoured several cheeseburgers and an ocean of orange juice during the hour-long session in a quiet dining room at the Madison Hotel in downtown Washington. He didn't say much, as Thompson generally directed the conversation. Later, across the street in the *Post* building, they toured the newsroom and the composing room, where Ewing seemed fascinated by the computer system used to set type and lay out the ads. Ewing smiled broadly and shook hands with anyone who came up to say hello—many did—and when the two huge men walked out of the building, Ewing was chatting animatedly about all that he had just seen. While it was obvious he was not an immediate candidate for a Rhodes scholarship, he seemed very much like a normal college freshman athlete trying to cope with a very complicated life. The tour of the *Post*, Thompson said, "is part of his normal education."

Ewing was taking a typical freshman load of five classes. He lived on campus with three roommates, including senior Ron Blaylock, a reserve guard on the team, in a large coed apartment complex. Georgetown had no jock dorm, but most players lived with at least one teammate. Ewing went to class in the morning and early afternoon and was in basketball practice from three to six every day. After dinner, there were mandatory study sessions for freshmen under Mary Fenlon's watchful eye.

"I've seen a mixture of happiness and depression," Thompson said two months after Ewing began classes. "He's been homesick. I'm sure there are things I don't know about, but I haven't observed anything really different from any other freshman. What's really pleasant is that he doesn't feel he has to be pampered. All this year's freshmen are that way. He's not spoiled, doesn't ask for things. It's too early to form a total opinion. I have noticed that he doesn't market his potential popularity. And that may be important because of the inordinate amount of attention that will surround Patrick."

Dr. Jesse Mann, a philosophy professor who had Ewing as a freshman, described him as "a very solid young man; very attentive, relating, engaging and not at all isolated. He seems to get along with the other students and he's an outgoing and pleasant youngster. Very genuine.

"I've read about all that special attention he was supposed to get here, but there's no special attention given to him in my [sixty-five-student Moral Development] class. He's got the same requirements as anyone else. He's come into my office twice and we've talked. He's got the personality of any Georgetown freshman. He's just a friendly overgrown freshman with a big smile."

Still, that was not the image Patrick Ewing would project over his next four years at Georgetown, at least not on the basketball court. Often he had the demeanor of a fierce warrior, with a scowling game face and a propensity to smack an opponent upside the head and retaliate quickly with flying elbows or fists. That became obvious in his very first game in a Georgetown uniform—a uniform that also would include a slight modification that season. Ever since high school, Ewing had preferred to wear a T-shirt under his basketball jersey, and the tradition continued his freshman year. "We played in a lot of unheated gyms," said his high school coach, Mike Jarvis, "and Patrick caught a lot of colds. He just felt better with that shirt on underneath."

Thompson did not start Ewing or two of his other talented freshmen, Billy Martin and Anthony Jones, in a preseason exhibition game against Cibona of Yugoslavia at McDonough Gymnasium. (Ralph Dalton, the fourth heralded freshman, had suffered a serious knee injury that fall and missed the entire season.) But with 16:23 left in the first half, Ewing, Martin and Jones entered the game, and the 2,718 in the stands roared their approval.

Within a minute, they were on their feet again. Fred Brown, a heady sophomore guard from the Bronx, saw that Ewing was being guarded by a much smaller man close to the basket. Brown lofted a lob pass that seemed impossible for anyone to reach before it hit high on the backboard. But in one moment Ewing soared up, hit the ball with his right arm and tapped it off the board for a basket that had to be seen to be believed.

"It didn't surprise me," Sleepy Floyd said that night. "I've seen it every day in practice for a month. It wasn't that big a deal."

Late in the game Ewing's temper flared, and it was not the first, or last, time that would happen. There had been several elbow-swinging incidents and near-fights in at least two high school all-star games involving Ewing the previous spring. And now, with 4:26 left against the Yugoslavian team, Ewing got frustrated with some pushing down low and responded with a shove of his own at Rajko Gaspodnetic before Fred Brown rushed in to separate the two big men. Thompson also came onto the court and spoke to his player. "I just told him it's going to happen and he should stay calm," Thompson said. But a minute later, 6-4 Alexandr Petrovic had a bear hug on Ewing. Unable to get the officials' attention, Ewing swung an elbow and whacked Petrovic on the side of the head.

"You never want that to happen," Thompson said afterward, "but the kid was pushing and holding him and the referee wouldn't call the intentional foul. At some point when you're held that long, you start to think maybe the guy wants to fight you."

Ewing's statistics were more than adequate. In twenty-two minutes, he scored 9 points, had 3 rebounds and 5 blocked shots. Still, the elbow incidents were troubling, but only his coach and teammates were able to get Ewing's version. True to Thompson's word, the big freshman center was not allowed to speak to the media when the game was over.

A week later, Georgetown opened its regular season in Anchorage, Alaska, of all places, as a participant in the eight-team Great Alaska Shootout, an event that is the highlight of the state's winter sports season. Georgetown went into the tournament with a number-five preseason national ranking, but that lasted all of one game. Thompson fussed that the Hoyas weren't that good anyway, and his team proved him right, losing to unranked Southwestern Louisiana, 70–61, in a first-round game.

Thompson started senior Ed Spriggs at center, with Floyd and Brown at the guards and seniors Eric Smith and Mike Hancock at the forwards. But Ewing entered three and a half minutes into the first half, and fifteen seconds later he scored his first official intercollegiate points on a slam dunk. He finished the night with only 7 points and picked up his fourth foul with 10:11 left in the game. Thompson chose not to put him back in, allowing Spriggs to finish up a game that saw the Hoyas fall behind by 10 at the half and never get closer than 6 the rest of the way.

The next night against the host team Alaska-Anchorage, Ewing made his first start. He scored 12 and added 6 rebounds in a 77–67 Georgetown victory, then scored 17 more the next night in a tough 47–46 loss to Ohio State settled by a twenty-foot jump shot by Buckeye guard Larry Huggins with four seconds left in the game. Thompson had been right—the 1–2 Hoyas were not the fifth-best team in the country at that point. But the season was young, and Thompson did not seem overly concerned, especially after a spirited team meeting in their Anchorage hotel "to air things out and get on the same page," according to Ron Blaylock.

"I never expected to lose any of these games," Thompson said. "But we have to keep going. This tournament was developmental. I keep telling myself that. Sometimes you need some courage."

And some patsies as well. Thompson always believed in a soft early-season schedule to prepare his team for the rigors of conference competition, and 1981–82 was no exception. The first opponent at the Capital Centre was San Diego State, and with close to nine thousand in the stands, Thompson used all his players in a 71–53 victory that was settled by a 20–2 Georgetown burst. There had been one scary moment, when Ewing was stretched out, facedown, on the Capital Centre court, the victim of a finger poked in his eye. Thompson walked out onto the court to check on his fallen player. "When I saw him smile," he said, "I turned and went back to the bench."

Afterward, it was obvious that Thompson knew this team was special. "One of the biggest things we're going through right now," he said, "is that these kids are so nice. Everybody wants so hard to do what I want done, to the extent they're thinking about it instead of reacting to it. They'll be all right. We'll make some mistakes, but that doesn't scare me. I've been in this business long enough to know that you've got to build a team. A team is not something that's hatched in December. Not the good ones."

And this was a very good team. The Hoyas demonstrated that by running off 13 straight victories after that dismal loss to Ohio State in

Alaska. Still, there were some lingering problems. In a victory over crosstown rival George Washington, Ewing got into a shoving and talking match with two players.

In the very last sequence of a 19-point victory over Western Kentucky, Ewing collided with Bobby Jones, a 5-10 point guard who was rushing over to commit an intentional foul. Soon, fists were flying again. "Patrick said that when the kid rushed in, he hit the guy as he was pivoting," Thompson said, defending his star freshman. "The kid reacted; that happens in an emotional game and this game was emotional and physical. The kids told me that Jones took a swing at Patrick. At that point Fred Brown came in and punched the kid." Brown's punch left Jones with a black eye, a cut lip and several loose teeth. Both benches cleared momentarily as time expired, and Thompson quickly moved in to get his team off the floor.

"We're not going to say anything about that," Brown said of his punch. "It was an impulse. The guy threw a punch at Pat." Replays also indicated that Brown's punch was a cheap shot, coming from the side and behind Jones, who clearly had no idea what hit him.

Thompson tried to minimize the fight in the postgame press conference. "If I thought it was getting out of hand, I would be concerned," he insisted. "But I think I have control of my team. I talked to the players about it. In fact, at first I thought Patrick threw the punch and I started to get upset with him. But it was Fred. . . . I'm not condoning what happened. My teams have never been known for starting brawls. But if someone throws a punch, you react."

The Hoyas' 11th straight victory over that span was far less controversial, but it clearly opened some eyes around the Big East Conference. In their first league outing, the Hoyas played the practically perfect basketball game, pummeling St. John's, 72–42, before 19,591 mostly stunned onlookers at Madison Square Garden in New York. This was to have been the ninth-ranked Hoyas' first major test since Alaska, going against an eighteenth-ranked St. John's team in a historic and hostile building on the road. A week before, St. John's had won the prestigious Holiday Festival, and the team was riding a 6-game winning streak of its own. But if Georgetown's young freshmen were nervous in the Big Apple, it hardly showed. Floyd scored on a breakaway basket off the opening tap, and Georgetown, applying fullcourt pressure from the start, never trailed again, leading by 26–4 early on and—incredibly—by 41–9 late in the first half.

"If a team could have a perfect game, I mean one you could use as a clinic, then Georgetown had it," St. John's coach Lou Carnesecca said when it was over, shaking his head in disbelief. "Their performance was something every coach would like to store and go back to when he needs it. I mean for passing, shooting, screening, quickness, defenses, shot blocking, rebounding and everything."

Ewing hit four straight free throws in the last minute to allow Georgetown's streak to continue in a 62–60 victory over Seton Hall, but the good times abruptly came to a halt a few days later at the cavernous Carrier Dome in Syracuse. Before 25,623, including an orange-clad masked man known as the Dome Ranger, it was Syracuse's turn to play a practically perfect game. The Orangemen hit 56 percent from the field, made 26 of 34 free throws and went right at Ewing almost every time down the court. Ewing picked up two quick fouls in the first four minutes and got his fourth with 17:38 left. Forced to the bench for a long stretch, Ewing finally fouled out with 1:40 remaining in the game, and he was not a factor, scoring only 6 points, with 6 rebounds. "He has to learn to play with fouls," Thompson said. "We missed him inside."

Three days later, it was the same story. Ewing fouled out again, scored only 8, and Georgetown lost to Connecticut, 63–52, at the Capital Centre. Five days after that there was another upset, this time to a badly outmanned Providence team coached by Joe Mullaney, Thompson's old college coach, who was taking a second tour at the school after a long run in the NBA. It was the first meeting between Thompson and his old mentor, and Mullaney used a special triangle defense to thwart the far more talented Hoyas on a night when Georgetown made only 21 of 58 shots and was outrebounded 34–31 by a much smaller team. The mentor had clearly outcoached his old student, and within six days Georgetown had lost three Big East games and was reeling in free-fall. With Villanova, the conference leader, coming to town, the Hoyas were in total disarray.

Thompson was trying everything. One day, he asked each player to get up in a meeting and say something positive about the basketball team. Then he took them back to the locker room to watch themselves on tape against St. John's. "That's the way we used to look," Thompson told them.

Clearly, they listened. The Hoyas pounded Villanova, 72–56, opening a 10–2 lead at the start, then scoring 39 points in their first 25 possessions of the second half to break open a close game. "I don't know why we did what we did tonight. I wish I could tell you," Thompson said. "I've pulled out everything. I told 'em, 'Let's win some games now and talk about life during the summer.' "

Once again, the Hoyas were off on another streak of devastating basketball—a 17-point win against St. John's, an 11-point win at Villanova, a 30-point win against Seton Hall and a 17-point drubbing of Syracuse at the Capital Centre with Bill Russell in attendance. Russell, whose daughter was attending Georgetown at the time, spoke to the team after the game. Thompson said he would also be around for a few days to tutor Ewing on "the psychology of blocking shots." Ewing did not look as if he needed much help this night. He merely scored 22 points, with 13 rebounds and 5 blocked shots. At one point, when Georgetown came from 9 back to go up by 20 with thirteen minutes to play, Ewing personally outscored the Syracuse team, 19–18, over a fifteen-minute span.

Georgetown faltered only once down the stretch thereafter, losing a bitter 80–71 decision at Boston College. It was Ewing's first trip back to his hometown to play a game, and the BC fans were not kind, taunting him with epithets, racial and otherwise, all night. Ewing did manage to score a career-high 23 points, but the Eagles were making 71 percent of their field goal attempts and they held Sleepy Floyd to just 7-of-20 shooting.

"I expected them to be hostile," Ewing said afterward. "I could hear some of the things they said but I just laughed. I didn't go up there trying to have a big game. I just wanted to win up there."

Said Thompson, "He handled the situation much better than I thought he would. He played real well, but I think Patrick will feel the same way I do. None of us will brag about our play against BC."

But over the next two months, the Hoyas would have plenty to brag about. In their next game, they pounded fourth-ranked Missouri, 63–51, in a rare McDonough game. Before the contest, Missouri coach Norm Stewart had joked, "I don't like playing in small gyms against big coaches." He was not laughing when it was over and the Hoyas had held his star center, Steve Stipanovich, to 5 points, forcing him to pick up three quick fouls before eventually fouling out midway through the second half.

Georgetown finished the Big East regular season with victories over Providence and Connecticut, leaving the Hoyas 23–6 overall and 10–4 in the conference, good for second place behind Villanova. Now it was on to Hartford, Connecticut, for the Big East tournament, and for Georgetown it was more of the same.

Freshman Anthony Jones came off the bench to score 19 points and Georgetown had another of its patented blitzes—a 24–2 run in the first ten minutes of the second half—to rout Providence, 62–48, in the first round. In the semifinals St. John's fell to Georgetown for the third time that season, in a game most notable for two more scuffles, once again with Ewing involved. The Hoyas prevailed easily, 57–42, after shutting down the Redmen defensively, forcing them to miss 13 of their first 15 shots in the second half.

And defense once again was the story in the final against Villanova. At halftime, senior cocaptain Eric Smith asked Thompson to ditch his zone in favor of man-to-man coverage once Villanova got past midcourt. "We don't vote on many things at Georgetown," Thompson said, "but I told them to go to it." The result was another typical run of 24–5 that broke the game open and gave the Hoyas their 6th straight victory, the Big East tournament title and an automatic bid to the NCAA tournament. In its infinite wisdom, the NCAA also decided to send Georgetown to the West regional, making the Hoyas the number-one seed. While some wondered why this newest beast of the East would be playing so far from home, Thompson had no complaints; the road to the Final Four in New Orleans would be so much smoother coming from the West because the opposition was not particularly daunting.

Though his first-round foe would be Big Sky Conference champion Wyoming in Logan, Utah, Thompson set up headquarters in Salt Lake City, an hour away from the game site. While he was there, Thompson picked up the newspaper one day and saw himself described as "the Idi Amin of college basketball" by Salt Lake City sports columnist John Mooney. If Thompson was offended by the comparison to the genocidal Ugandan dictator—as well he should have been—he didn't let on. "I have talked to Idi about that," Thompson said one day, "and he resents it. He says he is much better looking than I am."

Thompson's team waltzed through the West, knocking off Wyoming, 51–43, then making 64 percent of its shots in a 58–40 rout of Fresno State that saw the Hoyas limit the nation's top-ranked defensive team to just 4 field goals in the final fourteen minutes. And in the West regional championship game, with a performance Thompson later described as the finest by any team he'd ever coached, Georgetown destroyed Oregon State, 69–45, shooting an NCAA tournament record 74 percent from the field.

"Champions play when they have to play," Thompson said that day, chiding critics who had been carping all season about the Hoyas' inconsistent outside shooting. "Yeah, that's all I've heard all year—Georgetown can't shoot. I even got letters from people offering advice on shooting."

When it was over, Thompson made it a point to go over to each of his three graduating seniors—Floyd, Spriggs, and Eric Smith—and smother them in a bear hug on the sidelines as their teammates snipped down the net. In his tenth season, John Thompson at last was going to the Final Four.

"The great satisfaction," he said, "is that you think you're there so many times, only to be disappointed, and now you've made it because these players have worked so hard. We may not have the talent the 1980 team had. We're not great shooters, and we're terrible free-throw shooters. But when we have to do it, we do it."

A week later, Georgetown was back on the road again, far from the madding crowd of New Orleans, where the Final Four would be played in the Superdome before sixty thousand plus. This time, Thompson set up headquarters in Biloxi, Mississippi, ninety-seven miles away. "I didn't go to Biloxi for any advantage," Thompson said at his first press conference before his opening game against Louisville. "I went there for peace of mind. I just felt it would be best to get into an atmosphere where we could concentrate. They can come to New Orleans anytime to see Bourbon Street. This is a very important opportunity for us."

In Biloxi, Thompson's players were strictly off-limits to the press and, as usual, his practices were held behind closed doors. Biloxi had "a nice beach," senior Eric Smith told reporters the day before the Louisville game, "but I'm still trying to figure out if the city has a downtown. If Coach Thompson says we're in Biloxi, then so be it. Whatever is necessary to win."

At the same media session, Thompson was asked his reaction to being the first black coach in the Final Four, and he was clearly ready for it. "I resent the hell out of it [the question]," Thompson said. "It implies I was the first person competent enough to do this, which is a very misleading statement. There have been several people who were more qualified than I am to be here, but they were denied the opportunity. I don't take any honor and dignity in being the first black anything, anywhere. It implies that I was the first to have the ability and the intelligence, and I find it extremely offensive."

If Georgetown's players were apprehensive or nervous about their first appearance in the Final Four, it was not obvious in the locker room before the Louisville game. "We had a routine we went through that had started during the season," said Ron Blaylock. "Sleepy and I would do a little dance—we called it the Carolina shuffle. Anthony Jones liked to sing. He did a great Luther Vandross. We'd be telling jokes, staying loose, and it was the same in the Final Four. When the coaches came in with the scouting report, you'd start to focus and get serious. Before that first game, he [Thompson] told us we'd worked hard all year for this. He talked about pride and the work ethic. We also had this chant: 'We are Georgetown, we are Georgetown.' And that's what we said right before we'd hit the floor."

On this night, however, they did not look like the Georgetown team that had blitzed through its first three NCAA games. As well as they had played against Oregon State, this time they struggled, hitting only 18 of 41 shots with 18 turnovers. Fortunately, Louisville was just as bad in the face of a relentless Georgetown defense that clearly was the deciding factor in the basketball game. Louisville, which had been shooting at a tournament record 59 percent from the field, was held to just 19 of 48 shots against Thompson's stifling fullcourt defense.

"I can't remember us appearing to play so poorly offensively and still winning the game since I've been at Georgetown," Thompson said. "We had to strain for everything we got. . . . A lot of things happened out there we didn't like."

Still, the Hoyas had won despite their problems, and would be facing a North Carolina team that had knocked off Houston, 68–63, in the first game of the national semifinals. It would be John Thompson against his old friend and mentor Dean Smith, Sleepy Floyd against his old Gastonia rival James Worthy and Patrick Ewing against another heralded freshman, Michael Jordan.

Dean Smith had taken the Tar Heels to the Final Four six times before and had never won the title, with losses in three championship games. "It probably bothers me more than it does him," Thompson said graciously one day, "because I know he's one of the best to ever coach the game. It's far more difficult to get here than to win one game, and look how many times he's done that. He's an innovator. And beyond that, he has kept it all in perspective in a very competitive situation. He has a real concern for his kids."

There were so many intriguing story lines to choose from, but Thompson added an ugly one in his final press conference the day before the championship game. Almost casually, he revealed that the school had received a telephone death threat against Patrick Ewing shortly after the team's victory in the Big East tournament three weeks before.

Thompson was in the middle of a discussion about the pressures Ewing had faced that first year when he said, "I'll give you a perfect example. When we got back from Hartford, there was a death threat on Patrick's life."

There was an audible gasp from the three hundred reporters in the room, and Thompson went on. "It scared the hell out of me," he said. "You can say it's pretty common. But it was pretty common last year when the president of the United States was shot [the day of the NCAA title game], wasn't it?"

Thompson did not tell Ewing about the call until after the press conference. Thompson said he had told his players that the entire team had been threatened, and that athletic director Frank Rienzo had given him permission to discuss the incident at the press conference to spread the word to a national forum. But why now, on the eve of a championship game? he was asked. "Because tomorrow is the last game, and we're going to get out of here."

The phone call had come in to a university operator. "Please tell me Patrick Ewing's room number," the caller said, "because I want to kill him." The operator immediately relayed the information to the athletic department, and Rienzo consulted with the school's security chief as well as Washington police. Just to be safe, Ewing and seven other players spent their first two days back in town after the Big East tournament at a Marriott hotel across the Potomac River from the campus.

"He explained it to us," Eric Smith said. "We thought it was crazy that somebody would do something like that, but Coach told us he was going to put us in the hotel because he wasn't going to take any chances." Other precautions were taken. The team left for Utah a day earlier than planned, and a burly former Georgetown football player was assigned to travel with the team as an extra security man, sitting on the bench all during the regionals. A number of Georgetown officials also spent a great deal of time checking reporters' credentials outside the locker room after the Louisville game, and extra police officers were assigned to the team in Biloxi and New Orleans.

If the players were concerned, it hardly showed. "We didn't think much about it," said Anthony Jones. "I just thought it was a prank. I never really took it seriously. I don't think Patrick was laughing it off, I'm sure he thought about it, but he sure came ready to play that night. We all did."

"We knew what was at stake," added Blaylock. "In his speech before the Carolina game, Big John said the same thing: 'We've come a long way, do what we do best, just go out and do it.' When we left the locker room, we knew it was a mission. Patrick was pumped for prime time."

That quickly became very obvious. The first four times North Carolina shot the basketball, Ewing was called for goaltending. Hank Nichols, a veteran referee assigned to that game, said he can still remember thinking to himself, "Is he just going to try to block every Carolina shot and hope we won't make some of those calls? It was just amazing, and when I went back to look at them [on replays], there was no question that every call was the right call. There was no doubt about any of them."

Ewing later was whistled for a fifth goaltending call later in the half. Georgetown held a 32–31 lead at intermission, but 10 of Carolina's points came courtesy of Georgetown's fabulous freshman. "I didn't know if it was part of their strategy to intimidate Carolina or whether Patrick was just so fired up and ready to play," Nichols said. "But I definitely thought it was bizarre."

Despite the intimidation, James Worthy kept driving toward the basket and challenging the Hoyas, and Jordan was hitting regularly from the outside as the teams punched and counterpunched. Jordan gave Carolina a 61–58 lead with 3:26 to play when he came down the middle and softly tossed a left-handed lay-up high off the glass just over Ewing's reach, a breathtaking move from a young man just beginning to defy gravity as a freshman.

"I had the confidence I could do it," Jordan said of his stunning shot. "I knew he could have blocked it. I know I could have been called for a charge. I didn't want him to intimidate me. It was risky, but so what?"

Ewing answered right back with a turnaround jump shot, giving him 23 points for the night and cutting the Carolina lead to 1. At that point, the Tar Heels went to their famous four-corners offense, spreading the court and playing keepaway with the basketball. They ran down the clock until forward Matt Doherty was finally fouled. But Doherty missed the front end and Ewing's 11th rebound gave the Hoyas the ball and a chance to take the lead. Floyd, the all-American senior, wasted little time, hitting a short jumper in the lane for a 62–61 Georgetown advantage with fifty-four seconds left.

Once again, Carolina worked the ball around before Dean Smith called time-out with thirty-four seconds remaining to set up a final play.

Smith said afterward he expected Georgetown to deny the ball to his big men, so he told his players to take the first open shot they had. Jordan responded, sticking a sixteen-footer with seventeen seconds left, his tongue darting from his mouth as he let the ball fly.

The Hoyas had one more chance. Thompson was criticized for not calling a time-out to plot a final shot, but he said later, "I wouldn't have known what kind of defense Dean was going to use, so I would have been wasting my time setting up a play." Instead, Fred Brown hurried the ball up the court, but inexplicably threw a pass toward teammate Eric Smith on his right side. Worthy filled the lane between the two Hoyas, intercepted the ball and raced down toward the Carolina basket, smiling all the way. He was fouled with two seconds left, and though he missed both free throws, Georgetown had no time for a final play, and North Carolina had won, 63–62, giving Dean Smith his first and only national championship.

As the game ended, the television cameras panned the Georgetown sideline. There, a national audience watched as John Thompson at once embraced and consoled Fred Brown in a hug that defined John Thompson for many people as much as any action of his life. "I watched that scene that night," said Arthur Ashe, the great tennis professional, "and tears were streaming down my face."

Afterward, Fred Brown sat in the Georgetown locker room as wave after wave of reporters asked him about The Pass. He answered every question, until the last man left the room.

"I thought he [Worthy] was Eric Smith," Brown said, describing how he had heard Smith call for the ball a millisecond before he threw it in that direction. "I made a perfect pass but it was to the wrong guy. My job was to get it to him. I got it to the wrong man. It was their ball, their game, then. There ain't nothing I can do to recapture it. It's all over. I threw the pass that made us lose the game."

Still, it was left for John Thompson to put it all in perspective.

"I feel bad for Fred," he said, "but he's a tough kid. This is just part of his growing up. I told Fred that he had won more games for me than he had lost and he was not to worry. It was one of those human errors."

Later, Thompson had one more hug left in him. As he left the interview room with several of his players, Thompson bumped into Smith and Worthy in the hallway as the Carolina contingent prepared to face the press.

A photographer, Hugh Morton, tried to get a picture, but the two men had their backs to him. He tapped Thompson on the shoulder and asked if he and Smith would mind turning around. Thompson smiled and lifted Smith off the ground in an embrace that clearly was from the heart. His old friend had finally won a national championship, and with Patrick Ewing around for another three years, there would still be time for John Thompson and the Georgetown Hoyas to win one of their own.

13

John Thompson had heard all the stories about Michael Graham, knew all about his problems and his petulance. He also knew the bald man-child could win him a national championship. And so he did.

ALMOST FROM THE DAY PATRICK EWING HAD ARRIVED ON campus, college basketball aficionados had been clamoring for a matchup between the Georgetown giant and another towering presence 125 miles down the road at the University of Virginia. Patrick Ewing versus Ralph Sampson was a dream game that started to become a reality shortly after the 1981–82 season had ended.

John Thompson was not about to allow such a game during Ewing's freshman season, believing the youngster had enough pressure on him already without having to go up against the 7-foot-4 Sampson, two years ahead of him. But a few weeks after Georgetown's loss to North Carolina for the national championship, Georgetown athletic director Frank Rienzo and his counterpart at Virginia, Dick Schultz, began talking seriously about scheduling a game, finally agreeing that it would be played December 11, 1982, at the Capital Centre, Georgetown's home court but only a three-hour drive from the Charlottesville campus. Rienzo, as the athletic director of the host school, also would have the final say on television rights, and he held an auction, asking for bids from seven networks and syndicators.

The day after the Final Four had ended, one of those networks, Ted Turner's cable outlet WTBS in Atlanta, also was making plans to get involved in any future game between Georgetown and Virginia. WTBS president Robert Wussler and executive sports producer Terry Hanson met in a New Orleans hotel room with Russ Potts, a former SMU athletic director and assistant A.D. at the University of Maryland who was now in the business of putting together television deals for several schools.

Originally, Potts thought Georgetown-Virginia might be attractive enough to warrant placing the game in theaters around the country as well as on a fledgling pay-per-view system some cable companies were beginning to use, much like a heavyweight boxing match. But at the meeting with Wussler and Hanson, it was decided that Potts would represent WTBS in its negotiations with the schools for the game.

Potts was a shrewd good old boy from Winchester, Virginia, well versed in the art of the deal. Over the next few months he was in constant communication with Rienzo, and he also placed more than an occasional call to John Thompson. He had come to know Thompson a few years earlier when the Georgetown coach had asked him for advice on how to promote his own up-and-coming program in the 1970s, at a time when Potts was trying to fill up Byrd Stadium and Cole Field House in College Park, Maryland.

Thompson and Mary Fenlon flew down to Dallas for one meeting with Potts and several potential advertisers for the Virginia game, and a source in attendance that evening said it was a rather bizarre session, held over dinner in an exclusive private club. The source recalled that Mary Fenlon actually was tasting Thompson's food before the coach touched a bite to make sure it was cooked just right and wasn't too salty. He also said Fenlon told the assembled diners that Thompson was running low on a prescription for pills to control his blood pressure, and that unless it was filled that night the coach could have a serious problem. One of the participants immediately left the table and went looking for a pharmacy, delivering the medication to Thompson's hotel.

The source also recalled that Thompson was almost blatant in letting it be known that he wanted something for himself out of any deal, above and beyond what WTBS would be paying the two schools for the television rights. Many coaches were and still are in the practice of cutting side deals for themselves. A common practice involves Christmas tournaments: Coaches have been offered inducements to schedule their teams at such events. Come to our holiday tournament, the pitch goes, and we'll pay you $5,000 to talk to our booster club the day before your game. The $5,000 goes to the coach as a speaker's fee. No harm, no foul. "He [Thompson] wanted money out of it, no question," the source said. "That was made very obvious."

In the end, WTBS and CBS were Rienzo's two finalists. CBS was taking a somewhat arrogant stance, pushing for the game to be shifted to January 8 for prime-time exposure. It also was willing to up its original offer—from $510,000 to $635,000—if Georgetown would agree to move the date. WTBS, meanwhile, had bid $700,000 and was willing to play anytime and anyplace that suited Georgetown. And Russ Potts, according to another television industry source, also had arranged to sweeten the deal for the Georgetown coach by having a soft-drink company pay him $50,000 to do a few clinics. No one at Georgetown or WTBS would ever say that perk swung the deal to WTBS, but it certainly had to be a factor. Rienzo said that if Thompson had such an arrangement, he was not aware of it. "I don't think there's any connection between the clinics and Georgetown-Virginia in any way, shape or form," he said. "I would be shocked—my recollection is that's not true, wouldn't be true, couldn't be true." Potts declined comment, saying that he had called Thompson and "in the interest of our friendship" he preferred not to be interviewed for this book.

"Potts had the keys to the kingdom," said another source familiar with the negotiations. "At one point he said to the Georgetown people, 'If I can get something done for John . . .' WTBS never paid the company for the clinics. It was just a little perk thrown in for John. He'll say it had nothing to do with the decision, and maybe it didn't. It might be unethical, but it was not illegal, and that kind of thing goes on all the time in these deals. It was business, and John Thompson is a very good businessman."

The agreement between Georgetown and WTBS marked the first time that a major sports attraction would appear on basic cable television, and as *Sports Illustrated* media columnist William Taaffe noted, "It showed that for all their money and power, the major networks no longer can impose their will on every college athletic director with a game to sell."

The media hype in the days before the contest was intense, with one hyperbolic writer from *The Washington Times* comparing it to "Zachary Taylor vs. Santa Ana, Custer vs. Sitting Bull, Pershing vs. Pancho Villa." Whatever, Georgetown played hardball with WTBS, declining to make Ewing available for an interview that would be aired in the pregame show. Hearing that, Virginia coach Terry Holland also refused to let Sampson talk to the station. "We learned something from that," said Terry Hanson, who declined to comment on any of the negotiations. "Not having those two on the air really hurt our production. In every contract after that, we specifically had a clause saying that the players would be made available."

The game itself lived up to its billing, even if Sampson had developed a case of the flu that required him to be pumped with intravenous fluids after it was over. He hardly played like a sick man, outscoring Ewing 23–16, outrebounding him 16–8 and blocking 7 shots to Ewing's 5. There also were several memorable sequences involving the two big men, each trying to in-your-face the other as the game wore on. With the score tied at 59–59 with 3:48 remaining, Ewing had a lay-up blocked and Anthony Jones, in a terrible foul-shooting slump, missed the front end of a one-and-one. Virginia, meanwhile, though scoring only 1 field goal in the final 10:51, managed to hang on by making 9 of 10 free throws down the stretch for a 68–63 victory.

Sampson was gracious in victory. "I don't have enough words to describe Pat," he said. "He is a great, great player."

As the 1982–83 season continued, it also was becoming obvious that Ewing was a player under siege, particularly when the Hoyas left the friendly confines of McDonough or the Capital Centre. In the locker room he was known as Aloysius, his middle name, so that snoopy reporters could not find him in the training room or overhear conversations about him. And almost everywhere he went on the road, Ewing was subjected to vile language, racial epithets and crude signs and banners.

In a January game at Providence, a fan under a basket raised a sign that said "Ewing Can't Read" and Thompson pulled his team off the court until it was taken down. A few weeks later at the Palestra in Philadelphia, there were several more signs. One bedsheet read, "Ewing Is an Ape"; another said, "Ewing Can't Spell His Name." A fan was wearing a T-shirt that said, "Ewing Kant Read Dis." And when Ewing ran on the court for pregame introductions, a banana peel was thrown on the court.

"If we're playing away, it seems Pat is always the villain," said Billy Martin, a sophomore forward. "It has to do with the image Pat has projected of himself as an aggressive person. . . . The signs and the jeers don't bother Pat. They only make him play harder. Nothing bothers Pat. The more people yell at him, the better he plays."

On the court, he also was having a continuation of the problems that had beset him as a freshman. There were several pushing and shoving incidents that year, and in a game against St. John's at Madison Square Garden, Ewing twice scuffled with Kevin Williams, once punching him in the mouth and bloodying his lip as Garden fans booed loudly. After that game, Thompson, again trying to divert some attention from the fight, said he would tell Ewing to go turn professional and declare for the hardship draft if "he's going to be held, pushed and mauled like he was today."

A few weeks later, Thompson said Ewing was involved in so many melees because "Patrick doesn't complain, he retaliates. . . . I get a bunch of five-foot people writing me telling me I'm crying about this. Let them go out there, put up with what Patrick puts up with, and then see what they say."

Thompson also was incensed about the abuse from the stands. "A person who holds up a sign needs to be prayed for," he said. "It's been evidenced throughout history that keeping quiet about things doesn't help the situation. People probably said that about Hitler, too. 'Keep quiet and he'll go away.' I won't continue to sleep in peace and ignore it. . . . Patrick has been blessed with an outstanding ability to cope with those things. He is refreshingly tough-skinned about things. When I asked him before my TV show if he wanted to talk about it, he refused to talk about it. I can respect that."

Father Healy, the school president, was outraged. "It is cheap racist stuff," he said. "No one on the face of the earth can tell me if Patrick were a seven-foot-high white man that people would still carry those signs around. I'm a white man and I know it. John is a black man and he knows it. . . . This all strikes me as dreadful."

It struck the Big East office the same way. In mid-February, Commissioner Dave Gavitt sent a two-page letter to conference athletic directors and coaches detailing a number of improvements he wanted instituted in managing league games, including increased reaction to the derogatory signs and banners. Ewing's problems, Gavitt said, served as an impetus to the letter. "That was certainly a key part," he said. "I think it's despicable that any player or coach has to be subjected to those kind of signs. The people responsible at the arena have to be more alert to these things. Beyond that, we want security people and ushers to be more vigilant. Whether the signs are about Patrick Ewing, Villanova University or Joe Mullaney, no one should be subjected to them."

For a good part of the 1982–83 season, Georgetown was subjected to other problems. Four days before the start of practice, Fred Brown suffered a serious knee injury that required major surgery, and he was lost for most of the season, replaced by junior Gene Smith, a defensive specialist who had seen limited action as a sophomore because of a foot injury. Anthony Jones and Billy Martin, now sophomores, were struggling and more than occasionally in Thompson's doghouse. Dalton came back from knee surgery but was not the same player he'd been in high school, with limited mobility and no speed, though he was able to give Ewing a blow now and then in the games and pounded him daily in practice. The freshman class had several outstanding players, including guards Michael Jackson of nearby Reston, Virginia; Horace Broadnax of Turkey Creek, Florida; and forward David Wingate, another product of Baltimore's Dunbar High School and a shooter "with no conscience," according to Thompson. The coach had also added a bruising 6-8 forward from Mableton, Georgia, David Dunn, the last white player he would sign for his program until the 1989–90 season.

Bill Stein, meanwhile, had grown tired of the helter-skelter life that went with recruiting high school basketball players. He left the staff to accept the athletic directorship at St. Peter's College in Jersey City, New Jersey. Thompson added two new assistants, both former players: Craig Esherick had passed the D.C. bar examination but opted for basketball over the law, and Mike Riley was back in the fold, lured from his position as assistant headmaster at Gonzaga High School in Washington.

In December, both young coaches filled in for Thompson after the death of his mother. Thompson left the team for almost a week to grieve with his family, privately as always, and according to a friend he was obviously "very, very upset. He'd been taking care of her for so long. He actually would pick her up and carry her to the bathtub to bathe her every morning. She was always there for him. It just tore him up." In fact, a year later Thompson would say that Anna Thompson's death had so drained him emotionally that for the entire season he'd had a difficult time making himself concentrate on basketball.

The whole 1982–83 season was a struggle for Thompson and the young Hoyas. Though they were respectable enough, the graduations of Floyd, Eric Smith and Spriggs clearly hurt, and without Fred Brown to run the offense the Hoyas were inconsistent at best. They lost in the first round of the Big East tournament to Syracuse, struggled to beat heavy underdog Alcorn State, a small black school, 68–63 in the first round of the NCAA tournament, then were eliminated in the second round by Keith Lee's Memphis State team, 66–57, in a game that was not that close.

It had been a rebuilding season, despite the presence of eight returning players from the previous year. And while Ewing was a force on defense, his offensive skills were still somewhat suspect. It also was clear that Georgetown needed more help inside to crash the boards and to relieve the constant double- and triple-teams Ewing was facing in the paint.

That spring, Thompson knew exactly where that help was located: Spingarn High School, not far from the coach's old neighborhood and the playground where he once learned the game. Spingarn senior Michael Graham was a fierce 6-foot-9 presence who had shaved his head bald and been the scourge of Washington's tough Interhigh League for two years, leading Spingarn to a 47–11 record over that span. He also had a terrible reputation around the city, and Thompson was telling some of his friends he would have a difficult time justifying his pursuit of the talented but troubled youngster, even if he was exactly the kind of bruiser he needed to get back to the Final Four. Graham came from a broken home and as a teenager had lived off and on with one or the other parent or with other relatives. In Graham's senior year at Spingarn, he also had fathered a child, feuded openly with his basketball coach, John Wood, and was doing poorly in the classroom. In fact, he did not even have enough credits to graduate on time.

"Michael Graham was basically a scum bucket, and everybody in this city knew it," said Glenn Harris, a Washington sports broadcaster with deep roots in the black community. "He didn't have any grades, there was some talk about drugs, and he wanted to screw all the women. But he was no dummy, either. John knew that, and I guess he was willing to take a chance."

Thompson was not alone. The University of Maryland and several other schools also were pursuing Graham. In fact, Maryland coaches had watched him play fifteen times during his senior year, and at one point assistant coach Sherman Dillard said he had received an oral commitment from Graham that he would be attending Maryland the following fall. Even Graham's high school coach, John Wood, was shocked to learn that spring that Graham had quietly signed a letter of intent to play at Georgetown.

"With those youngsters, nothing will surprise you," Wood said. "A lot of times, these kids never tell you the truth. Where Michael wanted to go, that was his choice. I didn't like the method Georgetown used to get him. He got to Georgetown without me even knowing about it, and that's not right. That's all I want to say about it."

Thompson, meanwhile, insisted that he was convinced "beyond a doubt" that Graham could do the work and graduate from Georgetown. "I made it very clear to him that I'm not going to put up with anybody who is not going to work to get an education," he said at the time. With Thompson's help, Graham enrolled that summer in an Upward Bound program on the Georgetown campus and passed courses in English and math that allowed him to graduate from high school and be considered for admission.

Charles Deacon, the director of admissions, said that allowing Graham in was a difficult decision for him to make, but that Thompson and Sam Harvey, who ran the Community Scholars program back then, were very much in favor of Graham's acceptance. "The tough call for

Patrick Ewing and Ralph Sampson jockey for position in 1983. (The Washington Post)

him [Graham] was primarily the motivation question," Deacon said. "The way the process works, John and Sam would say, 'This is a student we think can do it, and has the motivation,' and the benefit of the doubt will go to them. But Michael's credentials were very marginal to get him in originally."

Even Father Healy got involved. "Yes, I was consulted because we had a sharp difference of opinion in the house as to whether Michael could do the academic side of it," he said. "Our best guy out there, Sam Harvey, worked with Michael for a summer, tested him and said he can [do the work]. It was a judgment call on my part. I backed Sam. I was only wrong on one thing: I should have held Michael out of playing as a freshman. I yielded to the argument that basketball was an integral part of his life, it's his pride, it's his thing and that it's better to let him play as a motivational tool than not play. Again, a judgment call. And I might do exactly the same thing again."

The start of classes was only a few days away when Thompson announced in late August two significant developments: Michael Graham had been admitted to the school, and junior forward Anthony Jones would be leaving to transfer to Nevada–Las Vegas.

"It feels great just being able to start over again," Graham said that day. "When I read the things people were saying about me, I thought it was another guy named Michael Graham. At one point, I never thought I'd get to college. My high school coach told me it would be impossible unless I got a GED [general equivalency diploma] or went to junior college. Then I got to talk to Coach Thompson and he told me to listen to him and I wouldn't be sorry. This is a chance to straighten out my life. In the past I just didn't want to attend school, so people thought I was a problem child. I was a problem, but only to myself; now I look to have a future. Mr. Thompson talked straight to me. He told me I had to get squared away. . . . I thought about guys in my neighborhood who stand around and talk about what they used to be. I don't want to be out on a corner five years from now telling about what I could have been."

Thompson had no problems justifying Graham's arrival on a campus that seemed so unsuited to such a questionable academic risk. "I asked a number of people, 'What kind of kid is this?' and ninety-nine percent—teachers of his, people he worked with—liked him as a person. . . . The most important thing for me was to know him, and not deal with his reputation." Of course, it also helped that Graham was 6-9 and would be of great help to his basketball team. Once again,

Georgetown's academic reputation was being stretched to the very limit to admit a student who had never in his life really been a student.

The departure of Jones also was somewhat academically related, but mostly he was leaving because he simply could not cope with Thompson's demanding system. He was not the first, or the last, to become dissatisfied at Georgetown, but he certainly was one of the few to talk about it openly. As a sophomore, Jones had struggled on the court and in the classroom, and in July following that season he announced that he would be taking a year off from school to "get things together." A month later, Jones had changed his mind and decided to start over at UNLV. As always, Thompson was hardly forthcoming about the reasons for Jones's transfer, saying that it was simply the best course of action for all concerned.

"I had dislocated my elbow in December that year," Jones said. "I wasn't playing much, and I was depressed about the way I was playing. And after the season, I pretty much slacked off on my studies, missed some classes, that kind of thing. John was shuffling people in and out a lot, and I was so used to playing all the time. That's his style, but that did not suit me as a player. I wanted to go more up-tempo."

Thompson tried to help. He called his friend John "Sonny" Vaccaro, a Nike shoe executive who was living in Las Vegas at the time and was good friends with the UNLV coach, Jerry Tarkanian. Soon Jones, Thompson and Fenlon visited Vegas—even then Thompson liked to play the slots—and the transfer process was under way.

A few months later, Jones said that he did not blame anyone but himself for his problems at Georgetown and that he had simply made the wrong choice of schools to suit his needs. "At Georgetown," he said, "there is always someone looking over your shoulder. I never could get relaxed there in any way. It's a pressure-type atmosphere on and off the court. It seemed to me like they [Thompson and Fenlon] had eyes in the back of their heads. . . . I am not a player who takes well to yelling. It was intimidating. I tried to put it out of my mind, but I couldn't. I was always worried about making a mistake."

If Jones had stayed, he also would have had to worry about another talented young player Thompson signed that year. Joining Graham in the freshman class was Reggie Williams, a silky-smooth 6-7 all-American and the consensus player of the year from the nation's top-ranked high school, undefeated Dunbar High School of Baltimore, coached by Bob Wade.

Williams had averaged 24 points and 13 rebounds in leading the

Poets to a 31–0 record. He said he selected Georgetown because of its business administration curriculum and because he would feel comfortable playing for Thompson. "Coach Thompson's philosophy is similar to my high school coach," Williams said. "Both stress academics and discipline."

With Williams and Graham in the fold, the return of a healthy Fred Brown and a talented cast of supporting characters for the most dominant big man in the game, Thompson was unusually optimistic about his 1983–84 team as he spoke to reporters at the Big East's annual media day in New York before the start of the season. "I feel good about this group, from the vibes I've gotten so far—how they're working together, their willingness to work hard," Thompson said. "I can get in there, chew them out and feel good that they are trying to get things done correctly. . . . I never had a feeling of bad vibes last season, but a feeling of understanding and sympathy because they were young kids. They played hard last year, but it was inexperience. . . . I felt I was making a cake from scratch, instead of going to the store and getting one of those ready-made packages."

It quickly became apparent why Thompson felt so comfortable. The Hoyas won 13 of their first 14 games, the best start in the school's history. The only blemish was a 63–61 loss in Chicago to De Paul, and judging from the celebration of the host team that day, one would have thought it had just won the national title. There would be only two more defeats the rest of the regular season, in fact, to Villanova in double overtime in January and to St. John's in early March. Still, the Hoyas were coming under increasing criticism for their rugged style of play, including a nasty incident in Springfield, Massachusetts, in which Ewing was ejected from a game against Boston College for fighting with BC point guard Michael Adams, about 14 inches shorter and 90 pounds lighter than the Hoya center.

Graham was not in attendance at the BC game; Thompson had left him home for academic reasons, the second time during the season that had occurred. But Graham was becoming a fixture in the Hoya lineup, and when the team began play in the Big East tournament, he was clearly established as the starting power forward.

Georgetown, the outright Big East regular-season champion, also prevailed in the Big East tournament, beating Providence, St. John's and, in the final, Syracuse in overtime. But in March of 1984, there was not so much talk of basketball as there was of "Hoya paranoia" and Georgetown's propensity for the cheap shot, the fist in the face.

After the Big East tournament, Curry Kirkpatrick, *Sports Illustrated*'s brilliantly acerbic basketball writer, described the Hoyas as "Coach John Thompson's plundering legions—Grandmaster Flash and the Furious Twelve is one of their milder aliases. . . . In New York, the Hoyas' MO was that familiar mix of public nonrelations, suspicion and silly security precautions—now known as Hoya Paranoia—and intense play."

Kirkpatrick praised Thompson as a "surprisingly bright, deep, discerning and articulate fellow who genuinely cares about his players' academic attainment—their graduation rate is very high." And then he buried him. "Nonetheless, on occasion Thompson plays the tough-guy role to the hilt, complete with such witty repartee as 'Get outta my face.' More often than not, his team, along with its leather-jackets-and-chains image, appears to slip into the same character. But of course, that's the point."

Said St. John's coach Lou Carnesecca: "They just completely destroy people and yeah, they scare the hell out of you."

In the championship game, Graham shoved Syracuse's Andre Hawkins to the floor after a battle for a rebound, then took a wild punch that missed. Referee Dick Paparo at first appeared to be signaling that Graham was being thrown out. But after a huddle with his fellow officials, he changed his mind. Syracuse coach Jim Boeheim, a notorious Big East whiner, seemed perfectly justified in declaring the officials "gutless" when it was over, and Kirkpatrick said the incident was "the inevitable result of the preposterous paramilitary atmosphere surrounding the team . . . and fostered by the insecurities and philosophies of Thompson. . . . Would that Georgetown abandon its foxhole mentality, the chips on the shoulders and all those flying fists and elbows so that the team can get on with playing pure basketball."

The following week, the bad-boy Hoyas opened play in the NCAA West regionals against SMU in Pullman, Washington. Thompson, as usual, kept his team ninety miles away in Spokane. He also responded angrily to Kirkpatrick's description of his team at a press conference the day before the first tournament game.

"We play basketball and we play aggressively," he said. "It's sometimes a question of how you define *aggressively*. If Chris Mullin [of St. John's] hustles, he's tough. If Gene Smith hustles, he's dirty.

"We play hard and we work hard at what we do. I resent very much any kind of accusation or implication that what we teach is dirty. I've seen altercations in intercollegiate athletics, and when you have grown men playing at an emotional pitch, there are going to be problems. But when you jump to conclusions and assume these things are being taught, I think you're being very petty."

Ewing was also asked about his style of play.

"Overaggressive? I'm overaggressive? I'm usually the one that had the concussion or got hit in the eye," he said. "I'm all scarred up and I'm the one who's overaggressive?" In fact, the week before the SMU game, Ewing had missed a day of practice to get his jaw x-rayed. He'd been hit in the face twice going up for rebounds, once against St. John's and once against Syracuse, and he could barely open his mouth to chew his food.

Still, there was no question that Ewing would be able to play against SMU, and with one stunning move late in the game he also managed to save the Hoyas' postseason. SMU opted for a deliberate slowdown offense and a packed-in two-three zone against Georgetown, hoping to keep the ball out of Ewing's hands and forcing the Hoyas to shoot from the outside. At halftime the strategy was working nicely, with SMU having taken a shocking 24–16 lead. Georgetown regained its composure and opened up a 6-point second-half advantage, but Thompson strangely decided to hold the ball and SMU sneaked back into the game. With fifty-one seconds left, the score was tied at 34–34.

Gene Smith, only a 64-percent foul shooter, was at the free-throw line, and his first attempt bounced hard off the rim. But Ewing had somehow managed to spin around SMU's 6-8 Larry Davis in the lane and got himself in perfect position to tap the ball through the basket. SMU came down and missed a shot that was rebounded by Michael Graham. When Michael Jackson hit a free throw with eight seconds left for a 37–34 lead, the Hoyas were home free.

"You can't describe greatness," Thompson said of Ewing's improbable basket at the end of the 37–36 victory. "I could coach for a hundred years and never map that out. It's like asking Bill Russell how he got that rebound with six guys around him. That's why he's a great player. He made the big play. He got around the guy for the ball."

In fact, Ewing had asked Thompson if he could take that spot on the lane near the basket, rather than go downcourt in his usual position as the last line of defense in Georgetown's press. "It's the first time I can remember something of that significance where we changed what we were about to do," Thompson said. "If I had told him, 'Hell no,' he'd have gone back and played in his regular spot. That's a sign of greatness, no question."

Still, Thompson was criticized that day by CBS announcer Brent Musburger for going into a delay offense with a 6-point lead. "When I have a team on the run, I don't go into a delay," Musburger told his national television audience on a day when he also criticized Georgetown's physical brand of basketball.

Thompson's response came a few weeks later, and he seemed to take great pains to mispronounce the announcer's name. "Well, Musburg never had anybody on the run," Thompson said. "He's never coached anywhere. He's never run anything, other than running his mouth. . . . I think I will take suggestions from people I respect. But it's true that I completely ignore the people I don't respect."

Before the start of the Western regional in Los Angeles, Thompson took another shot at the media. "I never thought I would turn to the sports pages for fiction," he said. "I'd like to meet this Georgetown coach they talk about. He must be a helluva nut." He also criticized the "herd mentality" of the nation's newspapers and magazines, decrying their use of the term *Hoya paranoia.*

"What disturbs me the most is that one guy writes what another guy writes without asking me about what he says. The mistake writers make is if they can't interview us, they interview the other writers. I can't predicate what I do for the fourteen or fifteen people I am responsible for on the needs of the media. My priority is them, not you. . . . But I was never St. John and I'm not the devil either."

Frank Rienzo, the athletic director, has another view of Thompson's so-called paranoia. "Van Gogh was a painter, Da Vinci was a painter, Michelangelo was a painter, and no one ever insisted that they paint the same way," he said. "John Thompson is a basketball coach, and why in America in this century should anyone be surprised that he wants to do things his own way, in the way that he thinks makes sense for his own program?

"Who cares where he stays on the road? I don't. He's staying where he thinks it's most appropriate for him to paint his masterpieces. And why is it that anyone thinks that they know better which color paint or which brush he should use? And so if he wears shoes that don't have shoelaces or he stays in a hotel that doesn't have a bar or that's eighty miles away rather than sixty-two miles away, what difference does it make other than somebody else thinks that you should stay sixty-one miles away and they think the perfect number is sixty-one?

". . . I sometimes feel sorry for people who can't step back and say they have their purpose and their goals and they are following them.

We have established what we think are our own goals and our own mechanisms for achieving them. There are at least two ways to do everything.

"We're not secretive, we're private. There's a difference. Why people don't connote that difference I don't know. We pay a price for that but we think the price is worth it."

Back on the basketball court the next day, Georgetown, despite shooting 28 percent in the first half, pulled away from Nevada–Las Vegas in the second half for a 62–48 rout as Ewing scored 16 points, had 15 rebounds and blocked 6 shots. Two days later, Georgetown won the West regional with a 61–49 victory over Dayton in a game marred by another deplorable incident involving Graham: With six minutes left, he turned and shoved Dayton's Sedric Toney to the floor after scoring on a slam dunk and was immediately called for a foul. Said Toney, "That was an exceptional cheap shot. There was no call for that."

Said Thompson, "I thought Michael made a mistake. . . . The referee called it correctly." But the brutal beat went on, and now it was on to Seattle for the Final Four, and John Thompson's team was clearly ready. In the semifinals, Georgetown would be facing a 29–4 Kentucky team with twin towers Sam Bowie and Mel Turpin and all-American forward Kenny "Sky" Walker, all three eventual first-round NBA draft choices.

Early on, it appeared as if the Hoyas would end their season on another frustrating note. Kentucky took a 27–15 lead and Ewing picked up three quick fouls, forcing him to miss the last eleven minutes of the first half as the Wildcats held a 29–22 advantage at intermission. But after that, it was no contest. With Ewing and the Hoyas playing their usual brand of hands-on defense, Kentucky made only 3 of 33 field-goal attempts in the second twenty minutes. Kentucky coach Joe B. Hall said it was "some kind of extraterrestrial phenomenon, that's the only explanation I have. Never have I had a team or seen a team shoot as badly as we shot the second half."

Georgetown, meanwhile, caught fire, hitting 13 of 21 shots in the second half and running away with a 53–40 victory. Ewing had scored only 8 points, but he played the entire last twenty minutes and was his usual intimidating self under the basket. "Patrick was the big factor," said teammate Horace Broadnax. "Just by being there, Patrick Ewing occupying space makes a big difference. If he wasn't there, we would have been lost."

The next day, an off-day before Monday's championship game,

Thompson was in fine form as he jousted with the national media. He was even wearing a button that read, "GEORGETOWN WHERE ARE YOU?" "Keep it coming," he said at one point, talking about the criticism of his program. "I love it. I love it. . . . Call me militaristic. I'm not ashamed of military people. It's an honor to be associated with the military. . . . That's a compliment. Please keep saying it. Please. . . . Discipline is the ability to follow directions in preparing people for life. Is that wrong? . . . Do you honestly think I look at my team and say, 'Fellas, they're all against us, let's go to war'?"

Still, that's exactly how it looked in the Monday-night final against the University of Houston, even if Georgetown would have to play without its defensive general, Gene Smith. Against Kentucky he had suffered an injury in the arch of his foot and he could barely walk the next day. It didn't really matter.

After a slow start, Georgetown outscored a Houston team led by 7-foot all-American center Akeem Olajuwon by 26–8, opening a 10-point lead at the half. When Houston got to 57–54 midway through the second half, freshman Reggie Williams began to take over, just as he would throughout his career at Georgetown. He followed his own miss with an offensive rebound put-back, then fed Graham for a huge dunk and a 61–54 lead, and the Cougars were in very deep trouble.

Williams made one more big play: He slipped behind Olajuwon and forced a jump ball that gave Georgetown possession. When David Wingate hit two free throws for an 8-point lead with less than two minutes remaining, it was time for the celebration to begin in the stands and on the sidelines.

As the final seconds of Georgetown's 84–75 victory ticked off, the cameras once again caught John Thompson hugging Fred Brown. This time, there were tears of joy in the eyes of both as Thompson told him, "We've got it, baby." Two years after The Pass to James Worthy, Fred Brown and his coach could exorcise all those demons and celebrate a national championship.

Brown had 4 points, 4 rebounds and 4 assists and had played tough defense on Houston's star guard, Michael Young. And there were other heroes this night. Ewing was named MVP of the Final Four. He had 10 points and 9 rebounds and helped hold Olajuwon to 15 points, well below his season average. Wingate had 16 points, guard Michael Jackson had 11 points and 6 assists and Michael Graham contributed 14 points and 7 rebounds. Thompson had been right: There had been a player in Washington the year before who could help him win the national championship, and at least on this night, his gamble on Michael Graham had paid off.

Williams scored 19 points, 13 in the second half, with 7 rebounds and 3 assists. It seemed as if the only time he faltered all night came after the final buzzer. Interviewed by CBS analyst Billy Packer as the star of the game, Williams stumbled, mumbled and seemed almost speechless trying to explain his play, adding even more fuel to the continuous contention of Georgetown critics that the school had sold its academic soul for the sake of a national championship. Never mind that Williams was an eighteen-year-old freshman appearing in the harsh glare of the national spotlight for the first time in his life and had momentarily choked up in the heat of the moment.

Years later, Williams said of that interview, "I look back and laugh at it. I know I'll just have to live with it. I'm not scared of making a mistake. If I make one, I'm accountable. But I won't make too many."

When the team gathered in the locker room that night for a final time, Thompson turned serious, telling his players to remember where they had come from. "There were a helluva lot of players who came before you who are not in this locker room tonight but who helped make this possible," he said, thinking of people like Merlin Wilson and Jonathan Smith, Steve Martin and Derrick Jackson, Craig Shelton and John Duren. "Don't forget all the people who got this program where it is now."

A few minutes later he gathered Mary Fenlon, Craig Esherick and Mike Riley in a small training room away from the celebration and enveloped all of them in another hug, thanking them for all they'd done for him and the players. "Just think, Mary, we did it," he said, turning toward Fenlon. "We did it with these two babies."

Later that night, *Washington Post* columnist Ken Denlinger saw Thompson in a deserted hotel lobby, and the coach paused for a moment to reflect. "The biggest thing that leaps out in my mind is all of the people, particularly of my race, who I felt never had the opportunity to experience what I have," he said. "I know I'm not more intelligent than they are, but they helped so much when all this adversity was going on.

"In L.A. [during the West regional], I'm walking down the street and a cabdriver stops and says, 'If I knew you were going to be around this much, I would have taken you home.' The maids in the hotel were coming up to me and telling me, 'Hey, you're doing a good job, don't let them get to you. Keep trying.'

"There were a lot of [black] coaches deprived of the opportunity I was able to get. Frank Bolden [of Cardozo], Dave Brown of Spingarn. They came out as high school coaches and that was the end. I don't think I'm any better than these men. And the college coaches. Big House Gaines and John McLendon; a guy at Elizabeth City whose name I can't recall just now. Those guys probably forgot more about basketball than I'll ever learn. I had more chances, and I hope they can take some pride in what I have because they contributed to it. The things that they went through, the things that they did, made my path a lot clearer, and I'm very much aware of that. I'm not interested in being the first or only black to do anything, because that implies that I'm also the first with ability. I don't want to be a part of that."

A week later, he also admitted that he had been obsessed with winning the national championship and that he was particularly concerned that Patrick Ewing would leave Georgetown without ever winning a title. "Patrick deserves that title," he said, "because he exemplifies what an athlete should be. It would have been a tremendous injustice if he hadn't gotten one. And I would have felt very badly because I was the pilot.

"The win will do me the most good psychologically," he said. "It will free me in some ways. A national championship was something I was obsessed with. It was something I selfishly and personally wanted to do. I wanted it very badly. I told my players all year that I had won every championship possible in basketball except one. I was on championship teams in junior high school and high school. We won the NIT when I was at Providence. The Celtics won the NBA title. I coached high school champions. I was an assistant coach for the [1976] Olympic team.

"After the Houston game, one of my players came over and said, 'Coach, you finally got that last one.' Now I have the period that ends all sentences: 'I won the NCAA.' "

14

In the middle of the court, Villanova's players and their supporters roll on top of each other in sweet ecstacy, celebrating perhaps the most improbable upset in the history of the NCAA basketball final.

Later, in the locker room, John Thompson tells his players they learned how to win a national championship the year before, and now it is time to show the world they know how to lose, with style and grace, as well.

GEORGETOWN'S DREAM SEASON WAS OVER NOW, BUT THE euphoria from the national championship lingered awhile, with a raucous on-campus rally to honor the basketball team upon its return from Seattle and a visit to the Rose Garden soon after to meet the president of the United States. On that glorious day, Ronald Reagan took special care to congratulate John Thompson for graduating most of his players, "which is something of a record in intercollegiate athletics these days. But it also says something about the coach's priorities. You never let these young men forget there is something more important for them being at Georgetown than basketball."

Everywhere Thompson turned, someone was waiting to honor him, and the coach was using the occasion to get on the soapbox and comment on a few of his pet peeves. Speaking at a team banquet, he stunned his audience by telling them, "Referees aren't the only ones who bet on college basketball games . . . and we ought to start looking at sportswriters who also bet on the games." He also defended Michael Graham's physical style of play, saying that while everyone had lashed out at Graham for taking a swing at Andre Hawkins in the Big East tournament final, no one mentioned that the Syracuse player once had been charged with rape.

That night, Thompson did not specifically mention Hawkins by name, but a few days later, questioned about his comments at yet another celebratory luncheon, Thompson elaborated. "What I was saying is that it was accepted that he [Graham] was picking on poor little innocent people not involved in things in the real world. I didn't mention the name. . . . There was more reaction made to Michael throwing the punch than to other things that have happened in the league that were worse. They jumped all over Michael for swinging more than they did to the thing regarding Hawkins. The way he was projected for swinging at him, you would think he was swinging at a helpless innocent. We received more ridicule for that than what was remembered from the problem he had in Hartford with that girl. Talk about a double standard."

Indeed, Hawkins and another Syracuse player had been charged with sexual assault and unlawful restraint, both felonies, in March of 1982 by a Villanova student after an incident in a Hartford hotel. But the woman eventually chose not to testify, and all charges were dismissed.

Thompson's comparison of Graham's swing to an incident involving rape seemed way out of line and terribly irresponsible, as did his comments on referees' gambling, a rather serious charge if true. At the luncheon, however, Thompson backed off a bit, admitting that he did not know of any referees who bet on games but "I've heard a lot of grumbling [by coaches] lately about referees betting. They ought to check it out. And they better just as well check out if what sportswriters write isn't influenced by their betting. Last year, at the end of the NCAA tournament, I heard coaches make the statement [about referees]. I don't know if it's true or not. But you better check on the officials."

That same day, Thompson also informed his audience at the elegant 1789 Restaurant that he had just spoken with Patrick Ewing to discuss his options. Thompson said he told Ewing that before he decided to come back to Georgetown for his senior year he would be wise to see how much he was worth in the professional ranks. "I think I scared him to death," Thompson said. "I said, 'We have to determine if you're going to go hardship.' He said, 'I'm not going to.' I said, 'We're going to look into it.' "

One NBA general manager said that Ewing and Akeem Olajuwon would be the first two picks in the draft, "period, exclamation point, no questions asked. They would be worth every bit what Ralph Sampson was, if not better, because of their competitiveness and combativeness."

Sampson had recently signed a four-year, $5 million contract, but that kind of money was of no immediate concern to Ewing. During Georgetown's championship season, his mother, Dorothy, had died, and he had every intention of fulfilling his pledge to her to graduate from college. He was not about to leave, and no amount could change his mind. "I guess it was just the way my mother and father raised me," he said. "They said an education is something you have forever, you know, that can't be taken away. And I always believed that. It was important for my parents that I get my degree and it's important to me."

The same could not be said for Michael Graham. Once the warm glow from the victory over Houston had faded into the reality of the spring semester, it was becoming increasingly obvious that Graham had no business being at Georgetown. Thompson was getting reports that Graham was skipping classes and not making up his work. At the end of the semester, Thompson decided that he would not allow him to play basketball at the start of the 1984–85 season, or ever, unless his attitude and his study habits changed. He did not even try to get Graham to enroll in summer school to make up his work and become academically eligible. Finally, on August 30, the coach announced that Graham had been dropped from the team roster. Though Thompson said Graham would remain in school on scholarship, he would not be permitted to play the next season because he needed to "develop greater responsibility and eliminate inconsistencies in his approach to academics."

Graham did remain in school, but not for long. Shortly after the Christmas break, Graham walked into athletic director Frank Rienzo's office and asked for his release from Georgetown so that he could attend the University of the District of Columbia, a mostly all-black commuter school across town. "Michael's biggest problem is academic motivation," Thompson said at the time. "The biggest thing that disappoints me about this is that I know, as well as I know anybody that I've ever had here, that Michael had the innate intelligence to do the work. His physical commitment has to catch up to his verbal commitment. Anybody who sits down and talks with him knows the kid is not dumb. That's what I found so refreshing when I first sat down and talked with him. I knew I was not talking to a dumb person. He's definitely a bright person, but a person can only be counseled by so many people so many times. He's twenty-one years old. He's getting to the point now where there's not going to be anybody to talk to. . . . The damndest thing is that if you sit down and talk to him right now, you would get the impression that he's going to make the commitment.

"I want to go on record as saying that kid has never been a bum, a hoodlum or any of that stuff. Michael's biggest problem is motivating himself to do his schoolwork. Whatever problem he's had with other people, I don't know. We didn't do any more or any less for Michael than for anybody else we've had here. It will still be my responsibility to provide an opportunity. If I had the situation to do over again, I would do it again." And why not? Graham at least had helped produce an NCAA championship. During a special faculty committee's annual review of students with academic difficulties that year, Father Timothy Healy, the school president at the time, said the general consensus was that Graham was among the brightest failures on the committee's list.

That self-serving contention may well have been the case, but Graham continued to make one blunder after another after leaving Georgetown. He never did play at UDC, an NCAA Division II power in the 1980s, opting to make himself eligible for the pro draft in May 1986. He was selected in the fourth round by Seattle, but was cut from the team. He has been knocking around the Continental Basketball Association ever since, getting closer and closer to that street corner he once insisted he was so determined to avoid.

Only John Thompson will ever know whether he was guilty of exploiting a troubled young man to win a national championship, as some suspect. And while there is every indication that he and the university went out of their way to change Michael Graham's life, clearly this was an experiment that failed miserably.

Thompson also would insist the following fall that Georgetown still could have won the championship without Graham, who had averaged 5 points and 5 rebounds a game for the season and had been named to the all-tournament team in the Final Four. "Yes, I think so," Thompson said. "If we go with one individual, Patrick Ewing caused us to win the national championship. I think he [Graham] was a major contributor."

And as Georgetown's 1984–85 season unfolded, it looked as if Graham would hardly be missed. For one thing, the Hoyas were actually cutting down a bit on the rough stuff. For another, they were playing a far different style of offensive basketball, looking to fast-break and allowing players like Reggie Williams, David Wingate and Michael Jackson to shoot anytime, from anywhere on the court. "We're [fast-] breaking more than we ever have since I've been at Georgetown," Thompson admitted. "The seniors have always heard me say, 'Slow down.' Now I'm saying, 'Let it go, shoot it.' The younger kids probably think this is the way I've always done it. . . . I realized that if we had to stand in and slug it out, we didn't have enough power. We've got to be quick. We've got to be able to move and run, and that will give the younger big kids more time to develop."

Georgetown, ranked number one in the preseason, blitzed through its first 18 games, outscoring the opposition by an average of 20 points and running its winning streak to 29 before St. John's held on for a 66–65 victory at the Capital Centre and Syracuse prevailed 65–63 a few days later before 32,229 slightly crazed fans at the Carrier Dome. That game was only four minutes old and Ewing was at the free-throw line when someone in the Syracuse crowd tossed an orange from the stands that splattered on the backboard just after Ewing had released the ball on his first shot. Thompson immediately pulled his team off the floor, and when order was restored, Ewing went back for his second attempt. Just as he went to the line, another orange hit the floor, and Thompson, livid now, again called his team to the bench and told referee Hank Nichols he was about to walk back to the locker room, perhaps for good.

"This was a very big game, on ESPN as I recall, with a lot riding on it as far as the conference race," Nichols said. "I chased after John and said, 'Hey, you can't just leave.' He said to me, 'I can, too.' I was a little desperate. I asked him to give me two minutes to straighten this out. He agreed. Then I went over to [Syracuse coach] Jimmy Boeheim and asked him to get on the PA to talk to the crowd. He did a great job. He told them that was not what he wanted and if it continued he was going to ask us to call technical fouls on his own team. Jim and John embraced at halfcourt, and that was the end of that." Nichols, in fact, said he never had a major problem with Thompson, though he was bothered by the Hoyas' style of play. "They were a rough team for a period of time—they would react to rough play quicker than most teams would," he said. "They were a little more aggressive than you'd want to see. Who knows why? The type of kid, the style of play. For a couple of years it was very tough to do their games. They were so protective of each other. If they got fouled hard, you always had to look out for the teammate who was going to come to their rescue.

"People who don't know John Thompson could be intimidated by him. But as an official, all he wants you to do is make the calls you're supposed to make. He always respected a guy who would stand in the middle of the chaos and make a tough decision. Even if it went against him, he'd respect you for making a decisive call. He came after me once in a while. They all try to push you to the limit. He might just yell louder because he's a big guy. But he never carried a grudge. When it was over, it was over. If you back away, he loses respect for you. In recent years he's been less prone to go after the officials than he was in his earlier days. His kids have always been good. I liked Patrick. He never said much. He just played. If he didn't like a call, he'd give you a look, but that's it. None of their kids give you problems. That's how he trains them."

Georgetown, meanwhile, would avenge both its defeats later in the season. The second meeting between number-one St. John's and number-two Georgetown was particularly memorable. No one could recall the last time the top two teams in the country had played that late in the regular season. And Thompson, the growling bear of the Big East, made a grand entrance sporting a Pepsodent smile and T-shirt knockoff of the ugly brown good-luck sweater Lou Carnesecca had worn all season. The crowd at Madison Square Garden, usually terribly antagonistic to the hated, hammering Hoyas, loved it, and so did Carnesecca. But none of the New Yorkers was laughing at the finish, when Georgetown had rolled to a 16-point victory. A win over Syracuse ended the regular season, with Georgetown claiming its second straight conference title, and the Hoyas kept right on rolling in the Big East tournament. Their semifinal victory over Syracuse was marred by a brief fight between Ewing and Syracuse guard Pearl Washington, perhaps just for old times' sake. And for good measure, the Hoyas drubbed St. John's 92–80 in the championship game, despite Ewing playing less than half the contest because of foul trouble. Even Curry Kirkpatrick was impressed with the Hoyas, declaring that "the entire NCAA field must be trembling in all the brackets" after three straight Georgetown blowouts. Of course, he was still on Georgetown's case about its physical play. He declared that Big East referees had been gutless for not throwing Ewing out of the Syracuse game immediately after the fight and that Georgetown had been allowed to get away with far too much banging and verbal abuse of its opponents. "Thompson so terrifies the Big East," he wrote, "and his team is allowed so much rope, that the result is a heated atmosphere brimming with animosity and nightly brawls."

Georgetown was ranked number one in the country going into the NCAA tournament, and this time the route to the Final Four in Lexington, Kentucky, had to be negotiated through the East. Georgetown mostly breezed through three straight games against Bucknell, Temple and Chicago-Loyola, then survived a scare in the East regional final by prevailing over Georgia Tech, 60–54, the final outcome not decided until Ralph Dalton hit two free throws with fourteen seconds remaining to assure the victory.

For Georgetown, it marked the third time in Ewing's four years that the team had advanced to the Final Four. For the Big East, it was an artistic and financial *tour de force*, with Villanova and St. John's also making it to Lexington, along with Memphis State, the first and last time three teams from the same conference had accomplished that feat.

Almost immediately, Thompson was embroiled in yet another controversy. In a telephone conference call with writers assembled in Lexington, each of the Final Four coaches was asked if he would be interested in the vacant University of Kentucky coaching job. Thompson's three rivals all said they were not. Thompson, who was staying with his team in Louisville, said, "I read in the paper here that before John Thompson got the coaching job at Kentucky, there would be a Martian in the White House." When he heard laughter in the background, Thompson said, "I fail to see the humor in racism and I never have. I read that column to my players because I want them to understand that very clearly." But Thompson, a bit too quick to invoke the charge of racism, had also misread the column, written by Billy Reed of the Louisville *Courier-Journal*. The premise of Reed's piece was to list ten people who had no chance to become the next Kentucky coach, including Phyllis George Brown, Sweet Georgia Brown and Bad, Bad Leroy Brown. Reed, a nationally respected writer, also listed eight qualified black coaches, but wrote that unfortunately they also had no chance to succeed Joe B. Hall. "I wrote that as a knock at UK," Reed said. "My point was that the situation has changed little since Adolph Rupp left and that the job is still closed to blacks, and that's sad. I was making a commentary on Lexington society. Racism is not funny, I agree with that. But racism is something to be made fun of and that was my intention. If John Thompson interpreted what I wrote any other way, I'm sorry."

Thompson did seem genuinely pleased to have his two old friends joining him for the Final Four in Lexington. He had known Carnesecca ever since little Looie had tried to recruit him out of high school. And Rollie Massimino, the wrinkled ringmaster of Villanova's program, was probably his closest friend in the conference, not to mention one of the brightest bench coaches in the country, despite the flailing arms, the loosened necktie and the shirttail over his belt.

The St. John's–Georgetown game in the national semifinals would be the teams' fourth meeting of the season, the final game matching Patrick Ewing and St. John's all-American Chris Mullin, a man many thought was the player of the year. Thompson, asked what his team would have to do to beat St. John's, said, "Stop listening to Looie's love songs. Sometimes you come to these press conferences, listen to everybody and think this is 'Love of Life.' I'm trying to get my game face on."

That was not a problem for Thompson or his team. Using a box-and-one defense to contain Mullin, the Hoyas opened a 4-point advantage at the half, scored the first 7 points of the second half and were never threatened. Mullin, hounded most of the day by David Wingate, managed only 8 points, with only one basket in the second half. Reggie

Williams had 20 points to lead all scorers, but reinjured a sprained ankle and limped off the floor toward the end of the game. Ewing had 16, and Michael Jackson was credited with 11 assists. Carnesecca was singing a melancholy love song when it was over.

"I put them with the great San Francisco teams with Bill Russell and K. C. Jones," he said of Georgetown. "And I put them with the great Kentucky teams of Alex Groza [1948–49], the great UCLA teams [of the 1970s] and the great Indiana team [1975–76] which won the title and produced five pro players. We tried everything. But when a club like Georgetown can perform at that level of proficiency, there's very little anyone can do."

Now it was Villanova's turn to try. The Wildcats had been quite proficient themselves in a 52–45 semifinal victory over Memphis State and were hardly fearful of Georgetown. They had lost twice to the Hoyas during the regular season, a 52–50 overtime decision in early January and a 57–50 decision a month later in Washington. Both games had been played with the Big East's forty-five-second shot clock in place, a factor that favored a Georgetown team that preferred to run and play at an up-tempo pace. Massimino was a master strategist who liked things slow and deliberate. The lack of a shot clock would allow him to have them just that way. Thompson, in fact, when asked why he had predicted Villanova to do well in the tournament weeks before, said, "I don't bet on the horses. I bet on the jockey."

Most of America was betting on Georgetown, a 9½-point favorite to win the first back-to-back titles since UCLA had accomplished that feat in 1972 and 1973. But Villanova had other ideas, and some emotional incentives as well. The day of the championship game, a former Villanova basketball coach, Al Severance, had suffered a fatal heart attack in his room at the school's Lexington hotel. His death had stunned the Villanova entourage, but had also become a rallying point for Massimino and his team. Also that night, sitting at the end of the bench, was Villanova's longtime trainer, Jake Nevin, confined to a wheelchair because of Lou Gehrig's disease. The basketball team had dedicated its season to the little bald man, and as the NCAA tournament wore on and the cameras focused in, it became increasingly obvious that their affection for him was no made-for-television sob story.

After taking his players to Mass the afternoon of the title game, Massimino sent them to their rooms for fifteen minutes to meditate. "I wanted them to think about the game and think about two things," he said. "One, not to play with the idea of not to lose, but to play to win.

Second, I wanted them to tell themselves they were good enough to win, that in a one-shot deal they could beat anyone in the United States."

Villanova definitely believed all of that, though it took the greatest shooting performance in the history of the championship game to accomplish a stunning 66–64 victory. They hit 22 of 28 shots (78.6 percent from the field), including an incredible 9 for 10 in the second half against a team that led the country in field-goal-percentage defense.

In the first half Georgetown moved to a 6-point lead twice, but trailed by a point at the half. In the final seconds of the first period, CBS cameras also caught Reggie Williams flagrantly pushing Villanova's Chuck Neverson in the face, definitely an unwarranted cheap shot. No foul was called, however, drawing the wrath of Massimino, CBS announcers and the capacity crowd at Rupp Arena that booed Georgetown lustily as the teams headed for the locker room.

The second half was more of the same. Georgetown had come back from a 53–48 deficit to take a 54–53 lead when Wingate drilled a bank shot with 4:50 to go. But Villanova sophomore guard Harold Jensen, playing the game of his life after an early-season slump, hit a jump shot, Villanova started making its free throws and suddenly the Hoyas were down by 5 points with eighteen seconds left in the game. Georgetown never did give up, but Villanova managed to inbound the ball with two seconds left and kill the clock for one of the most improbable upsets in the history of college basketball.

When it was over, the Georgetown players huddled at the foul line briefly, then stood at their bench and applauded respectfully as Villanova supporters mobbed their team on the court. In his final college game, Patrick Ewing had scored 14 points, but had only 2 field goals in the second half, and he got off a total of 1 shot in the last 13:09 against Villanova's suffocating two-three matchup zone defense.

Thompson had said the day before that his team's season would not be a disaster if it lost in the final. Asked the same question following the loss to Villanova, he said, "Thirty-five and three, must we dwell on the obvious? We played as hard as we could. We're disappointed, sure. We feel bad about losing. If I had to lose to somebody, I take some consolation that it's Rollie Massimino. . . . I don't want the players to hang their heads, run around and cry and make excuses. We know how to win, now we have to know how to lose."

Walking toward the Georgetown locker room when it was over, athletic director Frank Rienzo summed up the long night. "There comes a point when you concede you have come across a team of destiny," he said.

The Patrick Ewing era was over now, and what a sweet ride it had been: three Final Four appearances in four years, and the school's first national championship, not to mention all the fringe benefits that went with it. There was increased visibility for both the basketball program and the university itself. More of the best and brightest were applying every year to Georgetown, and the school also was attracting far more minority applicants than ever before from all around the country. "There was no question," said Charles Deacon, the admissions director, "that many minority students, not just athletes, were attracted to this place because of John Thompson and his team." The school also was profiting in fund-raising. In 1981, before Ewing arrived, Georgetown had raised $22.5 million in alumni and development funds. During Ewing's years, average annual fund-raising was $31 million. How much of an effect basketball had on that increase was impossible to determine, but school officials told *Regardie's* magazine in January 1986 that it had definitely been a factor. The magazine, in fact, estimated that the university's net profit—taking into account ticket revenue, television rights fees, money from the NCAA tournament, fund-raising, admissions fees and the sale of Georgetown paraphernalia—totaled $12.3 million. Considering that Ewing's scholarship had cost the school about $50,000, it seemed like a rather wise investment.

The basketball fund-raising arm known as the Hoya Hoop Club had also grown from its modest beginnings of raising $14,000 for Thompson's program in 1976 to raising $400,000 a year by 1990, pushed closer to that level during the Ewing years. There are now more than one thousand members who contribute at seven different levels, from associate members ($25 to $99) to the "Coach's Circle" ($5,000 and up), with preferential seating at the Capital Centre and for Big East and NCAA tournament games offered as incentives to the most generous givers. The money raised is used as a discretionary fund to provide improvements for the basketball program—locker-room renovations, weight-training equipment, training-room supplies and machinery—as well as to finance a highlight tape and the team's annual banquet.

Ewing's presence and the success of the team in the early 1980s helped swell the membership rolls and raised thousands of dollars for the program. Membership in the Hoya Hoop Club is about two thirds alumni, with the rest made up of other Georgetown basketball fans. But other than the preferred seating and special receptions after some games for the most generous contributors, club members are not offered many special privileges—a pin, a bumper sticker and the chance to see one practice a year. "John likes to keep his distance to avoid any appearance of impropriety with the boosters," said Pat McArdle, Georgetown's director of development for athletics. "There is no tradition here of glad-handing boosters, and that's the way he wants it."

Ewing's menacing demeanor and the hard-nosed style of play his teams exhibited also created a downside for Thompson and his program: In many quarters he was no longer St. John, the altruistic educator. By the mid-1980s he was Big Bad John, the head paranoid of a team that thrived on secrecy, intimidation and brutal physical play. In addition, the fact that a black coach had assembled an all-black team that in no way mirrored the racial makeup of the Georgetown student body hardly helped Thompson's image.

In truth, Thompson had recruited and signed a number of white players for his program through most of the 1970s. Though several had started, none of them had ever become a star, and for a good part of the 1980s Thompson left himself open to criticism that he was not even trying to get talented white players into his program.

Bill Stein, Thompson's chief recruiter from the day the program began in 1972 until 1982 when he left to become athletic director at St. Peter's College in New Jersey, told the *St. Petersburg Times*, "John recruits only certain types of people. I know he has refused to go after players who wound up as all-Americans. Whether someone is white or black has nothing to do with it. Whether a person can fit into his program, into the kind of style he wants to play, that's what matters. People can make a big deal about how he's a black coach with an all-black team. A white coach with an all-white team, that's acceptable. Nobody thinks much about it. A white coach with a black team, they'd say, 'What a great guy.' "

Father Timothy Healy, the school president, also had no problems with Thompson's racial mix. "What John does is recruit kids who play in his system," he said. "Obviously, he is more comfortable with black kids. That would be my guess, and it doesn't surprise me. I'm not uncomfortable with the team. Professional basketball players are mostly black. Basketball is a city game. Damn few farm kids come to play. If Alonzo Mourning were white, John would have gone after him."

Over the years, Thompson has also addressed the criticism. In a 1980 interview with *Sports Illustrated*, he was asked about growing concerns even then that he could not recruit white players and preferred not to coach them. "The first part, about recruiting, is true," he said. "Let me explain why. When I was at Providence College they had a pretty good hockey team, but the players were mostly Canadian. The hockey coach had a lot of trouble finding good American players. You understand what I'm saying? Basketball is a game that is taken seriously in the black community, especially in the cities. Black kids play basketball like Canadian kids play hockey. They start playing early, and they care about it a lot, generally more than suburban or rural white kids do. That's why they're so good at it. It's hard to find white kids with the same basketball background.

"About . . . not wanting to coach white kids—that is pure crap. If I can recruit a player who can help me, I'll coach him if he's purple and comes from Mars. I'll like and respect him as a man if he deserves it."

In another interview he said, "I don't know of any white player who qualified to play on my teams that I've turned down. . . . I'm not the person who makes the initial [recruiting] contact. The person who makes the initial contact [assistant coach Craig Esherick] now is, ironically, white. I go in after I'm told someone is good."

Thompson and his staff face a number of problems trying to recruit the best white basketball players. For one, there are not all that many of them to go around. "Hell," said University of Pittsburgh coach Paul Evans, "it's tough for all of us to recruit a white kid. I tried to go after Christian Laettner. Now, if you're the kid, where are you going to go, Pitt or Duke? The quality white kids are tough for any of us to get. Duke gets them, Carolina gets them, but who else does when you really think about it? You recruit where you recruit best. And if you are a good black player, who do you want to play for? If you are picking and choosing like John Thompson does, you'll pick the kids that will make you win. I think the guy gets a bad rap. How many white kids were on the Providence team last year [1989–90], one?"

Ed Tapscott, a former American University coach who also is black, wonders why "many of the same people who are now asking why he doesn't have white players neglected to ask Adolph Rupp why there were no black kids at Kentucky for so long. Georgetown's program has become a symbol for young black student-athletes. Many more want to be there than there are slots to play. He's been able to select youngsters, and I think he feels more comfortable coaching those kind of kids. But I believe he is more concerned with character than color of skin. If a kid can play his style of basketball and put up with his kind of discipline—and not everyone can—John Thompson would be interested, white or black."

Thompson also has claimed in the past that he has been blindsided by negative recruiting from opposing coaches who will tell potential white prospects that they will never play at Georgetown, that they will be tokens at the end of the bench because he will always favor the black players. One year in the mid-1970s, Thompson was recruiting a player in Canada and the young man's father asked him, "Why would my son want to come to an all-black school?" When Thompson told him that Georgetown was 99 percent white, the father said, "That's not what another coach told me."

In 1978, Jeff Bullis was a seventeen-year-old 6-7 forward from Bel Air, Maryland, who was being heavily recruited by Georgetown and James Madison in Harrisonburg, Virginia. The night he telephoned Madison's Lou Campanelli to tell him that he had finally decided on Georgetown, Bullis got an earful from a very unhappy basketball coach.

"The coach told Jeff he'd never play for Georgetown," Bullis's mother, Celeste Edwards, said at the time. "He said Coach Thompson was misleading him about where he stood with the team. He told him he'd be the token white player and he also brought it up to him how much time and money they'd spent on recruiting him. The last thing he said to him was 'God bless you, Jeff, you'll need it.' "

Two days after the telephone call, Bullis received a letter from Madison assistant coach John Thurston. He told Bullis, "You are the most deceitful young man I have ever come across. To have spent as much time with you as I did, I would think I deserve to hear your decision before I hear it on the radio. . . . You looked down your nose at us all year but didn't have the guts to tell us. But that just about sums you up."

Campanelli, now the head coach at the University of California, later denied telling Bullis that he would be a token. "That's his interpretation," he said. "It's something he'll have to live with."

Bullis went on to attend Georgetown and started a number of games as a sophomore. In his junior year, he was having dinner at the home of his aunt and uncle in suburban northern Virginia and had a few glasses of wine. That night in his dormitory room, Bullis could feel his heart beating rapidly, got short of breath and became extremely lethargic. Alarmed, he walked over to the Georgetown Hospital on his own and was eventually diagnosed as having had an attack of atrial fibrillation, which could be controlled by medication. He was given clearance to play as long as he stayed on the medicine and underwent periodic examinations. Shortly afterward, though, Bullis's role on the team began to change. Bullis and Thompson had never gotten along that well in the first place, and after he had broken training by sipping the wine during the season, "I was really in his doghouse.

"But it wasn't a racial thing between him and me, that was not the problem," Bullis said. "We just didn't see eye to eye on some things. I didn't feel the kind of camaraderie he had with some other guys. We just didn't hit it off, but it definitely was not racial. After that incident, it got bad. He lost respect for me, and as I reflect on it now, he was right to. The relationship was damaged. My senior year, I was having back problems and I went to him and told him I was hurting the team. He wished me luck and that's the last time I ever talked to him. I kept my scholarship, got my degree, and I was bitter for a while. But I'm over that now. When I reflect on it, going there was a good decision for me. I have no regrets."

Rick Weber, who was recruited by Thompson in 1976 and is now an assistant coach at Old Dominion, also recalled that "a lot of people at the time were telling me it was a mistake to go there because I was only being recruited because I was white. I never had the feeling with the Georgetown players or the staff, but other recruiters from some schools directly and strongly implied that. There was negative recruiting, most definitely. Even people in my own community were against it for that reason. It's an all-black team, they'd say, that kind of thing. There was always that undercurrent, people who thought that way."

David Dunn, a 6-7 forward from Mableton, Georgia, was the last heavily recruited white player on Thompson's teams in the 1980s. He arrived for the 1982–83 season, but left after his freshman year and transferred to Georgia. A Georgetown assistant coach had first noticed him playing in a national junior Amateur Athletic Union tournament in the summer before his senior season and the Hoyas beat out Creighton, Alabama and Bradley for his services. Dunn says that no other coaches brought up race to him during the recruiting process and that "once I got there, I never felt like I was the designated white boy. He built a lot of confidence in me. I was a green country boy from Georgia, and he tried to help me adjust. I think I was kind of a lost cause, though. I was very homesick. I'd never spent that much time in a place like Washington. I must have wanted to get closer to my family. Coach Thompson told me he didn't want me to leave, and I think I definitely would have played a lot there. But he also helped me transfer. He said he understood.

"All I can say about John Thompson is that I never felt like the man was in any way prejudiced to white people or players. He treated me the same way he treated everybody. I had no complaints with him or his program. None."

Still, not everyone agrees. Another Division I coach said he has heard stories about Thompson practicing negative recruiting himself, that he often uses his race to his advantage, emphasizing to black prospects and their parents that they would be far better off trusting their sons to a black man who really cares about them than to a white coach who will exploit them.

"Nobody will tell you that on the record," the coach said. "People are afraid of John Thompson—they're intimidated by him. He's a very powerful guy, and nobody wants to take him on. He's protected because most people live in fear of him. He's a very vindictive guy. Think about it: What chance would I have of recruiting a black athlete if I went public on John Thompson? He's a hero in the black community. I'd never get another black kid."

In 1983, the best white player in America was performing for DeMatha High School in Hyattsville, Maryland, playing for Thompson's bitter foe, Morgan Wootten. But Thompson never made an effort to recruit Danny Ferry for his program, not even a phone call to find out if the 6-10 high school all-American was remotely interested in attending the school.

"But that doesn't surprise me," Ferry said. "I had made it known early that I wanted to go the ACC [Atlantic Coast Conference]. I'm sure Coach Thompson knew that. When I was growing up, the Big East was just starting. To me, the ACC was the big conference. I liked the tradition. I knew about the feud between Coach Thompson and Morgan. I don't know the exact story; I never asked. But I'm sure that had nothing to do with them not calling. Everybody knew I wanted to go ACC. I'm sure that's why they never got in touch."

Danny's father, Bob, the former general manager of the Washington Bullets, said he never talked to Thompson about his son, and did not give Georgetown much thought. "Danny wanted to go away to school, and that was it," he said. "Georgetown alums would ask me all the time, but there was never anything from the basketball office."

In the early 1980s another talented white player, Tom Sheehey of Rochester, New York, had serious interest in Georgetown. His father, Dr. William Sheehey, had attended Georgetown's medical school, and an older brother had gone there and graduated from the law school as well.

"I wanted Tom to consider the school and he was interested," Dr. Sheehey said. "We even visited the campus on our own, I believe it was early in his junior year. We went over to the basketball office and we wanted to talk to John Thompson, but the secretary wouldn't let us in. I think John has a system where he can hear who's in the office. We did get to talk to Bill Stein. He indicated they weren't interested in Tom because they were recruiting Reggie Williams at the time. Bill also said they didn't recruit until the year before the kid is coming in. At that point, Tom indicated to us he was no longer interested in Georgetown. After that meeting, Georgetown never recruited him. Tom had been interested, but they weren't."

Sheehey wound up starting and starring for Terry Holland at the University of Virginia. He developed into a solid college basketball player and now plays professionally in Europe. "We were surprised [Georgetown had no interest]," Dr. Sheehey said, "but Tom was very happy in Charlottesville. I don't think he ever regretted that decision."

Only Thompson and his staff know for sure whether they pursued other white recruits after David Dunn. Thompson has always had a reputation for keeping his recruiting close to the vest and has rarely discussed the prospects he was interested in signing publicly, unless he felt that information would help him.

In 1989, Thompson did sign a white player, 6-7 freshman Mike Sabol of Gonzaga High School in Washington. Sabol had only averaged 10 points and 8 rebounds a game as a senior, and was not even considered the best player on his high school team. His coach, Dick Myers, said Sabol was looking at smaller-time schools like Fordham, Drexel and American University until Georgetown began showing interest late in his senior season.

"Mike was very surprised by it. We all were," Myers said. "It just happened so fast. I guess they needed a forward who could pass the ball and was a banger. Some of the other schools that were recruiting him were upset—actually, shocked is more like it. Why was Georgetown interested in this kid? Nobody has enlightened me about that. But he's a nice kid, and I hope he can be happy there. He was very caught up in being recruited by them. He was willing to sit just to be there."

There have been whispers that Thompson signed Sabol to appease some of his critics on and off campus who were concerned about the all-black team. Even Father Henle, the former school president who had hired Thompson in 1972, said it had bothered him back in the

1970s that most of Thompson's players were black. "It looked like we were making blacks hired gladiators," he said recently. "I would have preferred a better mix of whites and blacks."

Tom Matan, who played for Georgetown in the 1960s and is a member of the Hoya Hoop Club, says that some of his fellow alums have serious concerns about the image and the racial composition of the program. "To me, having a black coach, the racial mix is very natural," he said. "But it does bother a lot of people, there's no question about that. I personally think he runs a good program. The players are disciplined. It's been positive for the school. But people do talk about the racial thing."

Tommy Coleman, a Washington attorney who was on the selection committee that chose Thompson and who played for Georgetown between 1958 and 1961, also has concerns about the racial composition of the team but admits of Thompson that "his natural constituency is among black athletes. I don't think a good white player has to go into an environment where he is Jackie Robinson in reverse. It's easier for a white kid to go to another school."

And if there has been any pressure on Thompson from school officials to add white players, Bill Moore, a prominent member of the board of regents from Dallas, Texas, insists he is not aware of it. "There is always the occasional guy at one of our meetings who'll say something like that, but no one has ever told John who to recruit," Moore said. "I can't imagine John tolerating something like that, anyone telling him what to do. My own view is that the team under John has put the school on the map. If the best players are mostly black, that's great. If they can play and they can graduate, I'm all for it. He's done a helluva job there, just a helluva job."

15

I think there were a lot of
personal prejudices—as
opposed to racial prejudices—
exhibited before, during and
after the Olympics. One writer
told me that there were some
writers rooting against the
U.S. team because John
Thompson was the coach.
There's a sickness in that,
that someone could actually
root against his own country
because of the composition of
the coaching staff. No one
should dislike anyone that
much."

—George Raveling,
an assistant coach for the
1988 Olympic basketball team

JOHN THOMPSON ALWAYS WOULD REMEMBER THE FEELING he had that summer day in 1976 when he stepped onto the track inside Montreal's Olympic Stadium along with the rest of the U.S. Olympic team and felt a torrent of emotion sweep over his body. "We had heard and we had talked about how we, as Americans, would feel when they played the national anthem," Thompson once said. "But when we actually stepped onto that track . . . well, it's a feeling I can't describe."

Thompson had been an assistant coach on that 1976 American basketball team, and for years afterward he talked about the experience. He also thought he'd like to try it again, this time as the head man, and his dear friend Dean Smith was lobbying mightily for him in all the proper places. Dave Gavitt coached the 1980 team that never made it to Moscow because of Jimmy Carter's Olympic boycott after the Soviet invasion of Afghanistan. Bobby Knight, the preeminent coach in his profession, took the 1984 team to a gold medal in Los Angeles, though the triumph was marred by the absence of the tit-for-tat Soviet team.

So, as the Olympic selection committee gathered in May of 1986 to anoint the coach for the '88 Games in Seoul, South Korea, Thompson was considered the favorite for the job. After all, he'd been working with international basketball for years after '76, and had been a member of the Olympic player selection committee in 1984. He also had been a mover and shaker in the college coaching ranks, serving on the board of directors of the National Association of Basketball Coaches, and becoming the first black president of that organization in 1985.

So it came as no surprise to anyone when, on May 16, 1986, Thompson was selected to coach the 1988 Olympic team by a fifteen-man committee that included both Gavitt and Smith, both of whom had done some heavy-duty arm-twisting for their man for months preceding the final vote. Thompson, at that point forty-four years old, had beaten out a group of finalists that included Kansas coach Larry Brown; Denny Crum, coach of NCAA champion Louisville; Lute Olson of Arizona; and Eddie Sutton of Kentucky. Brown and Crum had provided his closest competition, but Thompson was the clear-cut choice.

"I don't win many popularity contests with some of the positions and stands that I take," Thompson said that day. "That's one of the reasons I'm very flattered that so many people said I should be the next head coach. . . . The judgment and respect that others have for you is very flattering. To have the opportunity to coach the Olympic team, to represent one's country in this way, is very exciting, a high, high honor. My goal is to work as hard as I can and bring back the gold."

Thompson still had his own Georgetown basketball team to coach, and he was hardly negligent in his duties. While the post–Patrick Ewing era left the Hoyas as just another top-twenty contender, Georgetown rolled up 20-plus win seasons in 1985–86, 1986–87 and 1987–88, with the 1986–87 team—also known as Reggie and the Miracles in Reggie Williams's all-American senior season—winning the Big East tournament and advancing to the Final Eight in the NCAA tournament before losing to Providence.

Thompson began his Olympic duties almost immediately, spending a good part of the summer of 1986 traveling in Europe to familiarize himself with some of the competition. In the summer of 1987, he and Mary Fenlon scouted Korea a full year before the Games in order to "look at the climate and the atmosphere and generally prepare ourselves for next year. I am a firm believer that the more preparation you do, the less likely you are to be surprised or distracted."

This was no joyride. Thompson was meticulous in his travels, checking on details like the size of the lockers in the dressing rooms and the length of the beds his players would be sleeping in at the Olympic Village. He even went to a U.S. military base to secure an alternative practice site for his team, just in case he was not happy with security at the Olympic facility. He also went to Europe that summer, mainly to scout the international referees who might be doing his games in Korea. "I want to see how they work, what they call, what they won't call," he said.

Thompson also was making all the right moves toward securing the premier high school player in America during the 1987–88 school year. Alonzo Mourning, a 6-10 center from Chesapeake in the Tidewater area of Virginia, had narrowed his choices to five schools in the fall of 1987— Georgia Tech, Maryland, Virginia, Syracuse and Georgetown. And Thompson held several aces up his extra-long sleeve.

Mourning had been a regular at Howard Garfinkel's Five Star camp since his sophomore year at Indian River High School, and recruiters had been hot on his trail ever since. He also was invited to the Nike/ABCD camp at Princeton University, another meat market that brought together 120 of the best high school players in the country while America's coaches flocked to watch. Sponsored by the Nike shoe company, the camp participants were selected by Nike's John "Sonny" Vaccaro, the man who first began using coaches to help market shoes in 1978. John Thompson signed up with Nike a year later for a fee of $5,000, and by 1990 he was the highest-paid man in the company's sixty-coach stable, at $200,000 a year. Thompson and Vaccaro had become close friends, and it was a relationship that was profitable for both men.

Vaccaro, a Pittsburgh native and a reformed gambler, always liked to hedge his bets. He had hired Mourning's coach, Bill Lassiter, to work at the Nike camp in the summers before Alonzo's junior and senior years. He made certain Lassiter's Indian River players wore Nike sneakers and carried Nike travel bags to hold their sweaty socks and jocks. Vaccaro also had named Lassiter to coach one of the teams in the annual high school all-star basketball tournament he ran in Pittsburgh every year, the Dapper Dan. Sonny Vaccaro and Alonzo Mourning had also become very good friends.

In November of 1987, during the week when Mourning had announced he would make his final decision on his choice of a college, Vaccaro just happened to be in Chesapeake, much to the chagrin of several coaches who firmly believed he was doing one final selling job for his pal John Thompson.

Vaccaro denies it. He says he was there by coincidence and had only been checking on a sponsorship deal with Mourning's summer-league team. He also insisted he never saw Mourning while he was in Chesapeake. "Look," he said. "I knew the kid, I spoke to him a lot. He liked my wife very much—I never denied that. But I did not see Alonzo Mourning that week, and I did not tell him to go to Georgetown. There's no way I can ever argue it. No one believes it. But I have never, ever, ever told a kid to go to a school. I never said anything to Alonzo. I could not bring myself to do it."

Bill Lassiter agreed. "There was absolutely no influence by Sonny Vaccaro," he insisted. "There is all kind of speculation on that, but it is not true. I have sense. Alonzo has sense. It didn't take anyone to tell us what to do. I'm upset that people still think that's why he went to Georgetown. People said Nike bought him. Well, that's not true. Hell, Alonzo's gone now and I still get shoes and equipment from them for my team. I'm not under contract to Nike. I'm poor. I'm broke. I haven't gained a thing out of this except to get some things for my players, and I resent it when somebody says otherwise."

On Mourning's day of decision, he called several coaches to tell them no, then picked up the phone and dialed John Thompson.

"Well," Thompson asked after Mourning told him how difficult it had been to give the bad news to the other coaches, "where are you going to school?"

"Oh," Mourning said, almost as an afterthought, "I'm going to Georgetown."

Mourning also called Sonny Vaccaro that day to tell him his final choice. "Sonny was real happy," Mourning told Bill Brubaker of *The Washington Post*. "When I called him to tell him I was going to Georgetown, he screamed, like he was saying, 'Yeah.' " Mourning also told Brubaker that Vaccaro had no influence whatsoever on his decision. Thompson said it wouldn't have bothered him if Vaccaro had been a factor.

"I hope that my relationship with Sonny helped me because Sonny is my friend," Thompson said. "But I don't think in any way Sonny aggressively went down there for the sole purpose of trying to out-and-out recruit Alonzo Mourning for John Thompson."

Thompson had one other big advantage in landing Mourning. When he met with the player in the fall of 1987, Thompson told him he had watched him on the court that summer "to see if I had the attitude and if I could adjust to different parts of the game to make the Olympics," Mourning said. "I was kind of shocked at first." Brubaker asked Mourning if he thought he'd have a better chance of making the 1988 team if he signed with Georgetown. "It probably would enhance my chances," he said.

It certainly did. When John Thompson finally gathered ninety-three of the nation's best players for the Olympic trials in Colorado Springs in May 1988, Alonzo Mourning was on the list of invitees, along with Georgetown forward John Turner, Georgetown starting guard Charles Smith and a pest from the past—little Gene Smith, the Hoyas' defensive ace of the early 1980s, who was now working for Nike himself in Portland, Oregon. If anyone wondered whether Thompson would be stressing defense and kamikaze hustle on this Olympic team, Gene Smith's invitation to the trials ended any doubt.

A Georgetown presence was very much in evidence in Colorado Springs. Mary Fenlon had been named an assistant coach, along with George Raveling, the Southern Cal head coach and Thompson's friend since high school days. Bill Stein was the team manager, and Craig Esherick and Mike Riley were there too, as unofficial assistants. And paranoia, particularly concerning the press corps that had come to cover the trials, also reigned supreme.

Practices were closed to the media by the ABA-USA, the governing body of American Olympic basketball. Executive director Bill Wall said the writers would be "a distraction," though he did allow more than fifty NBA scouts, shoe-company reps and several agents inside to watch the proceedings. "Interviews don't help the selection process," Wall insisted. "We don't need the publicity." Wall and his minions were so tight they even asked the Olympic boxing team, working out nearby, not to wander anywhere near the basketball team.

Thompson denied responsibility for the media lockout—"I'm labor," he said. "You'll have to ask management." And later in the week, after a number of frustrated newspaper writers simply left town, Dave Gavitt managed a compromise that allowed eight pool reporters to watch practice and report back to their colleagues. A number of papers, outraged by the media restrictions, refused to even cover the trials, including *The New York Times*, *The Boston Globe* and the *Philadelphia Daily News*. The U.S. Basketball Writers Association and the Associated Press Sports Editors vigorously protested and even considered legal action.

"I wasn't really sure to what extent John was really involved [in the decision to keep the press out]," said Malcolm Moran of *The New York Times*, president of the Basketball Writers Association that year. "The unanimous perception was that John was not entirely responsible. There was definitely an antipress feeling in the whole organization."

Yet the ABA-USA also ran the women's trials, which were open to the press, with almost total access to the players. Head coach Kay Yow told a number of reporters her final cuts before she even told her players so some journalists could file their stories and catch earlier flights back home from the trials. "It wasn't just ABA-USA and Bill Wall," said one reporter covering the men. "John's hand was very much in that policy."

Thompson had no control over the players who would show up for the trials. He was disappointed that several top stars—including Derrick Chievous of Missouri and Gary Grant of Michigan—had chosen not to attend, fearful that their pro stock might drop with poor play, or that they would suffer an injury that would hurt them in the NBA draft. Nor could he stop people from wondering, as Brent Musburger had the previous winter, whether there would be any white players on his final twelve-man roster.

Musburger, Thompson's old nemesis from the SMU game, had said on the air that "the number-one question" on sports talk shows in New York was "Is John Thompson going to put a white basketball player on the U.S. Olympic team?"

In response, Thompson said, "I think that's a very dangerous statement for anybody in Brent's position to make because I interpret that as saying there should be a quota of blacks on the Olympic team."

Still, when Thompson had finally selected the twenty players for the final Olympic camp on the Georgetown campus in July, there were several white players in the group, including an obscure swingman named Dan Majerle from Central Michigan and everyone's all-American, Danny Ferry from Duke.

But Ferry never made it to Seoul. Three days before the team was to gather in Washington for its final workouts, Ferry was playing at the Capital Centre with rookies and free agents trying out for his father's Washington Bullets team. In a friendly scrimmage, Ferry went up for a rebound, got bumped in the air and landed in an awkward position on the floor, his right knee hyperextended.

"I was scared as hell," Ferry said. "I went to Georgetown hoping it would get better. I saw their team doctor. Coach Thompson told me to come on in, work with the weights, stay in the training room and see how it progresses, then he'd make a decision. I did therapy on it twice a day, but it was not doable. The doctor said it could be another week, or another month. They were leaving for Korea in a month, and it was just not feasible for me to stick with them. He called me into his office and explained the situation. He had a month to put the team together, and he couldn't afford to wait. I told him I agreed with him. I told him I wasn't ready to jeopardize my future in basketball either. I don't second-guess him—not then, not at all now. As a matter of fact, my knee wasn't better in a month. I went back to school in September and started playing around September fourteenth. It flared up again. It took me about six weeks to get over it. It was definitely the right choice. How could I have played in the Olympics if I couldn't even practice?"

When Thompson finally did cut his team after a series of exhibitions around the country, only one Georgetown player remained—Charles Smith, his starting point guard. Alonzo Mourning had been impressive in both the trials and the tour—many coaches thought he truly deserved to be on the final team—but Thompson decided otherwise. Mourning was about to enter his freshman year and was hardly a great scholar to begin with. The first time he took the College Boards, he had failed to break 700. Though he eventually got a score of 840, Mourning clearly would be better off getting acclimated to college and going to class. The Olympic experience had improved his game immeasurably and had also served notice that he would be a force as a freshman that season, and for many years to come.

The U.S. team on paper seemed loaded with talent, even if Thompson had also cut Sean Elliott, the 6-9 Arizona all-American who had not played well in the trials; Oklahoma's Stacey King, who had been playing with a pulled groin since the trials; and Kentucky ace Rex Chapman, a prolific scorer in college who had suffered through a horrid shooting slump that summer. Still, with players like David Robinson of Navy, Danny Manning of Kansas and J. R. Reid of North Carolina in the front court and the nation's leading scorer, Hersey Hawkins from Bradley, to provide the firepower, the U.S. team was still considered a solid favorite to win the gold. Critics were saying that the team was weak at the point and that Thompson did not have enough decent long-range shooters. They questioned his decision to coach the Olympic team the same way he did at Georgetown, emphasizing an intricate fullcourt pressing defense that would be difficult to teach a team of all-stars in such a short time.

Thompson had other concerns. He was furious with the National Basketball Association for allowing two of its teams, the Milwaukee Bucks and the Atlanta Hawks, to play a series of exhibitions against the Soviet national team over the previous year. And he was critical of the Portland Trail Blazers for allowing Soviet center Arvidas Sabonis to spend months with them rehabilitating an Achilles tendon before the Olympics. "We're giving them the rope to hang us," he moaned. Still, the coach seemed confident enough. "We're going to win it," he said two months before the start of the Games. Others were not so sure.

There had even been talk that some of Thompson's Olympic players were not particularly happy being berated Georgetown-style in ruggedly physical practice sessions that summer. Manning, the college player of the year, was reportedly ready to leave the squad at one point late in the summer, asking his agent what the ramifications would be if he decided to walk away. Later in Korea, Manning denied the report, but other sources said he was not very happy.

Once in Seoul, the team was wrapped in Thompson's typical security blanket. Some players complained privately that they couldn't even see their parents. Practices, of course, were closed to the media, who had virtually no access to the players or the coaching staff save for brief and somewhat chaotic postgame sessions. Many reporters said that they had better access to the Soviet team than the Americans, and that the Soviets were far friendlier, even allowing several writers to ride their team bus to practice one day.

"The first day they [the Americans] were in town, I got out of a cab at the Hyatt Hotel and I saw George Raveling standing there with the team doctor," recalled John Feinstein, working for NBC at the time as a basketball commentator. "I said, 'How you doing, George?' He says, 'I can't talk to you.' It was like complete fear. Then I saw Charles Smith. I'd talked to him a lot when he played for Pittsburgh. I said, 'How are you?' He said, 'Fine.' I asked him about his trip, whether he'd been shopping. A lot of small talk. The next day, NBC gets a call from John. He says somebody spotted me trying to pump his players. He was pissed off. 'Don't do it anymore, stay away.' I couldn't believe it."

Mary Fenlon also got into the act. Bimbo Coles, a guard from Virginia Tech, recalled sitting down to lunch at a Korean restaurant with the team when a man approached with a camera. "Coach Thompson had this rule that no one could take pictures of us and we can't sign autographs when we're eating," Coles said. "So some guy comes up with a camera and starts taking pictures. We're all expecting Coach Thompson to jump up and start screaming at this guy. All of a sudden, she jumped up and yelled at him. I was so surprised. It was the damnedest thing you've ever seen. This calm, quiet, motherly lady yelling at this guy.

"Coach Thompson was always strict with us about the media during the whole thing. He gave us set times, like once a week, when we could talk to the media, and other than that we couldn't. There were always a lot of reporters outside the gym when we came out, but we couldn't say anything because of Coach Thompson. And I sure as heck wasn't going to talk to one and find out what he would do."

In the preliminary rounds, the U.S. team opened with a 44-point victory over Spain, then rallied from an 8-point deficit early in the second half to beat Canada, 76–70. Next up was Brazil, led by Oscar Schmidt, a gunning outside shooter who had scored 45 points to help upset the U.S. team in the Pan American Games in 1987. Thompson reminded his team of that loss by playing the game tape the first day they arrived in Korea. Though only three current Olympians had been on that Pan Am team, "it was very quiet in that room," said center David Robinson, one of the three. "Coach Thompson didn't need to say anything."

The Americans got an early scare from the Brazilians: They were trailing, 36–33, when Schmidt hit a three-point shot and was fouled, adding the free throw. But the Americans went on a 22–9 run, led by 8 at the half and kept increasing the margin. Schmidt scored 31 points, but his teammates wilted in the face of U.S. pressure and Brazil was routed, 102–87.

A 51-point victory over pitiful China in the next game was expected. But in the second half, the unthinkable occurred: Hersey Hawkins collided with teammate Jeff Grayer near the U.S. basket and strained his right knee. Hawkins, a 6-3 guard, was easily the Americans' best outside shooter. He'd been hitting 55 percent of his shots, including 62.5 percent of his three-point tries. Now he was lost for the tournament, a major blow to a team with precious few reliable shooters.

The Americans didn't miss Hawkins much in lopsided victories over Egypt (102–35) and Puerto Rico (94–57), but now it was time to face the Soviet Union in the semifinals of the medal round, and the Americans knew they had a serious problem. "Everybody was telling me there was no way we could lose," said Chris Plonsky, a Big East publicist who served as the team's media liaison. "I just remembered thinking to myself anything could happen. We knew the Russians were good. We knew this was not going to be easy."

That was obvious from the opening tip-off. Danny Manning, the team's second-leading scorer, picked up two quick fouls with 2:17 gone in the first half and left the game for the rest of the period. He did not score a point for the Americans, and played only seventeen minutes the entire game.

The American defense was mostly ineffective against a Soviet team that beat the press with precision passing from backcourt to frontcourt and deadly shooting from three-point range. The Soviets had no problem solving the American zone defense, and their shooters had uncontested shots almost from start to finish. Without Hawkins, the Americans had no outside presence to help them come all the way back from the 14-point lead the Soviets built up early in the second half. Georgetown's Charles Smith and J. R. Reid did ignite a rally that cut the deficit to 59–57 with 10:25 left. But the Soviets again took control and built the lead back to 71–62 with 4:58 remaining. The Americans twice got it to within 3 in the final minutes, only to miss shots or turn the ball over. Their play down the stretch was ragged at best. David Robinson led the Americans with 19 points and 12 rebounds, and Dan Majerle scored 15 but made only 5 of his 16 shots. No other American scored in double figures, and, of course, Hawkins never left the bench. To his credit,

Thompson would not allow him to play, even though Hawkins had told him that if he was needed he would give it a try.

The Russians, meanwhile, got 28 points from Rimas Kurtinaitis, and another 19 from Sharunas Marchulenis. Sabonis added 13, with 13 rebounds, including 2 in the final minutes as the Americans desperately tried to rally. Clearly, the Russians had learned their lessons well.

When it was over, the stunned American players quickly headed for the locker room, their coach following behind after shaking hands with a few Soviet players. But he also appeared immediately in the interview room and allowed his players to be questioned at length.

"I told the players I don't want any crying or anyone ashamed, unless you didn't think you did your best," Thompson said. "I figure they'll let us back in the country."

"After we lost to the Russians, I guess we all thought he would go off," said guard Mitch Richmond. "It was our first loss, and none of us knew how he would react. I didn't know whether he'd start screaming and yelling or throwing stuff. Some guys were probably afraid. But he calmed us down a lot. He just said we worked hard and it wasn't meant to be. That's all."

"He wouldn't let us get down," Hawkins said. "He refused to let us get down. He wanted everybody to know that he felt we gave a hundred percent and nobody should be ashamed because we just lost one game. He said everybody would forget about it sooner or later."

The Americans did come back and beat Australia for the bronze medal, but even before that game the long knives had been drawn by Thompson's critics in the press corps. Few American writers were feeling sorry for Thompson, not after all the indignities heaped upon them by his restrictive access to himself and his players over the previous five months, not to mention his perceived transgressions throughout most of the 1980s.

As one national columnist admitted, "There was not a sad face in the press box. There was a sense of just deserts. Nobody else at the Olympics had a system where you had to talk to people like this. It was boot-camp mentality. Even when the players were available, they were too scared to talk. Had he won, I know he would have gotten on the bully pulpit and said, 'You guys said I couldn't do it blah, blah, blah.' In the press section, people were giving each other low fives because they didn't want anybody to see them celebrating a U.S. loss. But there were no tears shed for John Thompson that day."

Or very many in the days and weeks following that devastating loss.

Listen to a sample of the opinions voiced by some of America's best-known sports journalists:

Leigh Montville, *The Boston Globe*: "Thompson's coaching included a number of bonehead decisions at all stops. He always seems as if he is trying to prove something. He is trying to show he is the boss and has his own mind and will not be influenced by anyone or anything else. He seems to revel in being disliked, feeds off it."

Jan Hubbard, *The Dallas Morning News*: "Thompson was too conservative. He should have played Manning until he fouled out. What was he saving him for? The 1992 Olympics?"

Dick Weiss, *Philadelphia Daily News*: "The international game is a game for the offensive-minded. That was something Thompson never grasped. The Americans' ball movement on offense was a disaster. The U.S. had only four assists and its patience was almost nonexistent in the final 10 minutes."

Dan Barreiro, Minneapolis *Star Tribune*: "Why must college coaches feed their own egos at the expense of their own team? Thompson picked a team to play the way his Georgetown Hoyas play. One problem: He wasn't playing St. John's or Villanova. He was playing mature, international teams, some of whom can handle defensive pressure. . . . The Americans ran an offense as stagnant as Seoul smog."

Terry Boers, *Chicago Sun-Times*: "He . . . gave us a team that gradually grew to be every bit as paranoid as Thompson's teams are at Georgetown. By forcing the players to live in the isolated world that he prefers, Thompson succeeded only in turning up the pressure to the point where no one was having any fun."

Barry Lorge, *The San Diego Union*: "He closes practices, isolates and gags his players, thinks the press ought to all be like Tass and generally acts as if his idea of Utopia would be preparing his program behind the Kremlin wall. With a vastly superior talent pool from which to select, Thompson came to the Olympics with a defense-oriented team flawed for the occasion."

The day after the game, Thompson was firm in insisting that he had done all the right things to prepare for the games. "I think if I had to do it all over again, every player I would select again, every staff member, everything that we decided to do," he said. "You make decisions and then you have to go with those decisions."

Bill Stein said the team "played as well as they could have. We just had a bad game. The guys were a little tight. Our boys had played sixteen games together. The Russians played something like a hundred twenty. They'd been together six years with one change in personnel. If we played those guys ten times, we'd beat them seven or eight. Too much was made of one game."

Many of Thompson's coaching colleagues have since stood up in his defense. Dean Smith and many others insisted that the improvement in international basketball has been phenomenal over the last decade and that American teams no longer are guaranteed victory anytime they walk onto the court, unless America professionals are allowed to compete. In 1992, U.S. pros, with a pro coach, will represent the United States in the Barcelona Olympics. In 1988, the Russians fielded an excellent basketball team, with a number of their players coveted by the NBA. They also played an almost perfect game against the Americans.

"A gold medal is not a given," Smith said.

"It's goddamned easy to second-guess," said Red Auerbach. "But I find it difficult to blame a coach for one game. I have no beef with what he did in the Olympics."

"We pick a college coach and give him freedom to do what he wants," said Iowa's Tom Davis. "If he wins, great. If he loses, he gets crucified. It's a no-win situation. If you win, you're supposed to win. If you lose, you did something wrong. John is a high-profile figure, and people came after him. I didn't think it was fair."

And yet some coaches also will say that Thompson may have made several fundamental mistakes.

"It's very tough to teach his style of defense," said Pitt's Paul Evans. "I don't know if you can coach his style of play in such a short time, get kids like that gung ho to play that style."

"This is not meant as a criticism of John Thompson," Duke coach Mike Krzyzewski said. "You can't count on Danny Ferry getting hurt, or Hersey Hawkins. Some other kids weren't available to him. The only thing I might have done differently would be to surround myself with all head coaches on the staff. Only a head coach can think like a head coach. I'd want guys involved in international experience, guys who have been in the pressure cooker, guys who are good teachers. It's the only thing I'd do differently."

"Most of the criticism I heard was on the guards he selected," said former Washington Bullets general manager Bob Ferry. "We're used to the pivot man dominating here. In international basketball, it's not that way. There is no true low post. It's a wider lane, and the game changes because of it. We've been slow to adapt to that. And we always underestimate that many of these players from other countries are great shooters. And if players can shoot, they can win. They are not necessarily great athletes, but they can shoot, and they've learned how to take away a team's inside game. We were going to press them. That works against the weaker teams, but as you move up the ladder, a lot of these teams can break the press. They're well trained. The bottom line is, if Hersey Hawkins is okay, we win the game and nobody says a word. But John got himself in trouble because he had no one to take his place."

There were other criticisms. David Robinson was still rusty after laying off basketball while fulfilling his Navy commitment. J. R. Reid was on the team only because of Thompson's friendship with Dean Smith. The same was said of Stacey Augmon, the team's defensive specialist from Nevada–Las Vegas—that he was there only as a favor to Thompson's pal Jerry Tarkanian. Meanwhile, great players like Sean Elliott, Stacey King, Rex Chapman, Sherman Douglas, Pooh Richardson and Brian Shaw (the last man cut) could have helped, but all were back home watching. Some said Thompson's paranoia had made the team tense and uptight, fearful of provoking his wrath.

There was a report in the *New York Post* that the Atlanta Hawks had given Thompson a ten-page scouting report on the Russians that was never used. "He ignored everything we covered," a source told the *Post*. "They didn't stop one thing we told them to look out for. Nor did John ever make a follow-up call to us." There was even some talk that several players had dogged it, more concerned about their pro careers and getting to NBA training camps healthy than they were about winning the Olympic gold.

Said one coach who has played against Thompson for most of the last two decades, "Knowing John Thompson as well as I do, he does not know how to use a big guy. Ewing was never an offensive force at Georgetown—he's been taught that in the pros. Alonzo Mourning is not an offensive force at Georgetown. His big guy in the Olympics, Danny Manning, never got the ball against the Russians. Someone told me he actually touched it nine times in that game. Not shot it. Touched it. Meanwhile, the guards were going one-on-one out there and throwing up these crazy shots. We never got the ball inside. You have to blame John for that."

To a man, though, none of his players will publicly blame John Thompson for that loss.

"I don't think he can be second-guessed," said Majerle, now a solid pro with the Phoenix Suns. "I don't know what any of us could have done different. I don't think you can blame John Thompson. He prepared us to the utmost. He ran us to death in practice, a lot of fast-break basketball and hours and hours of fundamental drills. He yelled at you—and I mean yelled—when you deserved it, but he praised you when you did something right. You can't fault the man for how he prepared us, no way."

"I thought John was a great man," said Jeff Grayer, now with the Milwaukee Bucks. "He worked hard and he really knew what he was doing out there. You knew the loss hurt him, but John never let us see the emotion. I don't know how he kept his composure, because it was the Soviets. But he acted like it was nothing special. He took the fall. He had to be hurting somewhere, but he patted all of us on the back and said, 'Good job.' "

"I'll give Thompson credit," said Danny Manning, now of the Los Angeles Clippers, who underwent reconstructive knee surgery during his rookie season, one of six Olympians who suffered debilitating injuries or serious health problems after the Games. "He was definitely a calming factor after the game. A lot of coaches might have gone off blaming people and making excuses, but John talked to us after the game, the whole team, when we were still together at the Olympic Village, and I know some of the guys saw him later separately. Hey, we played, we lost, we move on."

16

The quiet young man sits in the same seat on the same couch in the same office that so many talented basketball players have occupied over the years, but on this day in the fall of 1988, this chat is a little different.

Stay away from my boys, John Thompson tells Rayful Edmond, Washington's most notorious drug dealer. Don't play ball with them, don't hang with them in the clubs, don't be coming around to the games.

Within months he is indicted for drug dealing; within a year he begins serving a life sentence in a maximum-security federal penitentiary.

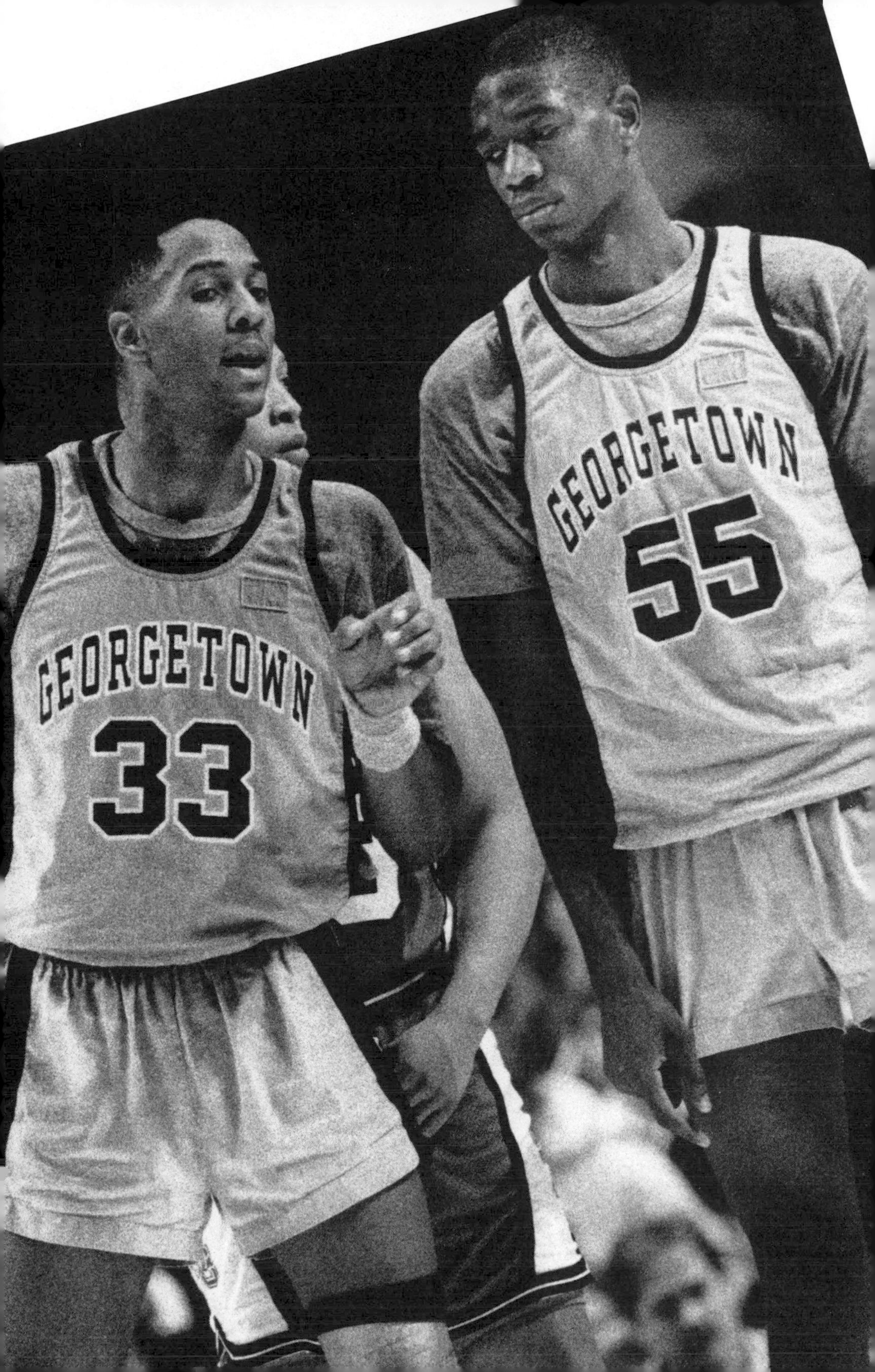
GEORGETOWN
33
GEORGETOWN
55

IF JOHN THOMPSON WAS DEVASTATED BY THE OLYMPIC LOSS TO the Soviet Union and the barrage of criticism that followed—most of it directed toward him—he was hiding it well in the days and weeks following his return from Seoul.

He made a short trip to Las Vegas and the slot machines to unwind a bit, but with the Games ending two weeks before the official start of practice at Georgetown on October 15, there was precious little time to look back, and every reason to press on with a team that once again was expected to compete for a national championship.

Thompson eased into his work in his own inimitable way, with Georgetown's full blessing. In the weeks before the start of the season in late November, Thompson generally stayed away from his office and his usual regimen of grueling twelve-hour days. He took few phone calls, scheduled no appointments or interviews and let someone else open his mail. He showed up for practice and left when it was over. He described his status as being on a leave of absence of sorts, avoiding the administrative end of his job and concentrating solely on basketball.

"I consider basketball a vacation because it's what I do and what I like to do," he told reporters at the Big East media day in November, his first formal session with the press since the Olympics. "I'm not a person who can go away for a long period of time and sit by the seaside— you know, look at the birds. People take vacations in different ways. But if I sense or if I see that, from the stresses, my temperament is changing or I'm picking on the kids or my nerves are going the other way, I'll say, 'Hey, Mike and Craig [assistants Mike Riley and Craig Esherick], you guys are good. You take this.' And I'll walk away from it. I'll disappear for a while."

Over the past several years, in fact, Thompson had taken an increasingly laid-back approach to his basketball team. He was still a fiery competitor on game days, and he could dress down a player with the best of them, but he also was relying more and more on Riley and Esherick, particularly on the recruiting end. Kenny Anderson of Archbishop Molloy in New York, considered the premier point guard coming out of high school before the 1989–90 season, said publicly that he would have gone to Georgetown if only Thompson had shown some interest. But Thompson, telling friends he was getting more disgusted with college recruiting and dealing with what he once described as those "snot-nosed little motherfuckers," never did. Anderson chose Georgia Tech, and led that team to the Final Four his freshman season.

At the same Big East media session, Thompson spoke at length about the disappointment of not winning the gold medal, and insisted he had not spent a lot of time dwelling on the loss to the Soviets.

"I think there are too many challenges in my life, too many times that you have to step into the arena, to harp on it, or to think about it," he said. "Certainly I think about it, and certainly I'm disappointed, but it falls in line with a lot of disappointments and a lot of successes. I don't think you ever go forward if you spend a heck of a lot of time on the things you're disappointed in. . . . I knew there wasn't a guaranteed win involved. And if I have an opportunity to jump into another arena that's just as competitive, I'll do it, because this is what I do. It's not something that scared me into a cave, or made me run around and feel ashamed. Competition is what I do this for, and what I like. The challenge is what I do it for."

Certainly, there would be more than enough challenges ahead for Thompson in the 1988–89 season. With Alonzo Mourning in the fold, and Charles Smith returning for his senior season along with a number of other experienced players, Georgetown was already a preseason top-ten selection. And there also were some promising new faces, including the coach's second son, Ronny, a star guard at Flint Hill Academy in suburban Virginia who had convinced his father they both could handle his presence on the team.

Two other players had come to Georgetown via nontraditional routes. In the past Thompson had mostly avoided signing junior college players, but nevertheless had added John Turner, a powerful 6-7 forward who had grown up in Glenarden, Maryland. Turner had first tried to get into Georgetown in 1985, but he had scored only 650 on the College Boards and he was not admitted. Instead, he attended Allegany Community College in Cumberland, Maryland, for a year, then transferred to Georgetown in 1987, sitting out a year as required by the NCAA.

The other new man had come to Georgetown from his native Zaire. Dikembe Mutombo, all 7-foot-2 of him, had been discovered by an Indiana high school basketball coach who had been in the African nation conducting clinics under a U.S. Information Agency program. The coach, Jim East of Merrillville High School, had seen Mutombo play and mentioned the youngster to Herman Henning, the cultural affairs officer for the U.S. embassy in Kinshasa and an old basketball coach from Chicago himself. Henning spoke with the boy's parents about the possibility of going to school in America, and they authorized him to serve as their go-between. Henning began looking at schools that might best serve Mutombo's needs. For one thing, he spoke fluent French and virtually no English. For another, he had only been playing the game for a few years, and he needed lots of fundamental help.

"I wanted a coach who had a good track record and could be patient with Dikembe because he was going to require a lot of work as a basketball player," Henning said. "I wanted a program with high visibility because this was a chance of a lifetime for the kid and I wanted him to be able to make the most of it. I also wanted a coach who had played center because I felt he would be more able to teach Dikembe than one who had been a guard. And I wanted a person whose word I could have confidence in because I needed to have a sure offer of a full scholarship."

Henning settled on John Thompson, who at first was not all that interested. Back at St. Anthony's, Thompson had once coached an African player, and it had been a frustrating experience teaching him the game. He wasn't at all certain he wanted to go through that again, especially with a player who did not understand much English. But Henning was persistent. He scrounged up a tape of Mutombo in a game televised by a Kinshasa station and sent that to Washington. Thompson became intrigued, if only because of Mutombo's size and raw skills, and eventually signed him, though it was decided that he would sit out a year while he adjusted to the U.S., improved his English and worked on his game.

But now, in 1988, Mutombo was ready to play, even if Thompson wasn't quite willing to allow him to meet the media, since he was a freshman subject to the January 1 rule. "He'll be a writer's field day when I let him talk," Thompson said. "You guys will love him. He's very cocky, very confident—he's outspoken. I told him when he talked to you guys if he didn't want to answer the question, say it in French because I knew all you well-rounded folks would understand."

Thompson's team began its season in Hawaii, and, with the usual patsy early schedule that included games against mighty Hawaii Loa, Hawaii Pacific, St. Leo, Shenandoah Music Conservatory and Mercer, the Hoyas opened up 9–0 before losing their first Big East game, a 94–86 decision to a Seton Hall team that would eventually go on to the Final Four and play for the national championship.

But basketball was not all that was occupying John Thompson's time this season. In early January, the NCAA held its annual convention and passed a piece of legislation known as Proposition 42. It applied to athletes who failed to score 700 (out of a possible 1,600) on the Scholastic Aptitude Test or 15 (out of 36) on the American College Test and who failed to achieve a 2.0 grade point average (out of 4.0) in a high school core curriculum of eleven subjects. Under a previous piece of legislation, passed in 1983 and known as Proposition 48, athletes who failed to meet those minimum standards could be accepted to college on scholarship, but were not eligible to compete in their first year. Under Proposition 42, passed almost routinely in a somewhat confusing session at the convention, students who did not meet those minimums would be ineligible for any financial aid administered by a school beginning in 1990.

Thompson, like many other black educators, had always been philosophically opposed to Proposition 48. He felt the College Boards were culturally biased against blacks and was against using them to determine eligibility for athletes. In fact, even the people who administered the SAT and the ACT had been opposed to using standardized tests as one of the two main standards for determining eligibility and admission for athletes. Still, while some of his players had been academically deficient upon arriving at Georgetown, a school whose average student scored 1,243 on the SAT, the coach had never signed a Prop 48 athlete for his program.

The Southeast Conference had sponsored Proposition 42 not so much for lofty academic reasons, but rather to level the playing field around the country. The University of Georgia, stung by a lawsuit filed by instructor Jan Kemp claiming she had been dismissed for protesting special treatment for athletes, had stopped admitting Prop 48 athletes in the mid-1980s. That also put Georgia at a competitive disadvantage with its fellow conference members, all of whom were allowing so-called partial qualifiers to get in and eventually become eligible for sports. Georgia had convinced its fellow conference members to adopt the same standards. Now the SEC wanted the rest of the country to go along, too.

When Proposition 42 was passed in January 1989, Thompson was outraged. For one, many people did not even understand what they had been voting for—even some of the black colleges had cast their ballots for a measure that would have its greatest impact on minority students who would not be able to afford college without institutional aid. A few days later, Thompson announced that he would walk off the basketball court when his team played a home game against Boston College at the Capital Centre on January 14 in protest of the NCAA vote. At a press conference the day before the game attended by Father Timothy Healy, the school president at the time, and athletic director Frank Rienzo, Thompson said he did not want his protest to be viewed as racially motivated. Still, when he was asked if he thought black athletes would be most affected by the new rule, he said, "De facto."

"I feel that had this been in existence when I started into school, I would not have been provided with an opportunity to get a college education," Thompson said. "I think it has been proven that there is a segment of our society, notably the low socioeconomic aspect of it, that statistics don't accurately reflect their abilities."

He said he was staging his protest "to bring attention to something that I think is a tremendous tragedy. I have every intention of talking to other people while I am in the form of this protest to try to identify what the reason for some of this was and also to try to get it changed in whatever sensible, reasonable manner I feel I am able to."

This was not the first time Thompson had used basketball as a vehicle to make his views known. Back in 1981, his players wore green ribbons on their uniforms to remind people that black children were being killed in Atlanta. "Basketball is my whole life," Thompson said at the time. "My happiness and my sorrow and my protests. People use what they have, and what I have is basketball."

Just before the tip-off of his team's game against BC, Thompson got up out of his chair and walked off the court toward the locker room to a standing ovation from the Capital Centre crowd, leaving the coaching duties to Esherick and Riley. He left the building and got into his car, driving around the city and listening to the game on the radio. He also decided to boycott the team's next game four days later at Providence. This time, he never left Washington, though his trademark towel was draped on an empty chair in the middle of the Georgetown bench area where Thompson normally would have been sitting.

Thompson's protest was generally applauded nationwide, though some cynics complained that it was a grandstand gesture and that Thompson's motives were not totally altruistic. Said one opposing coach, "I thought he was smart to do it. It endeared him to a lot of recruits and their parents. I believe he was sincere in what he was doing, but it sure as hell didn't hurt him or his basketball program."

Still, said Ed Tapscott, the black former head coach at American University, "no one else could have focused the debate better than John Thompson. People did criticize him for it, but it was a courageous stand, one he could have ducked if he'd wanted to. Somebody asked me if I would have walked out. I told him if I had walked, nobody would have cared. When John walked, the whole damned country stood up and took notice."

Indeed, Thompson's protest resulted in almost immediate reaction from the NCAA. A day after the Providence game, Albert Witte, the president of the NCAA, and Martin Massengale, chairman of the NCAA President's Commission, announced that they would recommend legislation that would postpone any changes in Proposition 48, including Proposition 42, until the NCAA had finished studying the relationship of academic success in college to high school grade point average and standardized test scores.

That was good enough for Thompson. The next day, he said he would be returning to the bench for his team's next game against the University of Connecticut "based on the fact that I think there is a sincere commitment to take [Proposition 42] back before the convention and to reevaluate what has happened. I feel very comfortable with the fact that, within the system, an honest effort is being made to rectify the problem that I had grave concerns about."

Still, some people had grave concerns about Thompson's stand. One of them was Arthur Ashe, the widely respected black tennis star, author and businessman who for years had been an advocate of not allowing black athletes to participate in sports unless they were academically qualified—at all levels. Ashe was very much in favor of keeping the academic standards of Proposition 48, and 42 if necessary, to send a message to black youngsters that they would not be able to get by in school simply because they were bigger, faster or taller than most of their peers.

"The seven hundred score encourages mediocrity," Ashe said. "It's a lousy goal and makes no sense. I have a tremendous amount of respect for John, but my feeling is that if you make it difficult for kids to get in [to college], you will go through two or three tough years, but you will get the attention of that black ninth grader: If you want to go to a major college on an athletic scholarship, you have to meet this standard. Will it ruin their lives if they don't meet it? No. They can go to a

Division II school, or a junior college, then transfer. We have to beat some of these kids over the head and say this has got to stop.

"My differences with John are severalfold. The cultural bias issue in theory makes sense. But it doesn't hold much water because seven hundred is so low. It's laughable. I don't know any schools in Division I that would have an incoming freshman class averaging seven hundred on the Boards. We're also talking about a graduation rate of less than twenty percent for black athletes in colleges. That's pitiful. We're exploiting so many of these kids. My feeling is that you tell these kids in the ninth grade this is what it takes to get in. If you don't do it, you can't get in. It's got to start somewhere."

Thompson did not take kindly to Ashe's criticism. "Arthur Ashe is not the spokesman for academic institutions in this country and has never been responsible to my knowledge for monitoring, baby-sitting, watching one kid for four years of his life, never mind for the eighteen years that I have sat there and watched them," he said. "I've said it before—seven hundred is far too low for many so-called minority students. But that's not the issue. The issue is whether you are using the instrument correctly. The instrument is being used incorrectly. It does have an effect on kids who are from low-income backgrounds simply because our educational system is based on money and politics. If individual institutions will have enough courage not to depend on national legislation and stand up for what they were founded for, that's all we have to do. End of story, problem is over and we don't need Proposition Zero."

In any case, the NCAA decided a year later that it did not need Proposition 42, at least not in the form passed a few days before Thompson's walkout. In January 1990 at its annual convention, the NCAA modified Proposition 42 to allow students ineligible for athletic competition to at least receive institutional aid so that they could continue their educations. They could not be on athletic scholarship until they demonstrated their ability to perform in the classroom, but they would not be denied the opportunity to stay in school.

There was no question that Thompson's protest had accomplished exactly what he set out to do in the first place: It had touched off a national debate on and off the campus, one that continues to this day as the NCAA monitors the long-term effects of Proposition 48.

Thompson had other triumphs that year as well. His basketball team, despite all the distractions, won the 2 games its coach missed, captured the Big East regular-season and tournament titles and won 3 straight NCAA tournament games before losing to Duke, 85–77, in the East regional finals, the sixth time Georgetown had been to the Final Eight since 1980.

Mourning was a singular sensation as a freshman, leading the nation in blocked shots as the Hoyas set an NCAA team record with a total of 309. On the few occasions Thompson used Mourning and Mutombo on the floor at the same time, basketballs were being swatted like so many pesky flies.

Mourning actually saved the Hoyas in the first round of the NCAA when he blocked a three-point attempt in the closing seconds to preserve a 50–49 victory over a plucky Princeton team in a game Georgetown was fortunate to win. Mourning's first year in college was a great learning experience for a player who seemed certain to dominate college basketball for as long as he decided to play. While Patrick Ewing had been a silent, glaring presence on the court, Mourning was an exuberant, animated athlete who also enjoyed the give-and-take with the media, once Thompson allowed him to speak. Apparently, he also enjoyed the life-style his celebrity status afforded, as Thompson learned much to his dismay a few days after returning from the Olympics.

Thompson was being told both by local law-enforcement officials and some of his friends around the city that John Turner and Mourning had been seen at various locations with Rayful Edmond III, the kingpin of a massive drug distribution network in Washington. Turner and Edmond had been childhood friends growing up in Glenarden, Maryland, not far from D.C. Turner had introduced Mourning, his roommate, to a young man who was a talented basketball player himself, but had taken a slightly different road to fame and notoriety. Though there was no indication that his two players were involved in any illegal activity—they saw Edmond socially in clubs around town and occasionally visited his house—Thompson ordered both players to avoid further contact with Edmond. He also put the word out on the street that he wanted to talk with Edmond to tell him to stay away from his players.

Edmond responded to the summons, showing up alone one day at Thompson's office in McDonough Gymnasium. "Do me a favor," Thompson said he told Edmond. "If you see anything going on out there, use whatever resources you have to stop it from happening." Later Thompson would insist he had no idea that the Edmond organization was thought to have been involved in at least thirty drug-related murders and was believed to have been responsible for supplying as much as 20 percent of the crack cocaine coming into the city. "Talking to Rayful, I didn't feel unsafe or threatened," Thompson told Dave Kindred, writing in *The Washingtonian* magazine. "Had he asked me to meet him somewhere, I would have gone there. I didn't focus on something possibly happening to me. . . . Those players are under my supervision, and I was trying to do that which my mother or my father would have done. If there had been a problem that concerns me, I could see my mother taking that apron off and going down the street and saying, 'Well, let me sit down and talk with this young man and find out just what this is about.' . . . He was as polite as anybody I've ever had an opportunity to talk with. He never gave me any form of disrespect or lip. He was extremely polite. Extremely polite."

The same could not be said for Thompson's message to his team in general and the two players specifically. He warned them in no uncertain terms to stay away from Edmond and his friends. He also advised them to avoid several clubs around town where Edmond and his gang were likely to be. Mourning, a country boy from Chesapeake, Virginia, apparently heeded Thompson's stern advice. Turner did not.

Not long after Thompson appeared on Ted Koppel's "Nightline" show a month after the season ended to tell the nation about his meeting with Edmond, the coach announced that Turner would no longer be attending Georgetown. Thompson had heard that Turner was still seeing his friend Edmond, had even attended a Washington Bullets basketball game with him at the Capital Centre. One day, after Turner spoke with Edmond at a playground in Northwest Washington, Turner said he got a call from his coach.

"Coach Thompson called me about an hour later," he told Bill Brubaker. "He said, 'I want you to get your stuff off campus by tomorrow.' " Though Georgetown had announced that Turner had withdrawn from school voluntarily for academic reasons, the player insisted otherwise.

"Coach Thompson said I can't leave the people on the street alone," Turner said. ". . . It cost me a lot [his friendship with Edmond]. But I don't think I made a mistake. Rayful is a good gentleman and a good young man. Rayful is a loyal buddy and a friend to everybody." And now he also is a convicted felon serving a life sentence at the federal penitentiary in Marion, Illinois. Mourning, in fact, was called to testify in Edmond's highly publicized trial in the fall of 1989, a few days before the start of Georgetown's basketball season. On the witness stand, he confirmed that Turner had introduced him to Edmond and other drug

Alonzo Mourning reacts to a call. (Cameron, The Washington Post)

dealers, but he said it was an ordinary friendship and he was not exactly certain what Edmond and his pal, Jerry Millington, another member of the gang, actually did.

"I never talked to him [Millington] about his activities," Mourning testified. "I didn't know anything about his activities. I've seen the beeper, yes, on him. On his side, I guess. I rode in the Pathfinder. From my remembrance, I think I went to the store. I didn't look in kitchen cabinets. No sir, I didn't think that was any of my business."

A few days later, Mourning would leave with the rest of his team for Hawaii to open the season. Turner, meanwhile, would end up at Phillips University in Enid, Oklahoma, an NAIA school where he was eligible to play basketball in his second semester.

Had Turner, a solid though hardly spectacular player, been made a scapegoat by Thompson, while Mourning, the superstar sophomore, was allowed to remain in school with no consequences from his dealings with Edmond and his murderous gang? Certainly it appeared that way. Could Mourning have been so naive that he did not know whom he was associating with, how dangerous they were and how much trouble he could get into with his coach and with the law? That seems hard to believe. Said one coach, "Who's going to win you a national championship, John Turner or Alonzo Mourning? That's all you have to ask."

Still, Bill Lassiter, Mourning's high school coach, insists this was the case of "a country kid who got caught up in the big-city life, and he has learned a very big lesson in his life. I think Alonzo knows now what kind of position he's in. I think it really opened his eyes. He knows that anything he does is going to be closely watched by a lot of people. It made him grow up real fast."

A lot of people were watching a game between Georgetown and the University of Connecticut in mid-January of 1990 when Mourning found himself at the center of yet another controversy. Mourning stood next to Nadev Henefeld, UConn's Israeli-born forward, as they toed the line on a free-throw attempt, when Mourning uttered an ethnic slur—"faggot Jew boy," he allegedly called him, according to two sources—in Henefeld's direction.

According to a report in *The National Sports Daily*, the remark was heard "clearly at courtside and on video replay." *Sports Illustrated* writer Alexander Wolff covered the game and made reference to the remark in his story, but the reference was deleted by editors when reporters and fact-checkers could not get anyone to confirm the incident on the record. Also, Georgetown's public relations director, Gary Krull, had placed an angry call to a *Sports Illustrated* reporter working on the story and another call to the magazine's managing editor, Mark Mulvoy, though Krull later insisted the university did not try to intimidate the magazine into deleting the reference to the incident.

A few days later, *Sports Illustrated* writer Curry Kirkpatrick showed the clip on a program he hosted on the Cable News Network. He said the tape seemed to indicate that Mourning had mouthed the ethnic epithet. "They [Georgetown officials] were angry at CNN," Kirkpatrick told *The National*. "But we played it to let the viewers decide. You can see [Mourning] forming the words." Another source, who viewed the tape a number of times, said he thought it was inconclusive.

To this day, Connecticut coach Jim Calhoun denies that Mourning uttered an anti-Semitic remark, though one UConn source says there was definitely some nasty language involved. "It was R-rated," said the source. "He called him a motherfucking white faggot. It's not like these kids have never heard that kind of talk. That's all he said."

"My own son, Jeff, is a ball boy and heard what he said," Calhoun insisted. "It was not very nice, but it was not an anti-Semitic remark. Unfortunately, Alonzo tends to negate a lot of his great play with some childish antics. He's got to learn that stuff doesn't get it."

Mourning and his teammates had lots to learn during the 1989–90 season. Over the summer, Thompson had decided he would start Mourning and Dikembe Mutombo together in a twin-towers alignment. He made the decision after having lunch one day with Red Auerbach, who told Thompson his opponents loved to see him use only one big man at a time.

But Thompson never seemed totally committed to the idea, nor could he settle on a consistent substitution pattern during a season many thought was his worst as a bench coach. The usual Georgetown pressure defense had serious leaks, and his own players had difficulty when the opposition pressed right back. As always, players were constantly being shuttled in and out of the games, but there seemed to be no rhyme or reason to any of it. A man might find himself getting twenty-five minutes one night and two the next.

In midseason, sophomore Milton Bell, a 6–7 forward who had been one of the nation's top forty players his senior year in high school, announced that he would be transferring immediately to the University of Richmond in his hometown. He was not playing very much, averaging 7.7 minutes, and he had not seen action in 7 of the Hoyas' 17 games. He also was struggling in the classroom and decided he'd be better suited at a place where "the academics are a little easier, so I can also concentrate on basketball."

Thompson caused another small stir himself in early March when he was thrown out of a game at Syracuse for picking up three technical fouls. It was the first time that had happened since the 1974–75 season, and Thompson seemed contrite when it was over. "It was probably my fault more than the officials' fault," he said at his postgame press conference. "I have respect for all three of those men. I probably let my competitive juices overflow. I made a mistake." It was a mistake that allowed Syracuse 5 points from the free-throw line and eventually cost the Hoyas an 89–87 overtime defeat. It also cost Thompson some respect on his own campus. One professor who asked not to be named said he felt Thompson had demeaned himself and his program by an uncalled-for display of temper, and it had not gone unnoticed.

Still, Thompson always seemed to have the Georgetown faculty and administration in the palm of his hand. Certainly, until he left following the 1988–89 school year to run the New York City public library system, school president Father Timothy Healy publicly backed Thompson every step of the way. John Thompson could simply do no wrong in Father Healy's eyes, and he often said so.

Interviews with a half-dozen professors also indicated similar support. Robert Lieber, a professor of government for eight years, said, "I like Thompson in the following sense: I respect him. Most professional and college coaches are nothing to write home about. Most of them are obsessive. Many of them glorify the least admirable aspects of human behavior. Thompson is a refreshing exception. I remember some years back he was doing an interview . . . at a time when Georgetown's principal rival was St. John's. Thompson described walking with the team into a New York hotel and seeing a local newspaper with a headline that read, "St. John's vs. Georgetown: It's War." And Thompson smiled, shrugged and said, 'Hey, it's not a war, it's a ball game.' So I think he has a useful sense of proportion."

Or Wayne Knoll, an English professor who's been there for nineteen years and serves as Georgetown's faculty representative to the NCAA: "[Thompson believes] Georgetown shouldn't shut the door on a student who is borderline or who has come from a disadvantaged socioeconomic background and also a poor academic background. It's worth it, he maintains, to give a person like that a chance. If he can't do it, he can't do it . . . you're gone. If, after judicious testing, it appears that a student with tutorial work and solid effort can make it, then why not, if it means that kid gets a chance to step out of poverty. Thompson knows all about that."

Thompson also knew a lot about frustration. His 1989–90 basketball season ended with a thoroughly unexpected 74–71 loss to Xavier of Cincinnati in the second round of the NCAA tournament. Just as he had done all season, Thompson shuffled bodies in and out all day trying to erase a 16-point deficit early in the second half. Georgetown rallied, but missed 5 of 6 free throws in the last 6:11 and watched the season conclude with a 24–7 record.

A few months later, there were two more defections of talented players. David Edwards, a fiery little guard who frequently followed a spectacular pass with a bonehead turnover, had played in every game. He'd been the leading scorer against Xavier with 19 points and seemed destined to be the Hoyas' point guard of the future. Michael Tate, the Washington area's high school player of the year in 1988–89, began the season as a starting forward and ended it planted firmly on the bench.

All three players—Bell, Edwards and Tate—had been unhappy with their roles and their playing time. All had been major stars in high school—all were used to being on the court, taking the big shots and making the crucial plays—and clearly they had problems adjusting to Thompson's system. Academics also had played a role. Bell had taken the SAT five times before scoring about 700, and Tate also failed to achieve that minimum the first time he took the test. Edwards said he had posted a 2.7 grade point average his first semester, and that grades were not a problem, though Thompson had announced his transfer was in his best interest "athletically and academically, to pursue his education elsewhere." Tate wound up at James Madison, Edwards at Texas A&M.

All three players also had been aware that Thompson and his staff had been busy assembling the largest recruiting class in the coach's tenure, adding seven players—two new point guards, three forwards and two centers.

"As I understand it, Milton was unhappy because of this playing time," said his high school coach, Frank Threatts. "He was also having some problems with his academics. And when you see people being brought in at your position, it said to him that Thompson wasn't satisfied with his performance. So he decided to go somewhere else. He saw no future there. I'm sure the other kids will tell you the same thing."

Thompson's future was also being widely discussed in the summer of 1990. There were reports that he had been offered the chance to become director of operations with the Boston Celtics before his friend, David Gavitt, was' named to the position. There also was some speculation that Nike was interested in Thompson for a top management position, as were the New York Knicks.

In mid-June, Thompson also was being wooed by the Denver Nuggets for a general manager's job with the possibility of a small piece of team ownership. The Nuggets had been purchased the year before by a group that included two minority businessmen—the only black ownership in any major American sport—and they were offering Thompson $700,000 a year and a 4-percent piece of the club if he stayed for five years. The total package was said to be worth $6 million, and Thompson agonized over the decision for several days.

He was not pleased that word of the negotiations had leaked out prematurely—two local television stations and USA Today had erroneously reported it was a done deal—and at one point he held a press conference to announce that he still had not made his final decision. Though he admitted he was considering Denver's proposal "far more seriously than any of the others," he said he wanted to speak with his staff, his players and the Georgetown administration before making up his mind.

Over the next three days, he did just that. There were reports that the only holdup involved Thompson trying to convince Georgetown officials to name Craig Esherick as his replacement. But school officials were saying privately that the longer Thompson waited on his response to the Nuggets, the better chance they had to keep him.

On June 23, Thompson called another press conference at McDonough Gymnasium to announce that he would be staying. "At this time," he said, "the timing is not right for me to leave here." The money was not an issue, he insisted. His friends were saying that Thompson had been concerned about the stability of the Denver franchise, an organization that had gone through four general managers in the previous two years. Even as Thompson was debating whether to accept the deal, Denver's team president, Carl Scheer, had swung two significant trades to improve Denver's position in the upcoming 1990 draft and Thompson was still not entirely comfortable with the fact that he would also have to deal with three different primary owners and a strong club president with an extensive NBA background. He had been told he would have absolute control, but he clearly had not been totally convinced.

Thompson had been consulted on Denver's predraft moves, but he had been disturbed by his conversations with Bob Wussler, the president of Comsat, a communications and cable television conglomerate that owned 62 percent of the Nuggets in partnership with the two black businessmen, Bert Lee and Peter Bynoe. Thompson had initially been approached about the job by Bynoe, and the two hit it off almost immediately. The same could not be said of Thompson's relationship with Wussler, a man he didn't know, or trust.

Wussler also told Thompson in no uncertain terms that he wanted to be informed ahead of time about any major moves Thompson would be making, particularly the financing of those moves.

"We had negotiated fairly and squarely," Wussler said. "It was not a question of money or ownership—that had been settled. We had difficulty with John regarding the fact that we were going to give him control, but we had to know about certain things before we read about them in the newspaper. Comsat is a publicly held company. I could not put our shareholders in a position where we have signed a player for twenty million dollars or thirty million dollars—and that's what the NBA is coming to over the next few years—without us knowing about it. John had difficulty accepting that. He did not want to operate like that, and I believe that's why he decided to stay at Georgetown.

"We wanted John Thompson in the job. We felt he had the discipline, the judgment, to run this ball club. But this half of the partnership needed more information—that was my view. And he was not willing to go that far."

"Everything has to be factored in," Thompson said. "And that's why I said before everybody has to have a comfort level and nobody can pay me enough money to go somewhere where I feel I'm going to fail.

"I never felt there was nothing left to accomplish at Georgetown, because I think I've always envisioned the challenge here much broader than most people. I've never viewed the challenge here . . . as being solely by won-lost record, and thank God I work for people who never viewed my responsibilities that way. I think when I see there is not a challenge here at Georgetown, it would be good for me to leave and go anywhere."

Most of his friends were stunned when he called the Nuggets to say thanks but no thanks. "To tell you the truth," said Sonny Vaccaro, "I'm shocked. I thought he was gone, and that's all I really want to say about it."

Frank Rienzo, Georgetown's athletic director, insisted he was not surprised that Thompson chose to stay. He had been through this before with his head coach, a man who had attracted a number of offers from other colleges and the pro ranks over the previous ten years. "The only difference here was that it had gotten out in public," Rienzo said, "and that put some pressure on him making a decision. John Thompson never does anything without taking his time and thinking about all the possibilities, but when it became public, that sped up the process."

Rienzo himself only a few weeks before had been approached about leaving Georgetown to replace Dave Gavitt as the commissioner of the Big East, but he eventually decided against it. He had always emphasized to the people working for him that they would be wise to explore other offers if they felt another job would appeal to them, and the Thompson case was no different.

He also emphasized that Thompson, in his dealings with the Nuggets, had made no demands on Georgetown to change his contract or improve his position at the school. "Not only did Georgetown feel it was inappropriate to make him a contract offer, John Thompson never intended in any way, shape or form that he wanted the university to change anything or do anything for him," Rienzo said. "There was never the slightest suggestion or inference to that effect. That was not on John Thompson's agenda."

There were other reasons to stay. With Mourning and Mutombo returning, Thompson could field a team in 1990–91 with two of the best big men in the country, a team that could contend for a national championship. He also felt an obligation to the school that had plucked him from relative obscurity in 1972 and given him free rein to mold a program from scratch. Washington was still home, and he also knew that there was still plenty of time to jump to the NBA. And it was not as if he needed the money.

John Thompson had been at Georgetown for eighteen years. His teams had won 423 games and a national championship. He was a millionaire coach making more than $300,000 a year on his contract with the school and pulling down another $200,000 from Nike, with more money pouring in from his summer camp, a weekly television show, product endorsements and speaking fees at $20,000 an appearance. His million-dollar residence was paid off and he was starting to invest in local real estate. Several years before, he had even purchased some property in Las Vegas, where he planned to build a home.

Still, at the age of forty-eight he also was becoming concerned about his own physical health and mental well-being. Once in 1985 he had collapsed after an NCAA game from dehydration and overall exhaustion, and the Olympic preparations had also taken a toll. For years he'd been on medication to control high blood pressure, and after the 1989–90 season he went on a diet and lost close to fifty pounds. He also checked into the hospital for three days of tests, admitting, "Basketball's a hypertension job." His friends said he had been deeply concerned about the results of that comprehensive physical, and was seriously thinking about getting out of coaching.

There may have been other factors in his consideration of the Denver job. Father Healy was gone now, replaced by Rev. Leo J. O'Donovan. Father Healy had demonstrated total trust in Thompson; the new man, though an enthusiastic supporter, was still mostly an unknown quantity. His friend Dave Gavitt was out of the conference as well, and Thompson knew that the NBA represented the cutting edge of international basketball. That's why Gavitt had left for the Boston Celtics, and that's why Thompson had been so tempted to join him.

Even before the Denver offer, Thompson had been telling people he had little more to prove, that he was concerned about the direction college sports were taking and that the stress and strain from coaching and recruiting were beginning to wear on him, even if he had pulled back somewhat since the Olympics and allowed his staff increased responsibility.

Yet coaching Georgetown also was a job he seemed to thrive on. Basketball was his arena, stalking the sidelines his stage, his whole life.

"I don't go to clubs, to movies, to dinner parties," John Thompson once said. "My entertainment comes from what I do here. My sister once told me I have no fun. But I do. To me, this is it. Sometimes I'm probably a sap, sometimes I yell or curse. Sometimes I don't. And sometimes I'm just a bastard. I'm just being me."

17

I want to be a winner, I want
my players to graduate and I
want to get rich. . . . The biggest con in education is kids
saying they were exploited. If
the kid doesn't get an education, it's his fault. Put yourself
in a position of power where
you create a need for yourself
that has an economic effect on
somebody. The world is not
black or white as much as it
is green."

—*John Thompson to* The Washingtonian *magazine, March 1990*

A FEW MINUTES AFTER HIS TEAM HAD EASILY DISPATCHED Virginia Tech in December of 1989, John Thompson walked into an interview room at the Capital Centre for his postgame comments. As he sat down, he heard a security guard out in the hallway carrying on a conversation, and he was not happy about it.

"Bill, Bill," he said, turning angrily toward the school's sports information director, Bill Shapland. And then he began to shout. "GOD-DAMMIT, I need someone to tell those people to shut the fuck up out there. Right now, tell them to SHUT THE FUCK UP."

A moment later, he turned back toward the assembled press corps and calmly dissected the basketball game, laughing and joking about an easy win, the play of his new point guard, David Edwards, and how impressed he'd been by Tech's Bimbo Coles, one of his former Olympians, whom he now praised as "the best guard in America."

The sudden flash of fury, followed so quickly by this placid, good-humored dissertation, seemed so odd, and somewhat unnerving to anyone who saw it. Yet his friends will tell you that was so typical of the John Thompson they have come to know. Many of those same people will also admit they don't really know him at all. They have an idea, a theory, an opinion, on what makes the man, what drives the man, but that's all. He's a very simple guy, says one friend. He's a very complex person, says another. Just when you think he's taking the money and running to the Denver Nuggets, he decides to stay at Georgetown.

It has been that way all of his life, and John Thompson can also tell you what he is not.

"I am not St. John," he once told me. "I do not go to confession seven days a week. I am not a father figure to my players. They all have parents, mothers and fathers, and I think you insult those people when you call me a father image to their sons. It is not my intention to be a crusader for this cause or that cause. I don't want to be a social worker. Let's take this education thing. They all say, 'Thompson is wonderful because he stresses education, education, education.' Well, they hired me to coach basketball. If I say I want my kids to get an education, it's perceived as an extraordinary thing, that I'm a martyr or something. Why should that be?

"Usually, there is a good guy or a bad guy. I'm not interested in being the bad guy. Who is? But I don't know if I'm the good guy either. I make mistakes. I get angry. Sometimes I work the kids too hard. I'm like any other coach—I'd love to have them concentrate on basketball. I have people on my staff who help me control those feelings. I need that check. I am not trying to be anything other than what I am, and I'm really not certain what that is."

I'm not exactly certain what that is either, but I've got a few opinions on some of the fundamental questions people have been asking me about John Thompson ever since I first met the man twenty years ago.

Is John Thompson a racist?

I do not believe he is.

Many are convinced otherwise. They insist he fields a mostly black team because he has an innate distrust of whites going all the way back to his childhood. And yet the record indicates otherwise. If the measure of a man is taken by the company he keeps, consider the following: John Thompson's best friend in the coaching business is Dean Smith. His two most trusted aides over the last eighteen years have been whites—Mary Fenlon and Bill Stein. His chief recruiter, Craig Esherick, is white. So are Georgetown's longtime head trainer, Lorry Michel; the team physician since 1974, Carl MacCartee; the radio play-by-play announcer from day one, Rich Chvotkin; and the longtime and long-suffering sports information director, Bill Shapland. His most loyal supporters on campus for most of his tenure—Father Timothy Healy, the former school president; Frank Rienzo, the current athletic director; and Charles Deacon, the director of admissions—are white. Two of his closest advisers over the years—Dave Gavitt and Red Auerbach—are white. So are his agents—Donald Dell and David Falk—not to mention his good friend Dan Rather, a loyal supporter of the program who calls more than occasionally. And when Thompson was leaning toward accepting the Denver job, it was Esherick he was pushing as his replacement, not Mike Riley, a black assistant.

He obviously cares very deeply about issues affecting minorities, as well he should. His stands on Propositions 48 and 42 are testament to that. He also tells his players there is one virtually certain way to overcome racism and escape the inner city: money. But John Thompson a racist? Emphatically no.

If he's not a racist, why are white players so few and far between on his teams?

The same question could also be asked of most of America's major-college basketball coaches. Heading into the 1990s, more than 70 percent of the players on major-college basketball teams are black, and the percentage is growing each year. The talent pool of white players physically gifted enough to play at the highest level of the sport is rather thin, and competition for the best players is fierce.

In Thompson's defense, many white players would prefer to go elsewhere and not play for a demanding black coach, though it must also be said that he has not gone out of his way to recruit white athletes. Danny Ferry grew up in his own backyard, but Thompson never made an attempt to talk to him. He should have. Still, in recent years Thompson hasn't been doing much recruiting anyway, of white or black players. He hates the process, finds it demeaning. But he does not hate whites.

Is he a bully?

At times he can be. He is an intimidating presence, a 6-foot-10, 270-pound bundle of belligerent bogarding rage and retribution who has also learned over the years how to use his size and his bellowing baritone voice to his full advantage. It is not a pretty sight.

Mike Freeman, a summer intern at *The Washington Post* in 1988, found that out the hard way. Freeman, a young black reporter, had been sent out to do an interview with Alonzo Mourning at a summer-league game before the start of Mourning's first year at Georgetown. Thompson happened to be in the stands watching, and when he saw Freeman talking to Mourning, he began screaming obscenities at the reporter. "He just got right in my face," Freeman recalled. " 'You sneaky motherfucker, I'll kick your ass.' He was using words I never even knew existed. He didn't want me talking to the kid because of his rule about freshmen. I had no idea, and when I told him that, he called me a liar. I couldn't believe it."

Bob Gibbons, who runs a North Carolina–based high school scouting service and publishes a newsletter with a wide circulation among America's college coaches, also remembers Thompson's wrath. In 1984, he jabbed Thompson in print about having no white players on his team. At the Nike camp that summer, Gibbons was standing in a gym when Thompson walked up, introduced himself and told Gibbons he did not appreciate what he'd written. Before long, the discussion became a shouting match, with Thompson doing most of the screaming. "He said to me, 'You're nothing but a motherfucking whore making his living off these kids,' " Gibbons said. "I gathered myself up and said, 'Well, how do you make your living, John?' Then he threatened me. He said there were ways to take care of guys like me. He started charging toward me. Fortunately, another coach grabbed him and restrained him."

In his own conference, Thompson has feuded with fellow coaches Jim Boeheim, Rick Pitino and Paul Evans, though all three insist they no longer have a problem with the head Hoya. His disdain for Brent Musburger has been well documented. He also tried to bully another old colleague, Bill Raftery of CBS, when the former Seton Hall coach criticized his team's roughhouse style during a game against Pittsburgh in 1987 that degenerated into a brawl. "John Thompson has to control his team," Raftery said on the air. "There are too many incidents over the years. It happens too often."

Thompson lashed right back on his own Washington television show, describing Raftery's remarks as "biased" and saying he was "unsuccessful as a basketball coach on all levels." He also insisted that Raftery had only given one side of the incident, that he never mentioned that the fight had been precipitated by Pitt's liberal use of hands and elbows, pushing and shoving. Thompson, as is often his style, was attacking the messenger instead of addressing the real issue at hand, and in the process he also was doing his very best to let CBS know he did not appreciate being criticized on national television. It was John Thompson, the raging bully, at his intimidating best.

When John Thompson is angry, he lets you know it. He yells at his players, his staff, his colleagues, referees, reporters, opposing coaches and players. He does it to give himself an advantage, an edge, and often his outbursts are coldly calculated. It's part of the package, but only one part.

There also is a soft and soppy side to the man: the John Thompson who cried the day his first recruiting class graduated; the man who lovingly cared for his mother over the last years of her life, lifting Anna Thompson in his arms to her daily morning bath; the man who once called a nervous young colleague who had just been named head basketball coach at a local university to offer encouragement and some advice.

"I will never forget that," said Ed Tapscott, the first black coach at American University. "This was a couple of days after I'd been hired. Like any twenty-eight-year-old in that kind of position, I was a little nervous, asking what I'd gotten myself into. One night I was up late, ridden with anxiety, and the phone rings. I hear a deep voice that I vaguely recognize, with a slightly bemused tone.

" 'Are you up? 'Cause if you're not up, you got no shot to beat me next year, young man.' John Thompson called me, and it was as reassuring a call as I've ever gotten in my life. I was struck by the kindness of it. He wanted to wish me good luck, and he had some important words of advice. I sensed he knew I was worried, and the gist of his advice was to believe in yourself and involve yourself with people who are loyal to you. After years of reflection, I realize now how fortunate I was to get that call, and how much it meant to me from a guy I hardly even knew."

That first year, Ed Tapscott won 20 games, including a victory over Georgetown. The next season, his team was dreadful, 4–19 at one point when Tapscott ran into John Thompson recruiting at a local high school game. Thompson asked him to sit down next to him. "He asked me how we were doing and I told him, 'We stink.' He says, 'No, no, no, how are you holding up under your change in fortune, how are the kids taking it?' I told him they were suffering with me. Then he reminded me that I was good enough last year to win twenty games. He said, 'Just ride it out and keep your kids up.' He didn't have to do that— we're not close friends by any means. When I hear all these other labels pinned on him, I always think back to the time when he took me under his wing as a young man and tried to help me. He'll never know how much that meant to me."

Can John Thompson coach?

No question here. The man's record speaks for itself—423 wins going into this season, a national championship, three Final Four appearances, four Big East Conference regular-season titles, fourteen times in the NCAA tournament, including twelve straight, sixteen consecutive postseason appearances.

His teams are disciplined, incredibly conditioned and thoroughly relentless, particularly on defense, where Thompson truly excels. The Hoyas have never been a sophisticated offensive team, and only when Patrick Ewing left the program and turned professional did he become a major scoring force. The same may also hold true for the team's current star, Alonzo Mourning, who has struggled in his first two seasons adjusting to Thompson's offense.

Thompson was not a great offensive player, and he is not a gifted offensive coach. But he does get results. Mitch Kupchak, the assistant general manager for the Los Angeles Lakers, also points out that very few of the eighteen players drafted by the NBA from Thompson's teams have been stars in the professional ranks. Ewing is an all-star. Sleepy Floyd a solid pro. Many of Thompson's best players—Craig Shelton, John Duren, Bill Martin, David Wingate, Reggie Williams, Charles Smith—have struggled in the NBA, disappearing toward the end of the bench on their way to relatively short careers. Kupchak believes it's a testament to Thompson's ability that he can keep his teams at the highest levels of the game without the best athletes.

John Thompson can coach, most definitely.

Did John Thompson blow the Olympics?

First, it must be said that American basketball teams are no longer invincible in international competition, not without professionals on the roster. The Americans lost to Brazil in the 1987 Pan Am Games. They lost to the Russians in the 1988 Olympics. They lost to Yugoslavia in the 1990 Goodwill Games, and in the 1990 world championships they lost to a Russian team in the preliminary round, then lost to Yugoslavia again. "It's not that we didn't play hard," said Mike Krzyzewski, the 1990 national coach, after the Goodwill Games. "But we are nineteen- and twenty-year-olds going against men."

Thompson had the same problem two years earlier. In hindsight, he also made a number of fundamental mistakes in 1988. He desperately could have used more outside firepower. He needed a coaching staff that did not consist of all his good friends, yes-men (and a yes-woman, Mary Fenlon) every one. He tried to pattern the Olympic team after his Georgetown team, relying heavily on pressing defense that never fazed the Soviets. He got no production from Danny Manning in the loss to the Russians and kept him on the bench too long. His team seemed to panic down the stretch in that loss, firing up desperation shots more often than not. At times his team looked scared and played scared.

John Thompson was the head coach. He must take the blame.

Is he too greedy for his own good?

Thompson's pursuit of the dollar has been almost as intense as his quest for a national championship. Money makes men free, Thompson is fond of saying, and it also allows him to have the kind of control he covets—complete, absolute authority to do it his way, just as Red Auerbach and Bill Russell taught him so many years ago. No one tells him anymore he can't sit in the front row at church. No one tells him anymore he can't shoot baskets at a whites-only playground. No one tells him anymore he can't live in a particular neighborhood or eat in a particular restaurant. No one tells him anymore his children can't go to any school their hearts desire.

Thompson believes money is the root of all power. "I think more change has come about because of economics, because people totally disregard color barriers if you have economic value," he said.

In America in 1990, it's hard to argue that philosophy with a man who pulled himself all the way up from poverty.

Does John Thompson have a competitive advantage recruiting players because of his ties to Nike?

Yes, with Alonzo Mourning the primary case in point. Thompson first met him on campus at a Nike-sponsored tournament. Mourning's high school team wore Nike products. He attended a Nike-sponsored summer camp; his high school coach was a paid counselor there for two years. The summer league Mourning played in used sneakers supplied by Nike, and specifically by Sonny Vaccaro, the Nike executive who is also a good friend of John Thompson's. Case closed, despite all the denials.

There is growing concern among college athletic officials—and even among coaches themselves—that shoe companies are influencing the recruiting process by offering free shoes, equipment and stipends to high school coaches, who then may steer top prospects toward college coaches affiliated with those very same shoe companies. Because of such concerns, the NCAA says it will soon be looking into the issue.

There are those who believe that college coaches under contracts to shoe companies should give back part of their earnings to their schools, perhaps even sharing endorsement money (in the form of a stipend) with their players who wear the shoes. Dean Smith has been an advocate of sharing the wealth, but that is now prohibited by the NCAA.

Thompson, always the capitalist, sees nothing wrong with the big money offered to coaches by the shoe companies, and finds it ironic that he's being criticized at a time when so few high-profile black athletes or coaches receive endorsement deals. He also says shoe contracts allow many smaller schools to keep high-profile coaches from moving to bigger institutions.

"Would P. J. Carlesimo have stayed at Seton Hall [without his shoe money]?" Thompson said. "No. Would John Thompson have stayed at Georgetown? No. Would Rollie Massimino have stayed at Villanova? No. In a competitive marketplace, the big state schools, particularly in the West, could have recruited the coaches with their big-time boosters."

Thompson was in the middle of a different sort of sneaker war last summer. Operation PUSH, the Chicago-based civil-rights organization founded by Rev. Jesse Jackson, announced a nationwide boycott against Nike. Operation PUSH claimed that while the company used high-visibility blacks like Michael Jordan, Bo Jackson, Spike Lee and Thompson as national spokesmen, Nike had a poor record in minority hiring, and had no blacks on its board of directors.

Thompson did not take kindly to the boycott, and also criticized PUSH for picking on a company he claimed had an outstanding record of providing funds for minority programs and had made major break-throughs in using black sports figures to endorse its products. Thompson tried to mediate the dispute, but PUSH went ahead with its boycott, even after Nike announced plans for a new affirmative-action program and a promise to add minority representation to its board of directors.

After years of corporate America failing to use blacks to endorse its products, it hardly seems fair to criticize Thompson for taking Nike's money and running to the bank. But clearly there are still troubling questions being raised by college academic and athletic officials about conflicts of interest and competitive advantages that may soon put an end to the gravy train.

Is John Thompson treated fairly by the media?

Thompson's relations with the print media in his hometown have been far less contentious than his dealings with the national press. He also has his favorite writers, and he knows how to use those writers to his full advantage.

He has never had any qualms about picking up the telephone and complaining to a reporter or his editor about a story that did not particularly please him. There is a widely held perception that the Washington media treat Thompson with kid gloves, and to a certain extent the coverage has generally been favorable. Yet he has had his share of harsh criticism on issues ranging from Ralph Dalton's name change to his team's physical style of play to the academic integrity of the George-town basketball program.

Thompson usually makes himself accessible to local beat writers, and while he will often return phone calls days later, frequently at the midnight hour, he generally does call back. The same cannot be said for his relations with writers from other cities, many of whom have simply stopped trying to reach him or his players and take great glee at aiming long-distance potshots at this very easy target.

I believe his critics went overboard after the Olympics in what seemed like a knee-jerk personal attack, but it must also be said that

Thompson probably brought a lot of that on himself. His media policies come from the Dark Ages by way of the Inquisition. A little more access and a lot less secrecy and paranoia would go a long way toward improving relations. But to expect Thompson to be molded by PR types seems highly unlikely.

Is John Thompson loyal to his former players and friends?

It depends on who they are and, in some cases, what they can do for him. Some of Thompson's players, particularly from his pre-Ewing days, are extremely bitter and haven't spoken to their former coach in years. His first three big-name signings from his own high school team—Greg Brooks, Jonathan Smith and Merlin Wilson—want nothing to do with the program, mostly because they believe Thompson lost interest in them once they stopped playing and left school. And yet their teammate Aaron Long, a seldom-used reserve, to this day remains a close Thompson confidant and speaks in glowing terms of his old coach.

Thompson's relationship with his stars is somewhat intriguing—and terribly inconsistent—as well. Patrick Ewing is still very much a presence in the program. Thompson speaks with him often, uses him to help recruit and gives him carte blanche to use Georgetown's facilities in the off-season.

But Sleepy Floyd, Thompson's first all-American, says he's lost touch with his old coach, for no particular reason other than the fact that he plays ball in Houston and was never that close to him to begin with. Similarly, Reggie Williams, Thompson's last all-American, hasn't had any contact with the program virtually since the day he graduated. When Williams was a free agent last winter after being dropped by the Cleveland Cavaliers, the Chicago Bulls were ready to sign him until general manager Jerry Krause called Thompson and asked him to put in a good word for his former player. Thompson told Krause he couldn't do it because he hadn't spoken with Williams for three years. And Thompson and Williams are represented by the same attorney, David Falk.

Thompson can hardly be expected to have close relationships with every athlete who ever came through the program, but several players have complained that Thompson, in addition to being inaccessible, has done virtually nothing to show his appreciation for their past contributions. Many schools, for example, bring back players from the past for special halftime or pregame ceremonies. Not Georgetown. "It's like we were never there," said one former player. "They don't even invite me to the team banquet, and I live ten minutes from campus."

Thompson's relationship with many of his old friends has also been strangely inconsistent. While people like Mary Fenlon, Bill Stein, Red Auerbach and Dave Gavitt have been constants in his life for years, many others who played significant roles in his success have fallen by the wayside. Jim Wiggins, the barber who was Thompson's shadow and closest confidant in the early years, is now a bitter enemy. Ron Watts, his pal from the Celtic days and the man he named his son after, hardly ever talks to Thompson. "We've just drifted apart," he said. High school recruiting maven Howard Garfinkel, a good friend and adviser in the 1970s, says Thompson turned on him years ago because he thought he was advising a recruit to go elsewhere, a charge Garfinkel vehemently denies. Bob Dwyer, his old high school coach, desperately wants to make peace with Thompson before he dies, but Thompson won't even return his telephone calls.

Joe Dean Davidson, the late Dunbar High School coach who sent Thompson some of his best players and once considered him a close friend, said he felt he'd been used by John Thompson, and "I wasn't the only one. I'll give him credit. The guy works very hard and earned what he got, but he walked over a lot of people to get there and never looked back. Some people view the way to succeed is to crush anyone else who may stand in their way. Others see success in their ability to help or promote their friends, like Bobby Knight did. He's had his people working all over the country as head coaches. How many of John's people can say the same thing?"

Do Georgetown players leave school with meaningful degrees?

Most yes, some no. There is no question that Thompson's players go to class and do their schoolwork. There aren't any gut courses in Basketball Theory or Principles of Folk Dancing. And it's no surprise that Thompson recruits basketball players, not scholars. Their lives revolve around ball, not books, just the way it is at most Division I basketball powers. Despite the hype, America produces few "student-athletes."

John Thompson exploits his players just as every college coach exploits his players. He uses them to win basketball games. The more games they win, the better it is for John Thompson. He'll make more money, he'll get more exposure, he'll keep his job and get offers of better jobs. It his players don't conform to his rigid rules and his demands, if they don't perform up to his standards, they are discarded like day-old bread. That's not just John Thompson's way, that's big-time competitive college basketball in 1990.

If his players happen to be exposed to literature, politics and foreign languages in their four years at Georgetown, good for them. If, like Ewing, they can get summer jobs working on Capitol Hill, that's fine, too. Thompson does stress the importance of getting a degree, and most of his players seem to go on to productive lives away from basketball. They are lawyers, teachers, ministers and businessmen.

And one of them is a hotel doorman. Tom Scates, the man-mountain of a center on Thompson's teams in the late 1970s, has been working as a doorman at a downtown Washington hotel—the J. W. Marriott— for most of the last decade. He's the doorman with the Georgetown degree. In response to an interview request, Scates replied, "Every time I talk to the press, they make me look stupid, so I'm not gonna comment. Nothing personal, you understand." Scates has also told his friends and former teammates he likes his job, makes $35,000 a year and has turned down several chances to work elsewhere in the hotel. Still, unfair as it may be, he'll always be the doorman with the Georgetown degree, a symbol of John Thompson's failure.

In September 1990, another former Georgetown athlete was in the headlines. And this was about failure, too. David Wingate, a starter on the 1984 championship team, was indicted in Howard County, Maryland, on six counts, including second-degree rape, sexual contact and assault and battery, in an incident involving a seventeen-year-old girl, who claimed he had intercourse with her and fondled her against her will. That indictment came two days after a twenty-one-year-old San Antonio woman filed a civil suit accusing Wingate of raping and sodomizing her in the summer of 1990.

The day after the indictment, Wingate was told by his employers, the San Antonio Spurs of the NBA, that he would not be allowed to return to the team. At the time, he was on the verge of signing a three-year, $2.25 million contract with the Spurs. Instead, this Georgetown graduate was facing charges that carried a maximum sentence of twenty years in jail.

Has Georgetown sold out to big-time college sports?

Of course it has, just as any school that maintains a high-profile, nationally ranked athletic program sells out, despite all the pious pronouncements to the contrary. As Murray Sperber wrote in *College Sports Inc.*, "Athletes are the only group of students recruited for entertainment—not academic—purposes, and they are the only students who go through school on grants based not on educational aptitude, but on their talent and potential as commercial entertainers. If colleges searched for and gave scholarships to up-and-coming rock stars so that they could entertain the university community and earn money for their schools through concerts and tours, educational authorities and the public would call this 'a perversion of academic values.' "

Georgetown's decision to allow marginal students into its program is a sellout as well. But what can we say about other sports at top "sports colleges" in America? Clearly Michael Graham had no business at Georgetown. Neither did John Turner. Professors who have these and other students in their classes can only shrug their shoulders. One psychology professor told me that he learned a long time ago it would be wise to simply accept the fact that some athletes did not belong in his class, and do the best he could to get them through. It's the price you pay for a top-twenty basketball team. And the evidence suggests that Thompson's record is better—far better—than the records of most other coaches in big-time college sports in this regard.

Is John Thompson good for Georgetown, and what's in it for the university to have a big-time basketball program?

There is no question that Thompson has been a godsend for Georgetown. His basketball program funds most of the school's athletic programs, and helps balance the department's budget. A good portion of the money earned from NCAA appearances goes into the school's scholarship fund and some also is used to improve athletic facilities. With NCAA Final Four teams scheduled to earn $3 million in 1991, that contribution to university coffers has the potential to be staggering.

More important, his team's constant success over the years has increased the school's national visibility and fueled intense interest in the university, particularly among minority applicants. Last year alone, the school had more than one thousand applications from black students around the country. When Thompson took over the program, there were fewer than one hundred black applicants a year. Similarly, the number of total applicants also has risen dramatically over the years, and school officials say the basketball team's rise to prominence in the national polls has played a significant role.

This is hardly an unusual phenomenon, by any means. When Doug Flutie was performing his miracles for the Boston College football team in the early 1980s, the BC admissions office was getting a record number of applications. The same was true at Villanova after the 1984–85 team upset Georgetown in the Final Four—suddenly, high school kids from all over America got interested in the little Catholic school in the Philadelphia suburbs. More applications also translate into a larger talent pool to choose from, allowing admissions officers to be more selective.

That, in turn, leads to a higher-caliber student body over the long haul. Even if the basketball players are not brilliant scholars, universities believe the trade-off is well worth the risk of accepting some academically marginal athletes.

A successful athletic team also helps draw a college community together. It becomes a rallying point for students, faculty and far-flung alumni, particularly when the team does well. Father Healy, the school's former president, spoke frequently about the "great pride and joy" the basketball team provided the Georgetown community—how successful teams were also part of the educational process, giving students an outlet to vent their emotions and blow off steam after a tough day in the classroom and the library.

And, of course, it doesn't hurt when appreciative alumni say thank you with their checkbooks, another fringe benefit from successful sports teams at almost every school in America.

Thompson clearly has fulfilled his end of the bargain. He wins games. He's never been found guilty of cheating by the NCAA. And almost all of his players graduate. And while he is hardly a candidate for canonization by any means, he's still head and shoulders above many of his colleagues in the world of big-time collegiate sports.

"I'm a great admirer of his," said Al Hunt, the Washington bureau chief of *The Wall Street Journal* and a Georgetown season-ticket holder for most of the 1980s. "The only area I have reservations about is how he prepares his kids for life after Georgetown. They're so sheltered there. But in my mind, John Thompson's glass is ninety percent full, ten percent empty."

Another view comes from James T. "Miggs" Reilly, the Washington attorney who was on the original selection committee that chose Thompson, even though he preferred DeMatha coach Morgan Wootten. "I still think Morgan was the right choice at the time," Reilly said. "And I don't agree with everything Thompson does. But he's turned that program around, and I'm proud of that team, I really am. I watch 'em play, and I root like hell for Georgetown. I have some concerns about some of the kids he lets in there, but if he can get them through, get them their degrees, then I'll just say God bless John Thompson, he's done what he's supposed to do."

So what's the bottom line?

It's all about contradictions.

John Thompson can call Ed Tapscott at midnight, but not return the telephone calls from one of his former players, Craig Shelton. He can rail at critics for exploiting his players, yet have no qualms about being paid $200,000 a year by a company so that his team will wear shoes and shirts with a Nike logo. He can talk about the importance of education, yet allow a Michael Graham and a John Turner into his program, then cut them loose when—surprise, surprise—they can't make it in the classroom. He can moan about the Portland Trail Blazers rehabilitating an Olympic foe, then two years later sign Vladimir Bosanac, a 6-9 Yugoslavian with the potential to eventually play for his national team, to a Georgetown scholarship.

It's also about power and control.

It's John Thompson's world, his ball. He works long, hard hours and expects the same from everyone around him. Accept it or leave. That's how he runs his life, that's how he runs his program. He makes no promises to his players. He sets down the rules and expects them to be followed. Coats and ties on the road. Freshmen carry the basketballs. You will sign John's book or face the consequences. Miss a class, don't bother to practice. Miss a bunch of classes, don't bother to come back at all.

The secrecy, the security, the paranoia are also part of the package. So are Thompson's relentless and occasionally unethical pursuit of the almighty dollar, his silly little fusses and feuds with so many people he's climbed over to get where he is, his almost fiendish fetish for the privacy of his family and his team.

And yet the system works for Georgetown, and especially for John Thompson. He wins basketball games, and does it within the rules. He makes a ton of money for his school, and has given Georgetown more exposure than anyone thought possible when he was first hired in 1972. Almost all of his players graduate and go on to productive lives.

But John Thompson's own life has been the greatest success story of them all: A poor black boy from the depths of the inner city rises above poverty and prejudice to reach the very top of his highly visible profession, earns a small fortune along the way and becomes a widely respected spokesman for his school, his sport, and his people, just as Anna Thompson always told him he could.

Acknowledgments

My friend and colleague, George Solomon, the assistant managing editor for sports at *The Washington Post*, generously allowed me the time to research and write this book, and I will be forever grateful to him. I am also indebted to *The Washington Post*'s executive editor Ben Bradlee and managing editor Leonard Downie, enthusiastic supporters from the start.

My agent, Esther Newberg—even if she is a fanatical fan of the University of Connecticut and an avowed Hoya-hater—demonstrated once again why she is simply the very best in the business. And Jack Macrae of Henry Holt is the consummate professional, an editor's editor whose advice and counsel were invaluable. Amy Robbins, Jack's assistant, is nothing short of miraculous.

To friends and colleagues who shared their notes, their old tapes and transcripts, their personal files, their knowledge, their memories and their Rolodexes, many thanks, especially to Dave Kindred, Jane Leavy, Bill Brubaker, Steve Berkowitz, Tony Kornheiser, Ken Denlinger, Tom Boswell, Michael Wilbon, John Feinstein, Shirley Povich, David Sell, Richard Justice, Angus Phillips, Christine Brennan, Sally Jenkins, Mark Asher, Doug Cress, Athelia Knight, Donald Huff, Bill Gildea, David Aldridge, Tony Cotton, Emilio Garcia-Ruiz, Al Hunt, Dick Weiss, Gary Pomerantz, Jeff Motley, Peter Land, Juan Williams, Glenn Harris, Jim Cohen, Larry Van Dyne and Curry Kirkpatrick.

Others who took up the slack at the paper in my absence and helped with the myriad details that go into producing a book include Sandra Bailey, Tony Reid, Sushant Sagar, Arthur Pincus, Don Beard, Don White, Bob Van Winkle, Pat McLaughlin, Steve Goff, Jim Brady, Maynard Clarke, Steve King, Kay Coyte and Diane Mattingly.

A good portion of the research was the result of tenacious interviewing by a young journalist named Andrew Salomon; Olwen Price transcribed hours of tapes with unbelievable patience and incredible accuracy, right down to "pause while he eats his hamburger." Molly Solomon and Karl Hente, at the time two talented students, helped to provide invaluable research from the Georgetown campus.

Thanks to Jennifer Belton and *The Washington Post*'s news research library; Jane Jackson at the Providence College library; Chris Plonsky of the Big East office; Rick Brewer, sports information director at the University of North Carolina; Gregg Burke, sports information director at Providence College and Bill Shapland and Chartese Dean, sports information directors at Georgetown, perhaps the most difficult SID jobs in America. Fran Connors and John Blake, former Georgetown publicists, provided vital material and were kind enough to submit to lengthy interviews.

To my family, especially my wife, Vicky, thanks for your support, your patience and your understanding during some very trying times; my mother, brothers, their wives, Vicky's parents and a dozen close friends kept me going by solid encouragement and useful advice. I'm happy to name them: Budd and Audrey Fenton, Hank and Nance Minchin, Toby and Barbara Merchant, Bobby and Gwen Dobson, Michael Sussman and Renee Licht, Nick and Bucky Slater, Vern Hosta, Helen Wiley, Dr. Juan Cortes-Quirant and Mary Jane Hill.

Index